The
America Online®
MONEY
Guide

The
America Online®
MONEY
Guide

Gus Venditto

The America Online Money Guide

Copyright© 1996 by Que® Corporation.

Library of Congress Catalog No.: 96-68991

ISBN: 0-7897-0865-5

98 97 96   6 5 4 3 2 1

Interpretation of the printing code: the rightmost double-digit number is the year of the book's printing; the rightmost single-digit number, the number of the book's printing. For example, a printing code of 96-1 shows that the first printing of the book occurred in 1996.

Screen reproductions in this book were created using Collage Plus from Inner Media, Inc., Hollis, NH.

CREDITS

President
Roland Elgey

Vice President and Publisher
Marie Butler-Knight

Publishing Director
David W. Solomon

Title Manager
Kathie-Jo Arnoff

Editorial Services Director
Elizabeth Keaffaber

Managing Editor
Michael Cunningham

Director of Marketing
Lynn E. Zingraf

Production Editor
Rebecca M. Mounts

Editor
Sara Rudy

Assistant Product Marketing Manager
Christy M. Miller

Strategic Marketing Manager
Barry Pruett

Technical Editor
Stephen H. Kovacs

Technical Support Specialist
Nadeem Muhammed

Acquisitions Coordinator
Tracy C. Williams

Software Relations Coordinator
Patty Brooks

Editorial Assistant
Carmen Krikorian

Book Designers
Barbara Kordesh
Kim Scott
Dan Armstrong

Cover Designer
Barbara Kordesh

Production Team
Stephen Adams
Debra Bolhuis
Erin M. Danielson
Joan Evan
Jessica Ford
Jason Hand
Daryl Kessler
Clint Lahnen
Michelle Lee
Ryan Oldfather
Casey Price
Laura Robbins
Staci Somers
Jeff Yesh

Indexer
John Hulse

Composed in **Frutiger** by Que Corporation.

ABOUT THE AUTHOR

Gus Venditto is the author of *Your Money, Total Personal Financial Planning on Your Computer*, and three other books. A regular contributor to *Internet World* magazine, his work has appeared in *PC Magazine, Home PC, Computer Life*, and *PC Week*.

ACKNOWLEDGMENTS

It may be a cliché, but it's the truth. This book wouldn't have been possible without the efforts of Kathie-Jo Arnoff. She saw the promise in the idea long before everyone else, and she was willing to push it.

Finally, a word of special thanks to Steve Kovacs for his online expertise and to Rebecca Mounts for her skillful editing.

WE'D LIKE TO HEAR FROM YOU!

As part of our continuing effort to produce books of the highest possible quality, Que would like to hear your comments. To stay competitive, we *really* want you, as a computer book reader and user, to let us know what you like or dislike most about this book or other Que products.

You can mail comments, ideas, or suggestions for improving future editions to the address below, or send us a fax at (317) 581-4663. For the online inclined, Macmillan Computer Publishing has a forum on CompuServe (type **GO QUEBOOKS** at any prompt) through which our staff and authors are available for questions and comments. The address of our Internet site is **http://www.mcp.com** (World Wide Web).

In addition to exploring our forum, please feel free to contact me personally to discuss your opinions of this book: I'm **Karnoff18** on AOL, and I'm **Karnoff@que.mcp.com** on the Internet.

Thanks in advance—your comments will help us to continue publishing the best books available on computer topics in today's market.

Kathie-Jo Arnoff
Title Manager
Que Corporation
201 W. 103rd Street
Indianapolis, Indiana 46290
USA

Contents at a Glance

Table of Contents

Foreword

The Personal Finance section on America Online may not look like the cornerstone of a revolution, but it has become one in a very short period of time. Americans have shown a growing desire to take control over their personal finance, and we've helped millions to do just that.

Visitors to AOL's Personal Finance section receive the type of up-to-the-minute information that until a few short years ago was available only to institutions, like stock brokerage firms and investment bankers. At any time of the day, our customers receive reports on the markets that are accurate and timely. They don't have to wait for a newspaper to deliver the news a day later; they can read it and act on it the same day opportunities become available. More than a third of America Online's subscribers visit the Personal Finance channel on a regular basis.

America Online devotes an enormous amount of resources to providing the services you'll find in the Personal Finance area, but all of it is focused on two goals. We provide members with timely, reliable information, and we give them the tools they need to manipulate that information.

These two ingredients—information and analytical tools—can be an unparalleled advantage in helping you to reach your own goals. *The America Online Money Guide* can be an additional tool in maximizing your own personal wealth. I hope you'll find this book provides that extra bit of insight that can help you turn these tools into the right formula for reaching your own personal goals.

—David Baird
General Manager, Personal Finance
America Online, Inc.

Introduction

You don't have to spend much time online to sense that the traditional ways of doing business are changing, almost by the hour. Exciting opportunities are opening up all around us, offering unique ways to make money, increase the return on investments, and improve our savvy as consumers.

It all seems wonderful, but there's a big problem. It's all happening too fast. Banks, stockbrokers, and stores are urging you to visit them on the Web. Newscasts report that gossip circulating on the Internet is driving stock prices up. And more data is going online every day than the average library can hold.

Many of these new services promise to help you save more or increase the return on your investments. But who has the time to investigate these new opportunities?

Get More from Your Time Online

As someone who's been living and working in cyberspace for over a decade, I know how hard it is to keep up. But it's been my job—first at *PC Magazine* and more recently with *Internet World* magazine—to know the latest trends and test the latest products. So I'm always among the first to visit the new message boards, Web sites, and newsgroups.

While I'm often excited at what I find online, all too often I'm disappointed. Many of the new online features are little more than advertisements for companies that have been around for years; there's nothing new or exciting about the services they're promoting with a Web site. Some are loaded up with graphics that take forever to load, and others seem to have pages and pages of information, but little of it has anything of value. So much for saving time!

On the other hand, when I do find a service that delivers hard facts, it makes the long hours of searching worthwhile. Gold really does exist, buried deep under mountains of Web pages and bulletin board messages.

Achieving Your Own Financial Goals

I realize there was a need for a book that could help the average American use these valuable resources in their own life. But rather than list them like a phone book, I wanted to reveal the full value of these resources and so I've shown how they fit into the decisions all of us face over the course of a lifetime. You can jump from chapter to chapter if you're looking for help in a specific area, but you'll find the book is actually a step-by-step plan for using these financial tools to achieve your own personal goals.

All of us need to make our savings work a little harder, to make sure we have enough for retirement and to meet the major expenses we'll face along the way. If you follow the book, chapter by chapter, you'll find that you're building on a solid foundation of knowledge about the available opportunities. You'll learn how to get debt under control, build

your own investment portfolio, and plan for the future with realistic projections. This isn't a complicated stock-picking scheme. The book just takes the most widely accepted strategies that have been used for years by financial planners and shows you how to execute them by using your personal computer. You could hire a financial planner to do all of this for you, but I think you'll feel better if you're the one in control of your future. After all, no one can work for your best interests as well as you can.

One thing I've learned in my research is that there's no connection between the amount of attention an online resource earns and the quality of its information. Many jewels are shining in relative obscurity. This book is my effort to help cast some light on these overlooked treasures.

Some of the resources on America Online (AOL) and the Internet are truly groundbreaking, and when you know how to use them, you can be a better consumer and a smarter investor.

Detailed reports on stocks and mutual funds provide the same type of financial data that used to be sold for subscriptions that cost hundreds of dollars a month. Government sites provide straightforward advice on how you can protect your rights. And a broad range of online stores make it possible to compare prices with a few keystrokes for just about anything. You can even buy a car online, saving hundreds of dollars in the process. (Go ahead and kick the tires in a dealer's parking lot, but before you sign on the dotted line, be sure to read "Shopping for a Deal on a New Car" in Chapter 10.)

But finding the good stuff is only half the battle. Online information comes in many forms; some information can only be read while you're connected to America Online, other reports are easy to download, and others can be saved for your own personal use by using the techniques shown in this book. And once you've saved this information on your system, you'll get more out of it if you open the reports with a spreadsheet and apply some simple formulas.

You don't need to be a spreadsheet whiz to use the book; in fact, you can download all of the spreadsheets discussed directly from America Online. If you want to customize the spreadsheets further, you're welcome to do that. But if all you want to do is use these spreadsheets to help you make financial decisions, you can do that very easily, without bothering to look at the detailed descriptions on how each spreadsheet works.

Building Your Plan, Chapter by Chapter

The book is organized around the most important financial issues affecting most Americans. While the first chapters will help you master America Online and spreadsheet techniques, the following chapters concentrate on specific financial challenges: investing, shopping for interest rates, saving for college, planning for retirement, and buying a house.

You'll find recommendations on the best places to go and detailed instructions on how to accomplish each task.

The first two chapters show you how to use the two most important tools at your disposal: an account with America Online and a spreadsheet. Whether you've been using these two for years or are just getting started, you'll find tips on how to get more from these tools with less effort.

Every portfolio needs to devote some resources to growth stocks. Chapters 3 through 5 show you how to invest without exposing yourself to more risk than is necessary. First, you'll learn how to research companies with America Online's vast financial databases. From learning about the fundamentals of investing to analyzing a company's profit and loss statement, you'll find that the same information available to professional stock pickers is at your fingertips; the numbered instructions will show you how to use it for your own gain. Once you've got the basics under your belt, you'll be ready to venture into some of the hottest stock-trading talk imaginable. In Chapter 4, you'll learn how to navigate among the message boards where active investors share their own tips and are willing to answer questions. Chapter 5 shows you how to save money on commissions by trading stocks, mutual funds, and options directly through your America Online account.

No financial plan should have too much risk, and so Chapters 6 and 7 explain conservative investments: mutual funds, government bonds, money market funds, and certificates of deposit (CD). You'll find out how to download unbiased comparisons on the performance of any mutual fund. Whether you want to do your own analysis or just want to refer to up-to-date "Top 10" lists, Chapter 6 provides detailed steps on how you can research mutual funds. And before you renew a CD, be sure to read Chapter 7. You're almost certain to earn a better return on your money once you know how to find savings bank interest rate comparisons.

Chapter 8 shows you how to manage your investments, using America Online's up-to-the-minute portfolio tracking software and a spreadsheet that can analyze the results.

In Chapter 9, you'll learn how to manage debt and credit problems; whether you're struggling with debt or just want to keep your record clean, you'll find out how to obtain a free report on your credit history.

Saving money on big purchases is the focus of Chapters 10 and 11. Many online services make it possible for you to compare prices around the country in less time than it takes to drive to one store. These two chapters provide clear instructions on how you can compare products and prices without leaving your home.

Chapters 12, 13, and 14 help you prepare for some of the most important goals in your life: buying a house, saving for college, and planning for retirement. You'll be better able to meet these expenses if you know how to accurately project the costs you'll face—even if they're decades away. These chapters show you, step-by-step, how to use a spreadsheet to meet those expenses. You can download the spreadsheets from America Online and begin using them right away.

Finally, Chapter 15 will help you look ahead, showing you ways to spot new opportunities.

How To Use This Book

The book assumes you already have an account with America Online or you've just obtained the disks and are preparing to open an account. (You say you were planning to sign up but you lost the disks? Call 1-800-827-6364 and ask America Online to send you a new set of disks).

And while you will gain more from using the book if you own a spreadsheet program, you don't need to have advanced spreadsheet skills. The examples in this book are built with basic spreadsheet functions and detailed instructions are provided. If you don't own a spreadsheet, there's no need to be left out; Chapter 2 provides instructions on where you can find one on America Online that you can download at no cost (beyond normal connect charges).

The book is designed to work equally well for Mac and Windows users. Although the screens show a Windows 95 system, you'll find all of the techniques described work the same on Windows 3.1, Windows NT, or a Mac.

The spreadsheet examples are shown in Microsoft Works for Windows 95, but all of the instructions were carefully constructed to work with the other leading spreadsheets: Claris Works, Microsoft Excel (for Mac and Windows), and Lotus 1-2-3. When there are differences in the way the different spreadsheets perform, the distinctions are explained in the following chapters.

Updates Online

Finally, because the world of online information is constantly changing, the book is being supported by a site on the Web. Use the America Online keyword

http://www.mcp.com/que/desktop_os/ money

You can download the spreadsheets discussed in the book, and link to the many Web sites that are described. See Appendix A, "Online with the Money Guide," for further information.

And if you have any questions (or compliments), you can reach me directly at AOL. You'll find me in the ZDnet section where I host a message board. Use the keyword **zdnet**, select Mingle and look for the message board "MoreMoney, Less Work."

This unique combination of online elements, spreadsheet tools, and an interactive Web site is something you may not have tried before. But this a unique age and new ways of doing things are emerging.

Taking Charge of Your Financial Future

We live in a time when the opportunity to control our own financial future has never been greater. Financial institutions are reaching out to consumers with new products that provide new ways of managing money, and new opportunities to increase personal wealth. And financial publishers are broadening their services with lower prices for high quality information.

At the same time, changes in the world economy are putting more pressure on all of us. Guaranteed pensions are becoming a distant memory. Inflation is a constant threat. And financial security is enjoyed only by those who know how to create wealth for themselves. Learning how to take advantage of these new opportunities is a necessity. The alternative is a progressively lower standard of living.

You've already made the investment in technology. Now it's time to make it work for your financial future.

GusVend@aol.com
Westchester, New York

1

America Online: Filled with Facts, Opinions, and Opportunity

To get the most from America Online, you'll want to avoid wandering from one menu choice to another. This chapter will help you find the resources that can make you a better manager of your finances—and your online time.

America Online appeals to millions of people for millions of different reasons. Some users spend hours meeting new people, reading the news, and keeping up with hobbies. There are thousands of screens that are filled with millions of words, not to mention tens of thousands of graphics. It's fun, fascinating, and you can come away feeling renewed.

But when you're thinking about managing your own money, most areas within the service will seem like a distraction. Whether you're researching an investment opportunity or planning a major purchase, you don't want to be entertained as you find the hard facts that can help you make a decision.

In Chapters 3 through 15, you'll learn about the online services you can use to accomplish specific tasks. You'll find detailed instructions on how to find the right information quickly and advice on how to use it once you've got it. Chapter 2 explains spreadsheet techniques you can use to make the most of that information (and in the following chapters, you'll find some examples of spreadsheets you can download or build yourself to help with financial decisions). After you've finished your financial chores—quickly and efficiently—you'll be free to enjoy the rest of America Online (AOL), without feeling guilty.

This chapter will show you how to use America Online itself, concentrating on the features you'll use in your personal financial journey. You'll learn the basic techniques for using:

◆ E-mail

◆ Message boards

◆ Newsgroups

◆ Chat rooms

◆ AOL's Web browser

And you'll learn about some tips on how to squeeze more out of your online time, so you can keep your monthly bill low.

If you're an experienced AOL user, this chapter will cover some old ground but you'll learn some new tricks. The chapter is organized to make it easy for you to skim through and find the tips, without getting bogged down in instructions you don't need.

If you're new to AOL, this chapter will teach you everything you need to know as you improve your personal finances with information you'll learn online.

Starting with the Right Version

When you first begin to use America Online, you receive the software on a disk. You follow the simple

setup instructions to install the software on your hard disk, and from then on, you can forget about the software and just log on by clicking the AOL icon.

Occasionally, when you enter a new area, you'll see a message telling you that you need new software before you can use this area and that AOL is ready to download it now. If you agree, AOL begins the download process and automatically updates files on your hard disk all at one time. If you decline, (in Version 3.0) these updates will take place in the background as you move from screen to screen.

Even if you accept these offers to upgrade, that doesn't necessarily mean you are using the current version. America Online updates its software every few months with a major new edition. In the weeks following the upgrade, you will see invitations to download this major upgrade but you may decline; many people read the message that says the download process will take about 20 minutes and decide to pass on the offer.

▼ TIP

When you or another family member first start using AOL, be sure to read the help files on the Members menu under Member Services. It's free; AOL turns off connect charges while you read through the articles here.

If you fail to update your AOL software with a major upgrade, you'll miss out on some of the improvements to the system, and you may not be able to use all of the functions.

How To Upgrade Your AOL Software

Before you upgrade, you need to know which version of the software you're running. The following steps will show how to find out your current version number and then guide you to the Upgrade Center. Even if you just joined AOL, using disks that arrived in the mail or in a magazine, you should go through this process to be certain you installed the most current release:

1. After AOL has connected, you'll see the opening display. Move your mouse to the menu bar that runs along the top of the screen. Click Help; a menu drops down.

2. Click the About America Online option. A box opens, displaying the current version number. Figure 1.1 shows the box that displays under Windows 3.0. On a Mac, you select About America Online under the Apple menu option. (For the most precise details on the version, press Ctrl+R while the version number is open; you'll see more specific information about the software version.)

3. Note the version number and select OK or press the Enter key to close the About box. Now that you know the version of your software, you can check to see if AOL has released a higher version.

4. Connect to AOL by double-clicking the AOL icon. When the AOL software loads, enter your password and click the Sign On button.

5. Select Members, Member Services from the main menu. The screen shown in figure 1.2 opens.

6. On this menu, you'll find the AOL Software Upgrade icon. You won't find it on the list of services; the icon is sitting on the menu as shown in figure 1.2. Click this icon and a menu will open with information about the latest version.

7. If the version number is higher than the one you are running, select Download Now. You'll see detailed instructions on the steps you need to take in transferring the file to your computer and installing it to replace the AOL software already on your hard disk. You may want to make notes because AOL does not provide a way to print these steps.

FIG. 1.1

Be sure to use the latest version of AOL software; select the Help, About command to see which version you're running.

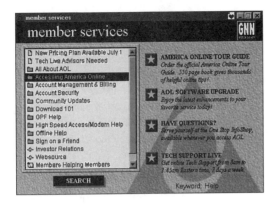

FIG. 1.2

AOL's Member Services can answer many of your questions, including whether you're running the most recent version of the software.

You'll have the option of downloading the file now or downloading later. If you choose to download now, AOL will suspend your connect charges while the file is transferred. After the download is finished, AOL will turn the meter back on, and you can continue to use AOL; you can complete the upgrade process at your convenience after you log off. If you choose to download later, you can use AOL services. When you decide to sign off, AOL will give you the option of transferring the file; however, connect charges will not be suspended during the download. After the file is downloaded, AOL will disconnect on its own.

To complete the installation, you need to exit from the AOL software and run the setup program that you downloaded; refer to the instructions that appeared online (see Step 7 above).

Why Things Slow Down When You Visit a New Area

One of the common woes of all AOL users is the "art download"—get a group of AOL users in a room, and within five minutes, someone will be complaining about "all of those art downloads." The problem is that all of those colorful pictures you see sprinkled throughout the system must move from AOL's computers to yours. When you first visit an area, the pictures are transferred and stored on your hard disk so that they can display faster on repeat visits. (Your computer can find and load images much faster if they're already sitting on your hard disk and if your computer doesn't have to transfer them from AOL's computers miles away.) So, art downloads won't get in your way every time you log on, only when you visit a new area. The art is essential to using the system; while a few of the graphics are decorative, many are essential icons that you'll use to navigate the system.

Some of the art is transferred without any notice, but when you use a service that has created a lot of pictures to illustrate its area, you will be asked whether you want to download the art all at once, as shown in figure 1.3.

It's nice of them to ask, especially because AOL will suspend your connect charges during this process. If you are hesitant about visiting this new area (you were curious about what's available here but you don't think you'd ever return), then select the Continue option. Connect charges will not be suspended when the art is downloaded. Art will download screen by screen, but you won't have to wait for everything to be downloaded at once.

▼ **TIP**

If your computer has a sound card and speakers, AOL will alert you when a file download is complete so you can turn your attention elsewhere while waiting; the computer will call to you when you can continue using AOL. Be sure Event Sounds are turned on from the menu under Members, Preferences, General.

The connect charges you save for the typical "free art download" are only pennies. If you may just visit this new area briefly and never return, you end up with several kilobytes worth of data on your hard disk that you never used. Don't be concerned about losing all of your hard disk space to the downloads; AOL sets a limit on the amount of space it uses. You can see this limit and adjust it from the command under Members, Preferences, Graphics.

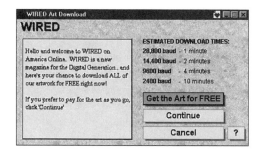

FIG. 1.3

Art for free: AOL suspends connect charges when you visit a new area that requires a large amount of graphic files.

Another reason you may have to wait when you visit a new area is a feature known as "tool on demand." In this case, the first time you visit a new area, AOL downloads the software code that you need to display the special menus and to perform certain calculations. For example, the first time you visit the stock-quote service or select the option to chart a stock's historical performance, AOL needs to download new software. This is done automatically without any option on how the files are transferred.

When AOL suspends connect charges, you'll see the message box shown in figure 1.4.

The message is necessary because you can be in several areas of AOL at once. For example, you can open the Web browser or visit a chat room while you're reading articles in a magazine section. When these free transfers are performed, AOL will close the Web browser or chat room software, and you'll need to start them again after the transfer is performed and connect charges are being levied again.

FIG. 1.4

Free software on the way: when you see this message, AOL is turning off the meter while it delivers new software.

Finding Your Way Around

AOL is designed to be easy to use. Click here, click there, and you're speeding around the service. Over time, you'll figure out how it's organized, but you'll spend hours wandering through one diversion after another. To quickly find the services you want to use, you'll need to understand the grand structure. Throughout the book, you'll learn time-saving tips. Efficiency begins just as soon as the meter starts running.

First Stop: A Hearty Welcome

The first screen you'll see every time you connect is the Welcome menu. If you have a sound board and speakers, you'll also hear a pleasant voice adding an audio greeting, too. If you have the proper hardware but don't hear "Welcome" when you log in or any other sounds from AOL, it's possible someone turned off sounds on your AOL setup. To see whether sound is turned on, select Members, Preferences, General. A check mark should appear next to Enable Event Sounds. If that doesn't fix the problem, check the speaker volume control and your operating system control panel for sound.

One of the first time-saving devices you'll want to employ is to check the status of your mail by reading the mailbox flag on the Welcome window. The mailbox flag is up (as shown in fig. 1.5) when you

FIG. 1.5

The Welcome screen tempts you to new diversions, but it can save time: when the flag's up, mail's in. No flag, no mail.

have mail waiting; click the mailbox and you can see a list of messages.

If the flag is not up, then you're only wasting your connect time by looking for new messages.

When you're interested in exploring AOL, an efficient way to get started is to select the What's Hot button that appears on the Welcome screen. When you select this button, you'll see a list of new services that have been added or updates made, as shown in figure 1.6.

Viewing this list is a good way to find new offerings that may interest you. The descriptions of the changes sound like advertisements, but don't let that turn you off. It's more efficient to read a summary of the newest offerings than to wander around looking for changes.

Beyond Welcome: The Channel View

If the Welcome menu is like the opening door to AOL, the Channels menu is like the main hallway of the house. From the Channels menu, you see the overall structure of the entire system. All of AOL's informational resources are represented here in logical categories, as shown in figure 1.7.

Until the most recent version, these buttons were listed on the main menu. With version 3.0, the channels moved to their own separate menu and a few

new channels were added (this is an example of the things you'll miss if you fail to upgrade to the current version). You can display the Channels menu by selecting the Channels button from the Welcome menu.

Just about all of the resources available for managing your money can be found on the Personal Finance channel; the Life, Styles & Interests channel has a few selections that can help in shopping for a car, electronic equipment, and other big purchases. And under Reference Desk, you'll find *Consumer Reports* and information that can help in shopping for a computer. Each of these services is covered in detail in later chapters.

FIG. 1.6

What's Hot on AOL? The monthly calendar has the answer.

FIG. 1.7

The Channels menu organizes all of AOL's informational resources into logical categories.

Keywords: The Fast Way To Travel Around AOL

Following the menu choices to find the services you're interested in is a good way to explore the territory, like a Sunday drive in the country. When you know where you're going, you can get there faster if you use the keyword command.

Keywords identify a specific area on AOL, and they're usually just one or two words long. For example, to find information about mutual funds, you can use the Personal Finance channel and scroll down the list on the main Personal Finance menu until you find The Mutual Fund Center.

But you'll get there faster if you use the keyword. Press Ctrl+K to open the Keyword menu. Then enter **mutual funds** as shown in figure 1.8. In a second, the Mutual Fund Center will open.

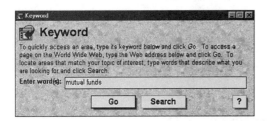

FIG. 1.8

Use the keyword command to cut through AOL's structure and open an online service quickly.

Keywords can be used for areas within AOL and on the Internet. When you use an Internet address for a Web site, an FTP site, or a Gopher server, AOL will load the browser and display that site. For example, to display the Web site where you can find the spreadsheets discussed in this book, use the keyword

http://www.mcp.com/que/desktop_os/ money

Many keywords are easy to remember. For example, **quotes** is the keyword to display AOL's stock quote service. Some areas have more than one keyword. For example, to find the U.S. Treasury Securities area, you can use **treasury bonds**, **treasury bills**, or **savings bonds**.

■ N O T E

Strictly speaking, a "keyword" refers only to the services provided by America Online, but the keyword command works the same way in displaying resources on the public Internet. To simplify the process of finding information, throughout this book Internet addresses are referred to as keywords.

With so many available services providing so much information, you can often find something just by trying different keywords. The following shows the resources you'll find when you use some common personal finance terms:

Keyword	AOL area
consumer	*Consumer Reports* maga-zine
markets	News summaries on major financial markets
money	Personal Finance main menu
mutual funds	Mutual Fund Center
stocks	Quotes & Portfolios

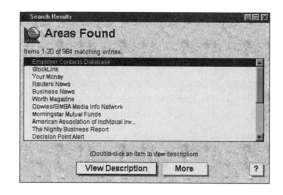

FIG. 1.9

The Search command may give you more than you bargained for.

Searching: An Imperfect Tool for Finding Information

While a keyword will often find a service on AOL, it may not show you exactly what you were looking for. And when some common financial terms are used as keywords, the results can be misleading (for example, "bonds").

One way to keep on digging is the Search option on the Keyword dialog box. You can search for any term by entering Ctrl+K to display the Keyword dialog box. After you type in a term, click Search. AOL will display a list of all the areas which mention this search term and the description that AOL maintains on the area.

Searching for a common term can display more information than you might want to see. For example, figure 1.9 shows the results of searching for "stocks"—964 areas within AOL were found.

And when you use a term that is a bit less common, you may be surprised at the results. A search on "bonds" for example, displays seven areas, including a few that have nothing to do with financial bonds, such as Electronic Schoolhouse. Further examination reveals that the description of Electronic Schoolhouse mentions, "the bonds that tie generation to generation."

Don't assume that the information you want is not available on AOL if you don't find it with the Search command. If the description in AOL's files of the area does not contain the words you enter at the Search command, it won't be listed with the search results. The information may be available on AOL with a slightly different description. Be persistent and try to rephrase your query.

Finding Text in a Document

Once you begin to read documents in a specific area, you may find you've got more than you bargained for. It's not uncommon to feel overwhelmed by the sheer volume of information in front of you.

The Find command can spare you from wading through a lot of text you don't care about. Any time a document is displayed in a window—for example a posted message in a message board, or an article in a news area—you can use the Find command to highlight a specific word or phrase:

1. Display the document you want to search.

2. Choose Edit, Find in Top Window. The Find dialog box opens.

3. Enter the word or phrase you want to find. If you are looking for a name or word where case

matters, click the Match Case box (for most searches, you'll get better results without checking this box). Select the Find button.

4. If the text is in the document, it will be highlighted, and the Find button will change to Find Next, as shown in figure 1.10. If you want to search again, click the Find Next button. If the text is not in this document, the message The text you entered was not found will be displayed.

Keeping What You Find

When you display a message or article you want to keep, you have the option of printing it or saving it to a disk on your system. Not everything you see online can be printed or saved, only information presented as text or pictures. You can not print

FIG. 1.10

Whenever text appears in a window, you can use Find to locate a word or phrase.

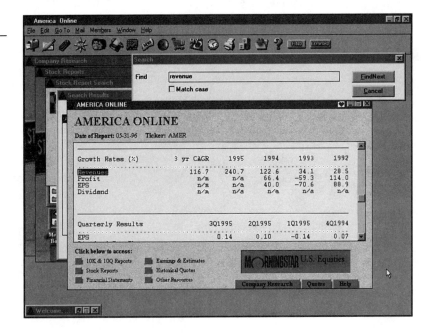

menus, including the graphics or lists of articles and files that appear on menus.

There are times when you won't be sure whether the contents of a window can be printed or saved. The only way to know for sure is to try and do it. Select File to open the file menu and then select either Print or Save.

If Print works, you'll see a Print dialog box that allows you to set the options for your printer.

If Save works, you'll be asked to confirm the file name and folder where the information will be stored.

If neither one works, you'll see a message box that reports: You must display text or a picture before using this function.

▼ T I P

Keep track of what you download so you'll be able to find it when you're offline. When you download a file, AOL stores it in a download folder within the AOL software directory. When you use the File, Save command to store a text document, your system will select the default folder but you should select a folder where you keep similar files.

You have one option but it's not a perfect solution. You can capture the entire contents of the screen to the system clipboard by pressing the Print Screen key. You can then paste the image into an application that can display graphics. Or you can do what I did in writing this book—use a screen capture program. You can download a shareware screen capture program from AOL's Computers & Software Channel.

Enter the Software Center and perform a search for "screen capture" to see a list of the programs available.

Retracing Your Steps— Quickly

Whether you use keywords or hunt through the menus to find services, you'll want to save the location with a shortcut for resources that you use often. AOL provides two ways to create a shortcut: the Go To menu and Favorite Places.

AOL's language in describing the two types of shortcuts may confuse you. You'll find the term "favorite places" used for the Go To menu and the separate Favorite Places menu; the two are not connected. You record and use each type of shortcut separately.

Go To Menu: Pull Down and Go

TheGo To Menu is a way to use shortcuts that will appeal to people who like using keyboard combinations. Press Alt+G to display the Go To menu and you'll find a list of popular online sites, including the online clock (which tells you how long you've been connected), the channels menu, and a list of services that you can choose.

When you install the AOL software, a number of sites have been recorded on the Go To menu but you can replace or add to these default sites with any you prefer.

FIG. 1.11

You can record the sites that will appear on the Go To menu by using keywords for sites inside AOL and on the Internet.

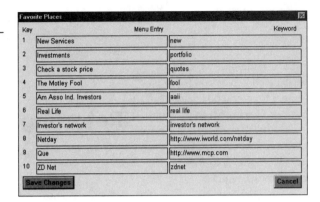

Key	Menu Entry	Keyword
1	New Services	new
2	Investments	portfolio
3	Check a stock price	quotes
4	The Motley Fool	fool
5	Am Asso Ind. Investors	aaii
6	Real Life	real life
7	Investor's network	investor's network
8	Netday	http://www.iworld.com/netday
9	Que	http://www.mcp.com
10	ZD Net	zdnet

Favorite Places

Save Changes   Cancel

Select Go To, Edit Go To Menu and a dialog box will open that allows you to edit the default places with your own selections. Figure 1.11 shows the dialog box after it was edited with the author's favorites.

On the left side, under Menu Entry, enter a description you want to see when the Go To Menu is used. You don't need to be limited to the official name, for example, My Portfolio, and you can use up to 30 characters. On the right side, you can enter any keyword including locations inside AOL or Internet addresses. An easy way to record the location of an Internet address is to press the right mouse button when you have displayed a site you want to record; a menu will open that gives you the Copy URL to Clipboard option. Select this option and then select Go To, Edit Go To Menu. Select the box where you want to record the keyword and select Copy, Paste. The correct keyword will be displayed.

The Go To Menu is easy to use but you can only record up to 10 sites at a time.

Favorite Places: An Expanding Folder

The Favorite Places folders performs the same job as the Go To menu, but it offers a number of advantages. You can record hundreds of sites, and you can organize the sites into folders. For example, in writing this book I created folders for each chapter. Inside a folder are sites that have information on a specific topic (see fig. 1.12).

Also, you can keep the folder open constantly and use it as a device for managing your online time. Once you've recorded the sites you like to see often, you can use it as a kind of road map so you'll be more efficient when you're online. Instead of rummaging through the Channels menus, you'll be able to quickly visit the sites you want to see if the Favorite Places folder is guiding your travels. In order to see other windows while the Favorite Places window is open, you may need to adjust the size of the window. Move your mouse to the edge of the Favorite Places window and it will become a sizing pointer; hold down the left mouse button and drag the border until the window is a better size. At times, you'll want to minimize it so it doesn't obscure the rest of the screen.

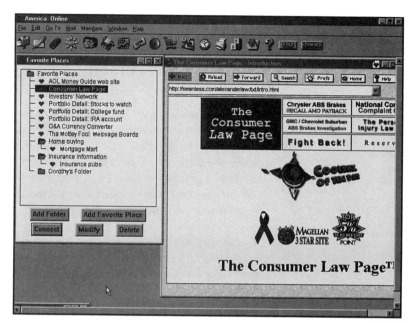

FIG. 1.12

You can create folders within your list of favorite places to help you stay organized.

You can open the Favorite Places folder by clicking the Folder icon on the AOL toolbar or by selecting Go To, Favorite Places from the pull-down menu. When the Favorite Places window is open, select the Add Favorite Place button to record either a site on America Online or on the Internet. As described previously for the Go To menu, an easy way to record sites on the Internet is to copy the site address (URL) to the clipboard by using the right mouse button.

You can also add a section to your favorite places whenever you see a Heart icon in the upper right corner of the window. Click this heart and the keyword will be added to your list of favorite places. (If your system plays sound events, you'll hear a "dropper" sound as this favorite place is dropped onto your collection.)

Creating a folder inside the main Favorite Place folder is easy; all you need to do is highlight the Favorite Places folder first and select the Add Folder button. Enter the name of the folder you want, then click OK. Then you highlight the new folder and select Add Favorite Places to insert items into the folder, or you can drag existing favorite places to the new folder. But placing the folder exactly where you want it is a little tricky. Be sure your cursor has selected the correct item or folder before you select the Add Folder button.

To create a folder that appears on the list of folders in the main folder directory, select the first item in the folder, Favorite Places, before you add a folder. But if you want your new folder to appear inside an existing folder, select an item inside the folder before you add the new folder. You can customize the names of places at any time. Highlight either the folder or favorite place item and select the Modify button. Enter a new name and click OK.

Customizing Your AOL Preferences

America Online gives you some control over your account and the way you're identified. You can select:

◆ A screen name to identify you to other members

◆ A password to protect access to your account

◆ A profile to describe your interests to other members

Each of these options can be changed by selecting Members, My AOL from the main menu (see fig. 1.13).

FIG. 1.13

The My AOL menu lets you control access to your account and the way others will see you.

A Screen Name Is Who You Are When You Want To Be That Person

Your first decision when you install AOL is to choose a screen name. This collection of letters or numbers is how you will be identified in e-mail, on message boards, and in chat rooms. Most of us can't use our real name: a screen name is limited to ten characters. And with over five million members already registered, many screen names are already claimed.

You were probably unprepared to select the perfect descriptor when you chose your screen name. You didn't know the question was coming, and after umpteen attempts, you ended up accepting AOL's suggestion of "mary2785."

If you want to try to claim a name that suits you better, you can create another screen name. The first name will remain on record but you'll have a choice of which name you use when you log in. You may want to have one name to use when you participate in chat rooms and another you'll use when you do your financial research.

Who Has the Name You Want?

Normally when you create a name, it's a matter of trial and error; if you choose a name that's taken, AOL will suggest a variation but it doesn't show you what else is available.

Now that you're an AOL member, you can do a little homework before you try to claim an identity that suits you better:

1. Connect to AOL and select Members, Member Directory. A menu of Member Directory options will open.

2. Select Search the Member Directory. A dialog box opens.

3. Enter the name you'd like to use and select the Search button. In a second, you'll see a list of people whose names include those characters. Figure 1.14 shows the results of searching for John Doe.

4. If the list is too long to fit in a single window, AOL will display only the first 20 matches. If you want to see all of the results, click the More button repeatedly until all are displayed. Then, you can scroll down to see the entire list.

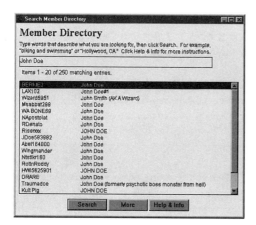

FIG. 1.14

You can find out if a name's already being used from the Member Directory.

The Member Directory shows you matches on more than the screen name. It also shows you people who use the name in their profile. Normally, the name used in a profile is displayed only when a user chooses to view another member's profile, so if the name is used only in the second column, it should still be available as a screen name.

Few people will know your real name, even if you do decide to record it in your profile; it will only be seen when another member displays your profile or searches through the member directory.

Creating Your New Identity

While it's easy to create a new screen name, keep in mind that the first name you selected will always be retained in AOL's records as the primary name (also called a master screen name) for the account. AOL will consider this to be the account holder. Screen names are designed to allow each member of a family to have a unique e-mail identity with unique settings, but an individual can choose to use different screen names for your own account.

You can create up to five screen names, but you must always log in with the primary name to create a new name or delete one of your additional names.

There are a few restrictions on the name you can claim. It must be 10 characters or less, it cannot be obscene, and a few prefixes are off limits. For example, screen names that begin with CAT are reserved for AOL staff members who work on the Community Action Team.

Here's how to add a new screen name:

1. Connect to AOL with your primary name.

2. Select Members, My AOL. The My AOL menu will appear, as shown in figure 1.13.

3. Select the button Set Up AOL Now; a menu will open with a list of choices.

4. Select Screen Names; the dialog box will change. Select Set Up Now. A dialog box will open, as shown in figure 1.15.

5. Enter the name you want to use and click the Create a Screen Name button.

6. If the name is accepted by AOL, you'll see a dialog box that asks you to enter a password that will be assigned to this screen name. If the name is already in use, AOL will suggest an alternate by changing the characters in the dialog box shown in figure 1.15. If you're willing to accept this suggestion, click the Create a Screen Name button and AOL will record the name. Otherwise, you should edit the name that appears in the box and select Create a Screen Name. You may need to repeat this process several times until you can find a name you're willing to live with.

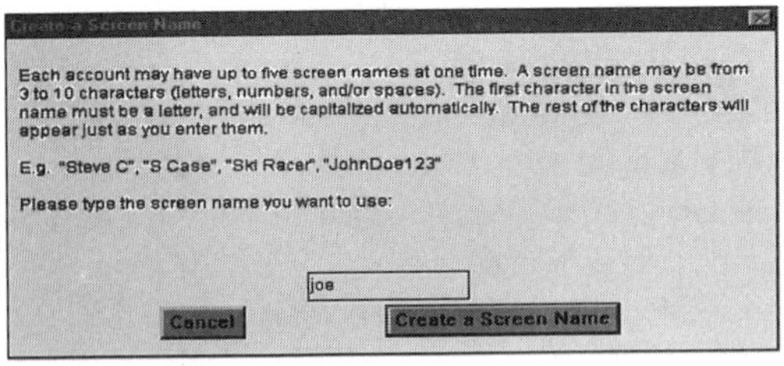

FIG. 1.15

Creating a screen name can be a process of trial and error.

You may need to be a little creative in how you enter the name. People create abbreviations by eliminating a vowel (for example, WiseGy). The easiest way to find a close match is to add a number to the name you want.

After a screen name is created, your Sign On screen will be updated. To log in under the new name, select File, Exit. A dialog box will give you the option to Sign Off or Exit. Select Sign off and AOL will disconnect but you'll then see the Sign On menu. Your new screen name will appear on the list of names.

Controlling Your Password

You must enter a password when creating a new screen name, but you may change the password later. For example, you could create an account for your spouse using a password you select, and then, when your spouse logs on, he or she can change it. Security experts recommend changing passwords routinely to safeguard your account.

To change your password, log on to AOL and enter the keyword **password**. You'll need to enter your old password before you can change it.

▼ **T I P**

When you're online, never ever reveal your password or credit card information. America Online has a policy of never asking members for this information while online. Only scam artists would ever ask for personal information.

Online Profiles: A Few Words About Yourself

Many AOL members never enter a profile for themselves. For the most part, it's never missed. But if you enter chat rooms, your online profile can be the difference between becoming the life of the party and remaining a wallflower. People who want to know a bit about you will read your profile; if something piques their interest, a conversation will start. And if you become an active participant in a message board, people will look for your profile. Creating the right profile will help you meet people who share your interests.

Profiles are always available for viewing by any member who looks for it. You can view a profile by selecting Members, Get a Member's Profile. A dialog box will ask for the name. Enter and select Go. The profile will display, as shown in figure 1.16.

Because it's easy to make a mistake when you type in a member's screen name, you may want to use copy and paste to grab someone's screen name. For example, if you're in a message board and decide you would like to know more about a message's author,

highlight the name, and select Edit, Copy. The name will now be in your system clipboard; select Get a Member's Profile and paste the name in the dialog box that appears.

To say a few words about yourself in a member profile, select Members, My AOL and click the Be Seen button. Choose the option Member Profile, then the Go There button and the menu choice Create/Edit Your Member Profile. You complete the profile by entering text in each box. Keep in mind that few people take the questionnaire seriously; have fun with it. Once you create an online profile, you can return to this menu to change it.

After you create the profile, you may occasionally want to visit a chat room without announcing your occupation and hobbies. The solution is to create a new screen name and log on in relative anonymity.

A few caveats: avoid revealing personal information in a profile that could be used by a scam artist. As a rule, always be general in revealing personal information while online. For example, enter your town, but not your street address. If your children have a separate account, be sure they are not revealing any personal information that could be used by someone trying to make personal contact.

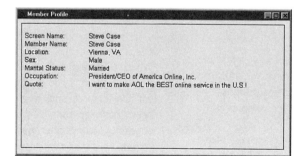

FIG. 1.16

AOL's president sets a good example. His profile is on file for anyone on AOL to read.

Sharing Opinions and Viewpoints with Other Members

Many people cite socializing as one of their most rewarding online activities. While much online talk is idle or purely social, many conversations are absolutely serious. Investor chats occur nightly (look for them in the Motley Fool area, under PF chat and elsewhere). And a number of message boards are devoted to specific personal finance topics. In later chapters, you'll learn where to find conversation suited to specific purposes, but the following pages will explain the techniques you can use to get the most from your talk time.

Chat Rooms: Live and Uncensored

A chat room can be many things: a party, a meeting around the water cooler, or a group of strangers passing the time. You can always find a chat, no matter what time of day, by selecting the People Connection button on the Welcome menu or by clicking the People Connection icon at the top of the screen.

You won't find many topics where people talk about their finances from this option, however; most chats revolve around purely social and sexual topics. On the main menu for Personal Finance (keyword: **money**) you'll find a listing for Personal Finance Chat Rooms. You'll also find Personal Finance oriented topics listed on the menus of personal finance areas. For example, the Motley Fool and Real Life menus

include chat options; the chats are usually scheduled for evening hours. You can enter these chat rooms at any time, but they're usually empty until the scheduled chat time nears.

When you enter chat through the People Connection menu, you'll find more casual conversation. When you first enter the Chat area this way, you will find yourself in the Lobby, with other AOL members who have just selected the People Connection icon. Most people go on to choose a more specific area using the List Rooms command on this menu. The List Rooms command shows dozens of chat areas devoted to specific topics about lifestyle issues.

Any AOL member can create a room with any topic he or she chooses; on a typical day, hundreds of members have done this. However, these member rooms are usually for sexually oriented conversations. You'll find them by choosing the Member Rooms option after you select List Rooms. Figure 1.17 shows a busy chat room and a list of member rooms.

▼ **T I P**

If you're new to chat rooms and a child shares the account, be sure to explore the People Connection at your first opportunity and decide whether you want to restrict your children's access to this area. You can do that by selecting Members, Parental Controls, Custom Controls.

When you enter a chat room, you'll immediately see a chat room, similar to the one in figure 1.17. But it will take a few seconds for the conversation to appear. Chat happens in real time with comments appearing seconds after the participants type the comments at their own keyboard. You'll need to wait a minute or two until the most recent comments arrive on your system.

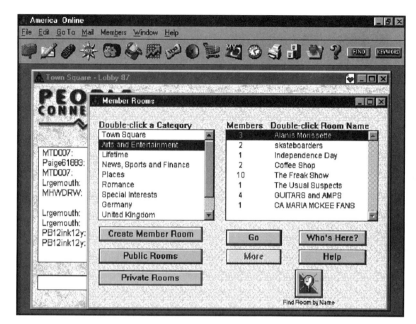

FIG. 1.17

Anyone on AOL can create a Member Room where the public is invited to chat about anything.

While you wait, you'll want to see who's checked in. On the right side of the chat window, a list displays the screen names of everyone who's participating. Before deciding whether you want to stick around, you may want to learn a little more about who's here. Highlight a name and double-click. A dialog box, shown in figure 1.18, will open to give you the option of sending a private message to this person or displaying the person's profile.

FIG. 1.18

To see who you're talking with in a Chat room, double-click the name and then Get Info.

Select Get Info and you'll see the person's online profile, if one has been created. Select Message and a dialog box will open, giving you the opportunity to begin a private conversation. Type a message in this dialog box, shown in figure 1.19.

When the message is entered, click Send and the other party will be notified that they have received an instant message. Don't be offended if you don't receive an answer. In a busy chat room, the other party may already be engaged in one or two other private conversations.

While instant messages are normally sent between parties in chat rooms, you can send one to anyone who's currently online by selecting Members, Send an Instant Message. If the other party is not connected to AOL, you'll receive a message back reporting that the member is not currently signed in.

FIG. 1.19

Sending an instant message begins a private conversation that only two parties can see.

Message Boards: Recorded and Moderated

To get answers to a question that's puzzling you, few modern inventions can match the message board. When you find a message board that attracts people who are knowledgeable in a field, you're able to find information that you'd have no way of finding elsewhere.

You may not always get the answers you're seeking, but you often will. Because message boards focus only on a specific subject, the people who read the messages are truly interested in the topic. As long as you take the trouble to find the message boards where your interests are discussed and spend a few minutes learning how to use them, you'll find that a wealth of knowledge is available.

Participating in a message board doesn't take much time. You can read and post messages in minutes. But you can't expect to receive an answer immediately. It may take days before someone responds to a question.

And while asking a specific question is one benefit of using message boards, another benefit is to gain a perspective that you wouldn't be able to gain

elsewhere. Message boards where a particular investment is discussed can help you decide whether you should buy, sell, or hold since some of the other participants are also people with an interest in that same investment. Be sure to keep in mind that some people may be posting misleading information in the hope of moving a stock price for their own personal gain. For example, someone who is hoping to sell a stock short will make disparaging remarks about a stock in the hopes of driving the price down. Others who own the stock will make overly positive remarks in the hopes of pushing the price up. You can gain valuable insight from a message board, as long as you use common sense.

You won't find a central list of message boards anywhere on AOL. To find boards that address a topic, first, enter a specific area and choose the message boards from the menu options. For example, if you're thinking about buying a sailboat, go to the Sailboat forum (keyword: **sailing**); if you're looking for help in investing, go to the Investor's Network (keyword: **investor's network**). Almost every resource within AOL maintains its own message boards. Throughout the book, you'll find specific discussions on many of these message boards.

Once you choose the message board option in an AOL area, you're likely to be confronted with a choice of many individual folders. Some busy areas have hundreds of message folders, and within each folder there are hundreds of individual messages. Some of the most popular areas have large groupings of message boards organized into folders.

When you display the main menu of the Investors' Network, for example, you see a list of more than 20 individual message boards, plus a separate main message board. Select one of these message boards and you'll find a long list of topics. The General Investment Topics message board has 50 topics, as shown in figure 1.20.

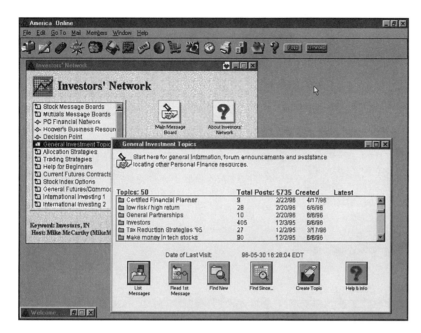

FIG. 1.20

FIG. 1.20

In a busy area, you'll find hundreds of topics; the Investors' Network has more than 20 message boards, and each one has dozens of topics.

Finding Information in a Message Board

When you first visit a board, you have plenty of reading material. But once you've caught up with the old messages, you can read only the newest material.

You navigate through message boards by selecting menu choices. Once you select a board, you'll be asked to choose between browsing through the folders or finding new messages (see fig. 1.21).

You'll need to browse folders in order to get a sense of what's talked about within. Some message boards have dozens of different folders, as shown in figure 1.20. Some message boards are so crowded that there are folders within folders. The Motley Fool, Investor's Network, and Company Research keep

individual message boards for hundreds of stocks, and when you select the stock boards, you first need to pick from alphabetical groupings before you see the board for a specific stock.

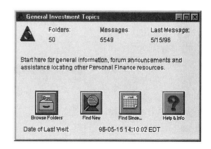

FIG. 1.21

When you visit a board, you have a choice between browsing all folders or finding only files posted within a certain number of days.

After you become familiar with the topics in a message board, you'll want to limit your reading to only the newest messages the next time you return to the board. When you enter the message board and find the dialog box displayed in figure 1.21, instead of browsing folders, select Find Since. The dialog box in figure 1.22 will appear.

You can enter any number (up to 99) but normally you'd enter the number of days since your last visit, counting back from today. You may not remember the date of your last visit, but AOL does; it displays the date (and time) on the menu that displays the list of topics. If you've posted a question and have come back in search of answers, you'll want to enter the date of your last visit.

▼ **T I P**

When you use the Find New and Find Since commands, you are limiting the messages you'll see in the folders that appear below your current selection. Be sure you've selected the folder you want to read before you select either option.

Once you've entered the number of days to count back, click Search. You'll see a list of messages that have been posted on the board since that date, as shown in figure 1.23.

FIG. 1.22

You can avoid seeing old messages by using the Find Since command in a message board.

FIG. 1.23

Once you've decided on how many days' worth of postings to read, you can scan through the subject of each message and the screen name of the person who posted it.

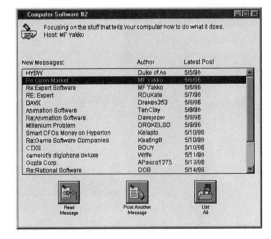

Take note of which topic you've selected before you select Find Since. If there are more topics nested below this topic, Find Since will display the messages posted in all of the folders below.

Whenever you have a list of messages—whether you're reading all messages or only messages posted after a certain date—you can choose to read only messages that seem interesting, or you can read one after the other.

To read a specific message, double-click the message and it will be displayed. When you're finished, close the window by clicking the close window button in the upper right corner.

To read the messages sequentially, select the Next Message button. After you've read a message, you can return to earlier messages by clicking the Previous Message button.

After you've visited a message board once, the next time you return you may want to use Find New. AOL software records the exact time of your visit to a message board. When you select this option, you'll see only messages that have appeared since your last visit.

You can still read messages that appeared earlier. Once you start to read a message, select the Previous Message option. You will be able to read messages that were posted earlier, even if they were posted before your last visit (or below the period you selected with the Find Since command).

AOL Mail: One-on-One Communications

While message boards and chat rooms are a good way to cast a wide net when you want to hear what other people think, sending mail is the best way to be sure you're reaching someone. If you read a note someone has posted in a message board and you want to pursue the conversation in private, copy the person's screen name to the clipboard by highlighting the name and then selected Edit, Copy. And then compose a mail message and use Edit, Paste to insert the name into the To: field.

You can send mail to anyone on AOL by using the Mail, Compose Mail command. To check to see whether anyone has read your mail, choose Mail, Check Mail You've Sent; then highlight the item and choose Status along the bottom of the screen. You can even send files to another user and exchange mail with people who have mailboxes on other online services. You'll want to record the e-mail addresses of frequent correspondents, using the Address command.

To send a message to someone outside of AOL, you need their full e-mail address (a user named, followed by the @ character, followed by the name of their mail domain if they're using the Internet or the name of the e-mail service). For example, to send a note to a friend with an Internet address, you might enter **gus@email.com**. (Internet mail systems do not distinguish between capital and lower case letters so there's no need to capitalize any of the letters in an e-mail address going to someone outside of America Online.)

To send a file with the mail system, use the Attach button in the Compose Mail box, as shown in figure 1.24.

When the Attach File dialog box opens, you can enter the name of the file if you want, but it's easier to use the dialog box to search through the files on your hard disk. You can send a file on any disk on your system.

While you are able to attach a file to any mail message, files sent outside of AOL may need to be converted with a uudecoding program when they're received. When AOL transfers messages to mail systems outside of AOL, it uses the MIME standard for transferring binary files. If the mail software receiving the message is compliant with the MIME standard, it should arrive in working order. But if the software used on your correspondent's system does not support this standard, the file is converted to the uucode format; your correspondent should be able to return the file to its original form by using a uudecoding utility.

Reaching the Internet from AOL

To judge by the AOL Channels menu, the Internet looks like it's just another group of services within AOL. In fact, the Internet is many times larger than AOL. Millions of pages of information are available on the World Wide Web; millions of messages are posted on Internet newsgroups, and hundreds of thousands of files are available for downloading from Internet FTP sites.

FIG. 1.24

When you attach a file to a mail message, you don't need to type in the name. You can search through the files on your system.

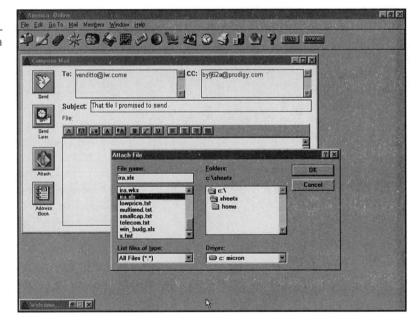

AOL allows you to reach any public site on the Web in two ways:

◆ The AOL Browser

◆ AOL's newsgroup reader

Throughout the book, sites within the Web and on newsgroups are discussed. If you're not familiar with the Internet, you should understand that the staff of AOL is only responsible for maintaining the quality of information within the AOL boundaries. AOL has no control over what's available on the Internet. AOL merely provides access to the public networks where these sites are located.

Internet Newsgroups

You'll find some of the most uninhibited, wide-ranging discussions you could imagine on Internet newsgroups. These newsgroups are similar to America Online message boards only in the sense that both are forums where messages are posted for all to read, and anyone who visits is welcome to respond either by e-mail or in a public message. But the similarities end there.

Most newsgroups do not have a moderator, or if there is a moderator, very little effort is made to control the types of messages being posted. As a result, just about anything goes on public newsgroups. Without a moderator, some newsgroup members feel free to insult other members. And even though a newsgroup is supposed to stick to a single topic, without a moderator, the discussion may wander around from subject to subject. A number of newsgroups are dedicated to distributing sexually oriented material or sharing dirty jokes; as a result, America Online gives members the ability to restrict access to either a particular newsgroup or all newsgroups.

▼ TIP

You can restrict newsgroup access for any user in your account by selecting Parental Controls on the main newsgroup menu (keyword: **newsgroup**).

There are over 20,000 newsgroups covering every topic imaginable, from the trivial to the serious. Many newsgroups are devoted to serious professional, scientific, and academic research, so you may want to review the list of topics. You could gain insight into your field by participating in a newsgroup that follows your specialty.

You can not reach every newsgroup available; while AOL gives members the ability to reach almost all newsgroups, some newsgroups are private and you need access to restricted servers. Also, some newsgroups on sexually explicit topics are not included on AOL's lists, although they can be accessed by typing in the newsgroup name with the Expert Add command.

AOL organizes access to all newsgroups in a central area (see fig. 1.25). Enter the keyword **newsgroups** to begin your journey into newsgroups.

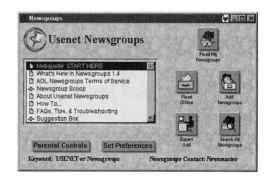

FIG. 1.25

You can reach all newsgroups from a central point on AOL.

The Newsgroup Hierarchy

Separating the meaningful from the trivial in newsgroups will be much easier when you understand the hierarchy. Newsgroups are organized into categories. Within the category, there may be a few groups or hundreds of groups that are divided into topics.

The most popular category, alt (for alternative), has 53 topics for "culture," including alt.culture.nudism, alt.culture.military-brats, and alt.culture.beaches.

Newsgroup names are punctuated with periods, with the category coming first, followed with the topic and any additional refinements to the topic. The naming system is for descriptive purposes only. For example, there's no real connection between the newsgroups called misc.invest.futures, misc.invest.stocks, and misc.invest.funds, aside from the fact that because some software programs allow users to post into several newsgroups simultaneously, you may find many of the same people participating in newsgroups covering a particular subject.

Occasionally, you may hear the term "usenet". Usenet was the original system for sharing messages in newsgroups, and it includes only a fraction of the many newsgroups that are now circulating on Internet news servers.

Subscribing to a Newsgroup

Before you can participate in a newsgroup, you need to "subscribe." The process of subscribing carries no obligation and incurs no extra cost. It simply means

that America Online will add the name of this newsgroup to a list that it keeps in your configuration. Once you've subscribed, you're free to view the list of subjects, read individual messages, respond to messages, or write new messages that others can read.

From the main newsgroups menu, you can read through the very long list of newsgroups by selecting the Add Newsgroup button or search for newsgroups with a specific word in the group title by selecting the Search All Newsgroups button.

You'll want to use Expert Add when you know the name of a group, and in later chapters you'll learn about some good newsgroups for specific financial tasks. Select the Expert Add button and type in the name of the group, as shown in figure 1.26.

Once you've added the group, you can read through messages by selecting the Read My Newsgroups button. AOL always tracks the messages you've read in a newsgroup, and whenever you view the list of your newsgroups, AOL will display the total number of messages in the group and the number unread.

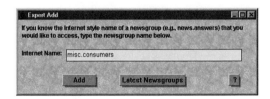

FIG. 1.26

Select the Expert Add button to begin reading messages in a newsgroup if you already know the name of the group.

You can go directly to any newsgroup with the keyword command. Enter **news:** followed by the name of the newsgroup. For example, if you use **news:misc.consumers** in the keyword dialog box, you will see the misc.consumers newsgroup.

The first time you view your groups, the same number will appear for both the total number in the group and the number unread. But when you return, you'll be able to gauge how many messages have been added to the group since your last visit. AOL gives you an option for "catching up" known as Mark All Read. You can use Mark All Read to save you from wading through all of the messages and waiting several minutes as over a thousand messages are transferred. You won't be able to read any of the old messages, but the next time you return, you'll have a more manageable number of messages.

When you select a newsgroup from your list, a window will display the current topics, showing the subject and the e-mail address of the person who wrote the message. Reading through newsgroups is similar to reading through message boards with a key difference. Newsgroup messages are organized into threads. When there is more than one message on a topic, you will see the number of messages on this subject, as shown in figure 1.27.

When you select a message in a thread, you will see the most recent posting, and the window will give you the option of reading the next message. The next message you read will be on the same subject, until you reach the end of this thread.

When you read messages in a newsgroup, you have the option of replying publicly so that everyone can read the message or replying by e-mail so that only the person who wrote this message will see your reply.

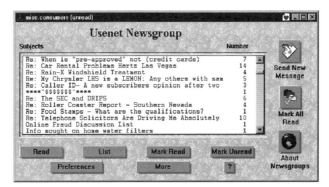

FIG. 1.27

Messages in newsgroups appear in threads; every message on the same subject can be read sequentially.

Browsing the Web

One of the richest areas available with your AOL account is the World Wide Web. Over 50 million pages are already available on the Web with millions more being added every month. Throughout the following chapters, you'll find discussions of many Web sites with valuable information for managing your finances.

▼ T I P

> The World Wide Web is open to anyone who wants to create a Web site. To create your own Web page, use the AOL keyword **personal publisher** and select the option Create/Edit My Home Page.

You can view pages on the Web in several ways. The easiest and most common technique is to use the AOL Web browser. This software is installed on your system the first time you access the Web. You may choose to use one of the other browsers on the market, but you'll have to put in a little extra work. The section "Switching Web Browsers" later in this chapter explains how to do it.

You can get a formal introduction to the Web by reading through the information available at AOL's Internet Connection (keyword: **internet**). Or you can jump right in simply by entering any of the dozens of Web addresses that appear through this book. Every time you see a keyword beginning with the letters "http://" in this book, the AOL browser will load and display the pages at the site.

Mastering the AOL Web Browser

Any time you enter a Web address in the AOL keyword command, a page on the Web is loaded and displayed by the AOL Browser (see fig.1.28).

One of the first things you'll want to do when you display a Web page is to maximize the browser by clicking the maximize button in the upper right corner of the browser window. You'll only see a small portion of most Web pages until you do this.

While you'll start from a single Web page, you can move to any other site on the Web without leaving this software. Most Web sites lead to other Web sites

FIG. 1.28

The AOL Web browser can display any page on the World Wide Web.

by including links; the most common way to move from one site to another is to select a link on a Web page. Any text that is underlined and appears in blue is a link; click this text and a different page or graphic will display. Many of the graphics on a Web page are also links; the only way to know if a graphic is a link is to move the mouse pointer to the graphic. If the arrow changes to a Hand icon, then this is a clickable image; click it and a different page will load.

▼ TIP

The AOL browser keeps track of which links you've selected. Links you've never selected appear in blue. Links you've selected at least once appear in purple.

A typical session with the Web browser will include many links to new sites, and so the icons that appear on the browser are designed to help you travel around the Web.

When you want to return to the last page you viewed, select the Back button in the upper left corner of the Web browser. The browser keeps track of all the pages you've visited since the browser loaded, and if you want to move ahead, select the Forward button. Some Web pages contain a lot of graphics, and they may take a long time to download. At times, you'll realize the page is not worth waiting for; click the Stop button and the browser will halt the download of this page.

You have a few other ways to display pages on the Web, other than clicking links. You can type the address of any Web site, FTP site, or gopher site in the location box which appears just below the Back button. If you know the address (often called URL for Uniform Resource Locator) of a Web page, this may be the fastest way to enter it. Be sure you include the

entire address, starting with the Internet protocol (http:// for Web pages, ftp:// for FTP sites, and gopher:// for gopher sites).

You can see a list of all the Web sites you've visited during this session by clicking the down arrow. Highlight one of these addresses and the browser will display the page. When you visit a Web site you want to remember, select the Heart icon that appears in the upper right corner of the browser window. The Web address will be added to your list of Favorite Places.

Fine-Tuning the Web Browser

You can improve the performance of the Web browser by turning off the downloading of graphics. You'll find most Web pages are displayed dramatically faster when you make this change. Select Prefs on the browser menu; the WWW Preferences dialog box, as shown in figure 1.29, will open.

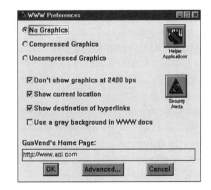

FIG. 1.29

You can speed up the AOL Web browser by turning off the display of graphic images.

After you've turned off graphics, you can move around the Web faster, but occasionally you'll find pages that you want to see in full. You can quickly turn graphics viewing back on to see these pages in full glory.

Select the Prefs window and click either Compressed Graphics or Uncompressed Graphics. Click OK to close the dialog box and select Reload on the browser. The page will now display with graphics. The two choices of graphics control how the graphics that are downloaded will appear during the download process. Select Compressed to display graphics gradually; select Uncompressed to wait until the entire graphic has been transferred before you see anything. This choice affects only graphics known as *interlaced*; most people prefer the compressed option since you can see a portion of the graphic more quickly.

Switching Web Browsers

Windows users can choose to replace the AOL browser with one of several browsers on the market, such as Netscape Navigator or Microsoft Explorer. But special software, known as a WINSOCK, may need to be configured. If you've upgraded your AOL software to the most current release and have never installed software for another Internet access program, you should be able to install another browser with a little extra effort. Be sure to install the correct type of browser for your system. For example, you may need to install a 16-bit version of the browser (many browsers are offered as 16-bit versions for Windows 3.1 and 32-bit versions for Windows 95).

Many systems will need to adjust the system configuration before a different browser will run. For example, if you are running Windows 95, a different

WINSOCK may have been installed that will cause conflict with AOL's version. Before you try to run a different browser, visit the Internet Connection, select World Wide Web, and read through the information about other browsers.

When you install a different Web browser, you'll need to switch out of AOL to open the browser. You won't be able to use AOL's keyword command to open Web sites with the new browser; using AOL's keyword with Web sites will load the AOL Web browser.

Different Browsers, Same Sites

Throughout this book, all resources on the Web are illustrated using the most recent version of the AOL browser (release 3.0). At some point, America Online will replace this browser. For the most part, there'll be very little difference in how you use these sites, and the descriptions of these sites throughout the book will not be affected in any significant way. The World Wide Web was designed to work with a wide variety of Web browser programs so the screens you see with the next version of the browser will be almost identical to figures in this book.

The reason AOL will be updating the browser is to gain access software being developed for the Web using Java and ActiveX. Aside from giving you access to these new applications, little is likely to change about the way you'll use the Web. Web addresses you save to your Favorite Places folder will still work. And the information you see in the browser window will be unchanged.

Keep in mind as you read the following chapters that pages on the Web change frequently. In most cases, the changes will be minor, and the information discussed in the book will still be there; many times when a Web site relocates, you'll find a link to the new location at the old address. If you do have difficulty locating a Web site mentioned in the book, enter this Web address in the AOL keyword command

http://www.mcp.com/que/desktop_os/ money/

This Web page will post updates to Web addresses mentioned in the book as they change.

2

Building Your Personal Finance Plan

Financial independence isn't an easy goal, but you're more likely to achieve it when you know how to crunch numbers like a financial expert.

If you're like most people, you've already made quite a few plans for your life. Some have already been realized, and others are still in development. You probably paid some attention to the place where you live. You certainly gave some thought to developing your career. And, if you're being completely honest, you'd admit to having worked out a strategy for finding the right spouse. That's at least three plans for controlling your own destiny. Maybe you didn't sit down at your computer and plan each step, but you did give some thought to how you would achieve your goals.

What about your personal finances? You plan well enough to make it from paycheck to paycheck, after all (maybe just barely some months). So you do have a plan. But do you have a strategy for investing your savings? Do you have goals or are you just hoping your next raise will put you on easy street? Do you even know how much you have saved or invested?

Whether you've already crafted an intricate investment plan or just have general goals (like having more money next year than you have today), a personal finance plan evolves with you over time and changes as your lifestyle changes. Some of the choices you make are based on your outlook. If you like to play it safe, you'll want to keep your money in savings accounts, certificates of deposit (CD), and money market funds. If you're willing to take risks, you'll pursue aggressive growth mutual funds and the stock of promising companies. Most of us will use some of each approach over time—usually a mixture of safe and aggressive investments. The fact is, over the course of your life, you should pursue a different strategy that helps you meet your goals.

A healthy financial plan is always in development. New investment opportunities, broad economic changes, and personal lifestyle choices all have an impact on our own strategies. One thing is certain, though. The world is not getting any simpler or safer, and the need to constantly evaluate your personal finance plan grows more important every day.

No one is qualified to make all of these decisions other than you. You can gain valuable advice from experienced investors, but no one shares your best interests other than the members of your family. In taking responsibility for your own future, you'll find it's a lot easier if you know how to make some of the calculations that experts make. America Online (AOL) delivers reams and reams of data and the regular doses of advice from financial experts, but to sort it all out, and compare it with your own situation, you'll need to use a spreadsheet.

In this chapter, we look at the fundamentals of personal finance, and see how you can use your subscription to America Online, a spreadsheet, and a few hours of your time to make progress on your current plan. And when your needs change, you'll be better equipped to make changes.

This chapter should help change your perspective so that when you browse among the hundreds of personal finance offerings on AOL, you'll be able to focus on the services that will help you increase your net worth. I can't tell you which stocks or mutual funds will make you rich, and I can't tell you which exact piece of information, out of the millions vying for your attention, are the most important for you to know. But I can show you how to use the available tools so you're thinking of your own personal finance goals.

From Simple Spreadsheets Come Great Things

You could spend a fortune on personal finance software without blinking an eye. Software stores have an entire section devoted to the category. There's Quicken to manage your checkbook. Managing Your Money to create an investment strategy. And a whole raft of other products for special needs. Most are good solid products (I couldn't live without Quicken). But the one tool you really should use is a spreadsheet. Chances are, you already own one. Most personal computers come with a spreadsheet either already installed or hiding somewhere inside the carton. Windows users who don't already have one can download a shareware spreadsheet from America Online's Software Center. (Unfortunately, Mac users won't find a shareware spreadsheet available for downloading from America Online, but you should be able to use any of the popular Mac spreadsheets for sale, such as Microsoft Excel or Claris Works).

To download the HOT spreadsheet, follow these steps.

1. Log on to AOL and enter the keyword **quickfind**.

2. When the Quickfind dialog box opens, enter **hotspred**.

3. A window will display the file listing for the HOT Spreadsheet. Select Download Now to begin the download process.

A spreadsheet is such a valuable tool in managing money, that if you haven't been using one to help you make financial decisions, you'll want to start right away. You don't need to become a wizard with formulas and macros to take advantage of a spreadsheet. Only basic arithmetic is needed to help you analyze most personal finance decisions. Once you take a few minutes to learn how to plug numbers into a spreadsheet and create simple equations, you'll find it's indispensable in helping you make big decisions.

Not only can a spreadsheet calculate spending totals to create a budget and compute percentages to estimate earnings on an investment, it can also show you a graphic representation of your financial situation. America Online offers financial data on many opportunities, and once you've downloaded them, you'll want help in finding the answers you need. You'll find it's much easier to use a spreadsheet's chart command to graph the numbers than to squint over rows and rows of numbers until you see a pattern. Graphing is available only with the commercial spreadsheets and is not provided by the shareware program, HOT Spreadsheet.

Choosing a Spreadsheet

Even though close to a dozen spreadsheet programs are on the market, each one is remarkably similar. One of the few differences is the file format used. Understanding file formats is essential in getting the most from your online time because data is distributed online—both on America Online and from Internet Web sites—in a few different formats.

You can use any spreadsheet program. While the example screens throughout this book show Microsoft Works, all of the spreadsheets will work in

Microsoft Excel, Microsoft Works, Claris Works, Lotus 1-2-3, or the shareware spreadsheet HOT Spreadsheet.

You can obtain a copy of the examples used throughout the book by downloading them from America Online. You'll be able to use the spreadsheets to help you make decisions by simply entering in figures and reading the results, without devoting much effort to the discussion of how the spreadsheets were constructed. But you'll be better equipped to create your own financial worksheets if you take the time to learn how each one was designed.

"Only basic arithmetic is needed to help you analyze most personal finance decisions."

▼ TIP

All of the spreadsheet files described in this book can be downloaded by using the keyword **http://www.mcp.com/que/desktop_os/money**. You can download the version that's best for your spreadsheet. Each file is available in the Lotus 1-2-3 WK1 format, the Microsoft Excel XLS format, and the Microsoft Works WKS format.

The way you use the spreadsheet is far more important than which one you use. When creating the type of spreadsheets you need to help you make basic personal finance decisions, all spreadsheets work in pretty much the same way. Most of the differences among the programs show up only when you delve into fancy formatting techniques and sophisticated analytical models. Managing your personal finances requires none of these fancy techniques.

One of these techniques, however, can make your use of online information more productive: Microsoft Works does not have the ability to parse text that you import. Parsing is a technique for converting text displayed in a table into spreadsheet columns that is described later in the chapter in the section "Analyzing Downloaded Data." If you're thinking of buying a new spreadsheet and you want to make the best use of online financial information, go for the higher priced brand (Excel or 1-2-3).

Spreadsheet Basics

Even if you've never created or edited a single spreadsheet, this section will tell you everything you need to know. While professional number crunchers have come up with some fairly creative uses for a spreadsheet, you'll be concentrating on just the classic designs for analyzing a financial situation. You start by learning how to create spreadsheets that track your monthly spending, and you learn the techniques needed to evaluate investment opportunities. Much of the financial information available on America Online is available for downloading onto

your system. Once you're comfortable with a spreadsheet, you'll be better equipped to whip it into shape for your own analysis. This short tour may be a slight over-simplification of a spreadsheet's powerful arsenal, but the goal is to help you get up and running quickly.

The main part of the spreadsheet is a grid where you store information in separate boxes, known as *cells*. A group of cells is known as a *range*. Cells that run from top to bottom are known collectively as a *column*. Cells that run in a line from left to right are called a *row*. Headers identify each column by letter and each row with a number, creating an "address" system. Each cell is named for both the column and row it's in, starting with A1 in column A and row 1; this name is known as the cell address. Figure 2.1 identifies the major spreadsheet elements with a screen capture from Microsoft Works, but the same principles are used in Lotus 1-2-3, Microsoft Excel, and HOT Spreadsheet.

A cell can hold either a number, a label that identifies those numbers, or a formula. Formulas are used to work some form of magic on the other cells. Spreadsheet formulas can provide statistical, logical, date,

FIG. 2.1

The major parts of a spreadsheet.

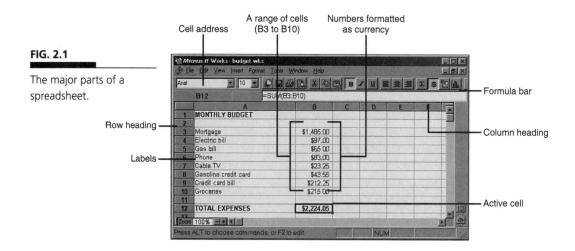

and other esoteric functions but you won't need very many of them for managing your personal finance. A group of financial functions can help project returns on investments; Chapter 13, "Planning Ahead To Meet College Costs," and Chapter 14, "Planning for Retirement," show how some of them are used.

You enter data in a spreadsheet by clicking a cell, and then typing. As you type, characters appear both inside the cell you've selected and above in the formula bar. Whenever you need to make a change, click the cell, then move your mouse up to the formula bar and make changes here.

Normally, personal finance spreadsheets require only a few basic arithmetic operators: the plus sign (+) for addition, the minus sign (-) for subtraction, the slash (/) for division, and the asterisk (*) for multiplication.

You begin a formula with a unique character so the spreadsheet knows that this cell should be treated differently from cells with labels and numbers. The equal sign (=) is used in Excel, Works, and HOT Spreadsheet, while the @ sign is used in Lotus 1-2-3.

You also need to separate cell addresses in formulas because many formulas don't work on two distinct cells, but they work on a series of cells, which is known as a range. Microsoft spreadsheets separate the beginning and end of a range with a colon (:). Lotus spreadsheets separate cell addresses with two dots (..).

Table 2.1 shows the most basic formulas for both the Microsoft and Lotus families. Fortunately, the most recent versions of many spreadsheets are forgiving and will automatically convert formulas entered in their competitor's syntax into the correct formula.

A few other formulas can be valuable. The PMT (payment) formula can show the installments required to pay off a loan, and the FV (future value) formula can project how an investment will increase in value. To use these formulas, you start with the same principle used in the SUM formula, but you need to supply cell values for other values, such as the number of years for the calculation and percentage rates. You'll find the specific format for each formula in the spreadsheet's help screens, but this book guides you through everything you need to know. If you're interested in learning more about building your own spreadsheets, you may want to refer to other books on the topic, such as *Special Edition Using Excel for Windows 95* or *Special Edition Using 1-2-3 for Windows 95* (both published by Que).

TABLE 2.1   Some Typical Spreadsheet Formulas

	Microsoft Formula	Lotus Formula
Add two cells	=B2+B3	@B2+B3
Subtract one cell from another	=B2-B3	@B2-B3
Add a range of cells	=SUM(B1:B3)	@SUM(B1..B3)
Combining formulas	=SUM(B1:B3)-B4	@SUM(B1..B3)-B4

Taking Stock of Where You Are

Most people follow a very simple financial management plan. They get paid; they spend. If there's anything left in the bank the day before payday, they think the plan's working. Of course, there's a better way. Building a solid financial future absolutely requires that you invest a portion of your earnings on a regular basis. If you're not doing that already, you need to get started right away.

You say you don't have any extra money right now? That excuse won't fly here. Your goal is to gain some control over your financial future, and you start by recognizing that you can make decisions about where your money goes.

Now that you know how to use a spreadsheet, you can create a budget to show you where the money is going and how much should be available for investing. No need to tally up every stick of gum you bought and assign it to categories. Start by looking

at the major spending and record each item separately. Use figure 2.1 as a guide. A good way to start is to get your checkbook and record all of the checks you wrote in a recent month, using general categories to identify each check.

You can build your own version pretty quickly, but you can download this spreadsheet from AOL by using the keyword **http://www.mcp.com/que/ desktop_os/money**.

Follow these steps to create your own budget spreadsheet.

1. Run your spreadsheet and begin a new file.

2. In the first cell, A1, type the label **Monthly Budget**.

3. Press the down arrow twice and type a label for one of your budget categories, such as "mortgage."

4. Press the right arrow to move the cell pointer in column B. Enter the amount you paid for this category.

5. Repeat Steps 3 and 4 until you've entered most of your major expenses.

6. You'll find it's easier to work with your numbers if you format the amounts to display currency. Highlight the column where your amounts are recorded by clicking the column header labeled B. All of the cells in this column should be highlighted. Now select your spreadsheet's Format menu command and choose a currency style. All of the amounts should appear formatted as currency.

7. In a cell below your last expense, enter a SUM formula that includes the cells in your range of expenses, for example =SUM(B3:B10). If you use a Lotus spreadsheet, begin the formula with an @ symbol rather than =.

8. Now create a section for income, recording each paycheck or other significant amount of income, using the same structure as you did for expenses.

9. After each monthly income amount is entered, record a SUM formula that covers only the cells with income amounts (for example, =SUM(B15:B18)).

10. Now you need to subtract expenses from income. In an empty cell in column B, subtract the cell with the total for expenses from the cell with the total for income. In the sample shown in figure 2.2, the formula is =B20-B12.

11. Save your work by selecting File, Save.

You now know what *should* be left over at the end of the month—what economists call "discretionary income" or the money you control after fixed expenses are paid. It's about how much you should be investing.

Once you've tried this exercise, you're bound to discover new expenses that you face each month and should include. This is where the power of the spreadsheet becomes apparent. You can insert a new row by placing your cell pointer where the new row should appear, and then choosing Insert, Row from the main menu. Type the new expense category and amount into this row. Once you've finished inserting the amount, the spreadsheet will update the totals for expenses and discretionary income. The spreadsheet formula will be adjusted to reflect the change you made to the spreadsheet's structure. If you look at the formula by selecting the cell, you'll see that the spreadsheet changed the formula.

Changing Spreadsheets, Relatively and Absolutely

Normally, when you insert or delete cells that are covered by a formula, the spreadsheet will update

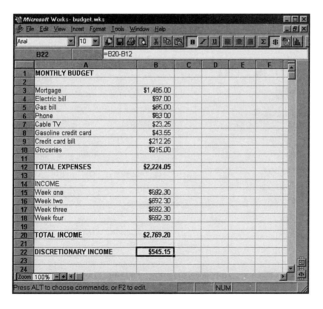

FIG. 2.2

Creating a simple budget spreadsheet is a good way to take control of your financial destiny.

> "Knowing what you have and where you keep it will help you make better financial decisions."

the formula to note the changes to the spreadsheet structure. There are exceptions you should be aware of. When you use cell references as shown above, the cell address is considered *relative*, meaning that the location is stored in relation to other cells. When you insert a row, you're not changing the relationship between where the formula is stored and the range of cells; the formula will adjust itself to the new relative cell reference. But because some spreadsheet designs require that a formula remains unchanged, *absolute* cell references are sometimes used in formulas so that the formula always uses the contents of a specific cell, even if new rows or columns were added. Absolute references are indicated with a dollar sign ($) in front of the row and column. For example, the address B12 would be treated as an absolute reference if it were identified as B12.

Tallying Your Savings and Investments

One of the best ways you can help improve your future prospects is to get organized and stay that way. Knowing what you have and where you keep it will help you make better financial decisions. Monthly bank statements, savings account passbooks, and quarterly investment reports from mutual funds are a rich source of information that you should be recording. Keep the original documents in a paper folder, if you want, but you'll get more from the information if you take a few minutes every month or two to enter the data in a spreadsheet.

▼ **TIP**

The spreadsheet function PMT can be used to calculate the payments you need to make on a loan, or to project the return you'll receive on an amount that earns interest. The spreadsheet function FV can project the future value of an investment when you make contributions on a regular basis, such as a retirement plan.

Once the data is entered into a spreadsheet, you'll be able to compare your return on an investment with opportunities you encounter. You can display your assets in charts, calculate the actual return on your investment, and project the return you should be earning two, three, or more years from now. You can also print out multiple copies. If you have any concerns about losing your records, you can keep different sets in different locations (one in the office, one in a drawer in the house, another in the attic).

You'll also have printed records that may prove essential if you're ever incapacitated. It's not the most pleasant topic—and most people would like to just forget about the possibility—but one reason to keep good records is so that your affairs will be in relatively good shape if the unforeseen happens. A surviving spouse or family attorney won't know which financial institutions you've been using, and the assets you've been working hard to acquire could be lost to your family for years if you don't make some effort at staying organized. Keeping recent financial statements in a filing cabinet is one good step but entering important data in a spreadsheet, and then printing out copies once or twice a year is even better.

▼ **TIP**

Contrary to many people's assumption, spreadsheet records can also be much more durable than paper records. Create extra backup copies of your data on floppy disk, and then keep them in several places: your office, a safe deposit box, and the attic. You might lose one copy to a fire or theft, but you're not likely to lose all three backups. Floppy disks are inexpensive, and it doesn't take much time to create a duplicate.

And, the fact is, if you own a mutual fund, you'll end up typing all the information you receive on periodic statements sooner or later. The year you sell shares, you'll need to make a full accounting of your capital gain or loss on your federal tax return. Since mutual fund dividends and capital gains are dispersed as shares in the fund, you'll need to know how much each share was worth when you acquired it. You'll need to subtract the purchase price of each share from the selling price in order to calculate your capital gain or loss. Normally, mutual funds report this on quarterly or annual statements and sitting down with these forms years after you received them is not a fun way to spend an afternoon. You might as well record the information as you go along so it can help you create an accurate picture of your net worth.

Basic Asset Management: Tracking a Mutual Fund

An asset management spreadsheet is easy to build, now that you know how to enter the formulas for basic arithmetic operators. You will want to track every savings and investment account you own by using this basic principle. As an example, let's see how to create a spreadsheet that tracks the performance of a mutual fund.

The easiest way to create the basic spreadsheet is to use the printed mutual fund statement you receive in

the mail as a guide. The spreadsheet, MutualFd, which you can download from the AOL Money Guide Web site is one way to do it; this spreadsheet is based on a mutual fund statement for a fund that reports monthly earnings. This fund is a bond fund, so the earnings are expressed as dividends. Stock funds report the dividends earned as well as capital gains, but they usually report on an annual basis, not monthly.

You can download MutualFd by using the AOL keyword **http://www.mcp.com/que/desktop_os/ money**.

The process of building the spreadsheet to track a stock fund is similar, as long as you use the printed statement as your guide.

1. Run your spreadsheet program and open a new file. Enter a title for this fund (for example, Dreyfus Tax-Exempt Bond Fund). You'll want to create separate files for each fund you own.

2. In row 2, enter headings for the types of amounts you'll record, using the table on your mutual fund statement as a model. The headings will require more space than the amounts that will appear below, so you may want to use two rows for the headers, entering a portion of the header wording in each cell, as in the figure 2.3.

3. In column A, record the date of the statement, not the date when you sit down to type it in, but the exact date that the financial institution issued the statement. To display the dates properly, you'll need to use your spreadsheet's column format. To do that, first highlight the column by clicking the column header, then select the format, number, and date command.

4. Columns B, C, and F will be dollar amounts. You can format all of these columns at the same

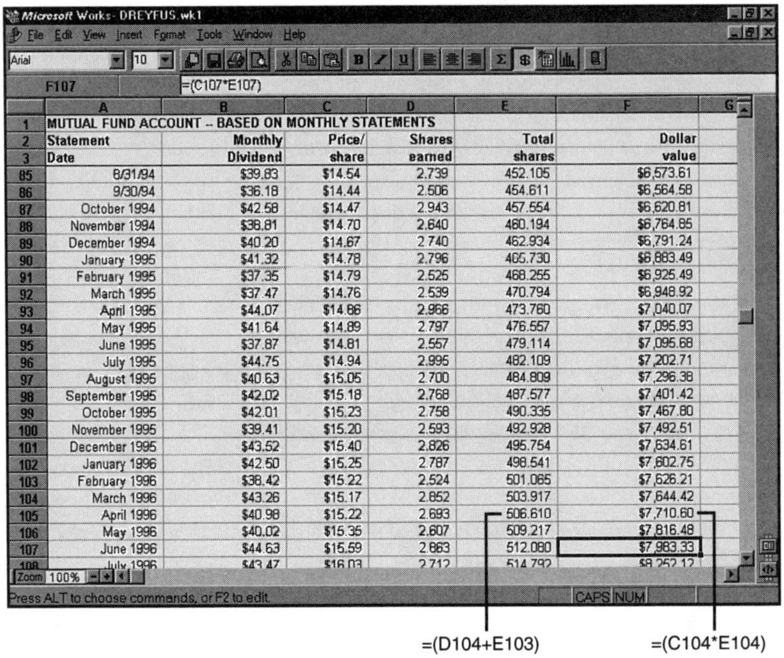

FIG. 2.3

A spreadsheet for tracking mutual fund earnings.

	A	B	C	D	E	F	G
	Microsoft Works - DREYFUS.wk1						
	File Edit View Insert Format Tools Window Help						
	Arial ▼ 10 ▼						
	F107 =(C107*E107)						
1	MUTUAL FUND ACCOUNT -- BASED ON MONTHLY STATEMENTS						
2	Statement	Monthly	Price/	Shares	Total	Dollar	
3	Date	Dividend	share	earned	shares	value	
85	8/31/94	$39.83	$14.54	2.739	452.105	$6,573.61	
86	9/30/94	$36.18	$14.44	2.506	454.611	$6,564.58	
87	October 1994	$42.58	$14.47	2.943	457.554	$6,620.81	
88	November 1994	$38.81	$14.70	2.640	460.194	$6,764.85	
89	December 1994	$40.20	$14.67	2.740	462.934	$6,791.24	
90	January 1995	$41.32	$14.78	2.796	465.730	$6,883.49	
91	February 1995	$37.35	$14.79	2.525	468.255	$6,925.49	
92	March 1995	$37.47	$14.76	2.539	470.794	$6,948.92	
93	April 1995	$44.07	$14.86	2.966	473.760	$7,040.07	
94	May 1995	$41.64	$14.89	2.797	476.557	$7,095.93	
95	June 1995	$37.87	$14.81	2.557	479.114	$7,095.68	
96	July 1995	$44.75	$14.94	2.995	482.109	$7,202.71	
97	August 1995	$40.63	$15.05	2.700	484.809	$7,296.38	
98	September 1995	$42.02	$15.18	2.768	487.577	$7,401.42	
99	October 1995	$42.01	$15.23	2.758	490.335	$7,467.80	
100	November 1995	$39.41	$15.20	2.593	492.928	$7,492.51	
101	December 1995	$43.52	$15.40	2.826	495.754	$7,634.61	
102	January 1996	$42.50	$15.25	2.787	498.541	$7,602.75	
103	February 1996	$38.42	$15.22	2.524	501.065	$7,626.21	
104	March 1996	$43.26	$15.17	2.852	503.917	$7,644.42	
105	April 1996	$40.98	$15.22	2.693	506.610	$7,710.60	
106	May 1996	$40.02	$15.35	2.607	509.217	$7,816.48	
107	June 1996	$44.63	$15.59	2.863	512.080	$7,983.33	
108	July 1996	$43.47	$16.03	2.712	514.792	$8,252.12	
	Zoom 100%						
	Press ALT to choose commands, or F2 to edit				CAPS NUM		

=(D104+E103)   =(C104*E104)

time. Select the header for column B, hold down the Ctrl key, and select each of the other columns until you've highlighted every column where a dollar amount will appear. Choose your spreadsheet's Format, Number command. Choose one of the dollar formats. You can choose between a currency format that displays cents or one that rounds the number off to whole dollars. Federal tax laws allow you to round off dollar figures so you may want to simplify your record keeping by rounding off the dollar amounts. Format columns D and E using this same procedure, but choose a format that displays three decimal places.

5. The first three columns in our sample state-ment—monthly dividend (B), price per share (C), and shares earned (D)—are amounts you copy directly from the mutual fund statement. Of course, in building your own statement, follow the statement you've received in the mail.

6. The cells in the next two column are calculated by the spreadsheet from formulas. While your statement probably displays the cumulative total, it's a good idea to enter a formula in your spreadsheet to calculate the amount since it will save you typing in the long run and help you avoid typing errors. In the first row of your new spreadsheet, there's nothing to add since you're starting with the initial amount, but from then on, you will want to add the shares you've just earned to the shares you owned at the time of the last statement. The formula in cell E107 in figure 2.3 is

=(D107+E106)

7. The next column, F, calculates the value of the current holdings by multiplying the share price (column C) by the number of shares now held (column E). As shown in figure 2.3, the formula entered in cell F107 is

`=(C107*E107)`

8. Once you've entered the figures from your statement and copied the formulas into each row, be sure to save the file. Use a name that helps to identify the mutual fund. You can use this file as the basis for recording information about your other funds. When you open this file to track a different fund, keep the formulas intact and replace the dollar amounts for that fund. Be sure you use File, Save As and give the file a different name.

Building this spreadsheet isn't as tedious as it seems. Each formula needs to be entered just once. From then on, it can be copied and pasted into the next cell. As explained earlier, a spreadsheet uses relative references when you move cells or insert new ones, so the actual formula is updated every time it is copied so it will calculate the values correctly.

To copy a formula, first select the cell containing the formula, choose Edit, Copy, move your mouse to the new cell, and then choose Edit, Paste. You can also copy the contents of one cell into many cells if you hold down your mouse just when you select the destination cell and then drag the mouse until you've selected a longer range of cells.

With your mutual fund data safely recorded, you'll be able to print out a copy whenever you want, or use other spreadsheet features to analyze the numbers. A few examples follow.

One little treat you owe yourself after all your hard work is to create a chart. Spreadsheets can draw a graphic picture for your numbers in the blink of an

eye, and when your investment is producing healthy returns, no sight will be more beautiful than a chart of your growing returns. The exact process of creating a chart is a bit different for each spreadsheet, but the basic technique is to highlight the range of numbers you want to see charted and then select the chart command. Figure 2.4 shows a chart for the mutual fund report created in figure 2.3.

Extending Your Spreadsheet To Calculate Capital Gains

One analysis you'll need to make is a calculation of your capital gain in the mutual fund when you sell shares. You'll need to report the gains (or losses) on your tax return for that year. In calculating capital gains, you determine the amount earned on each share by comparing the purchase price to the selling price. Since the shares you own were bought at different prices, you need to make a separate calculation for every transaction. This would be a tedious chore if all you had were a calculator and a pencil. But if you've been recording the transactions on a spreadsheet, it will take about a minute to calculate the capital gains.

Before you calculate your capital gains, you need to know the price you received per share.

1. Open the Mutual Fund spreadsheet.

2. In column G, enter a heading for Capital Gain.

3. In the first row where you've recorded fund earnings, enter the formula that will calculate the capital gain. This formula includes the price you earned for each share. Assuming you earned $16.50 per share and you began entering data in the 4th column, in cell G4, you'd enter

`=(D4*16.50)-(D4*C4)`

FIG. 2.4

A beautiful sight: a growing investment.

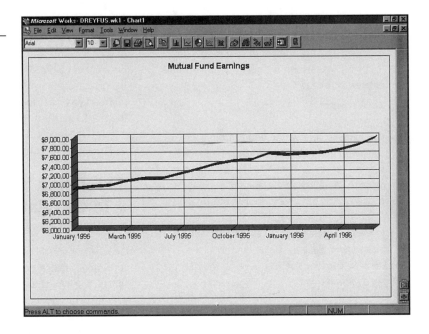

4. You can then copy that formula into all the cells in column G where the formula should appear. Highlight the cell containing the formula, select Edit, Copy, and then select all of the cells below by clicking the first cell, hold down the left mouse button, and move your mouse until you've highlighted the entire range. Release the mouse and select Edit, Paste. Figure 2.5 shows a spreadsheet in the middle of a procedure for copying a formula to other cells.

Basic Technique: Calculating Your Returns

The most important number to look at when evaluating any investment is the return—the amount this investment is returning to you. Don't confuse this with capital gains; the return is a concept that applies to any investment, from a savings account to a stock. Capital gains is used to determine your earnings for tax purposes; return is often a calculation of how much you would have earned *if* you sold.

In comparing investments, return is usually reported on an annual basis to make it easier to compare investments. In AOL's Morningstar Fund Reports, the annual return is reported for every mutual fund. This number is considered an essential barometer in gauging the performance of a fund. If you have any doubt that a mutual fund is a better investment than a CD, compare the two returns. A mutual fund's return is based on the change in the price of the fund plus earnings that the fund distributed to shareholders during the year. The CD's return is calculated as the cumulative interest it paid over a year.

To calculate the return in a spreadsheet, the earnings over the course of a year are divided by the total value at the beginning of the year. So if a mutual

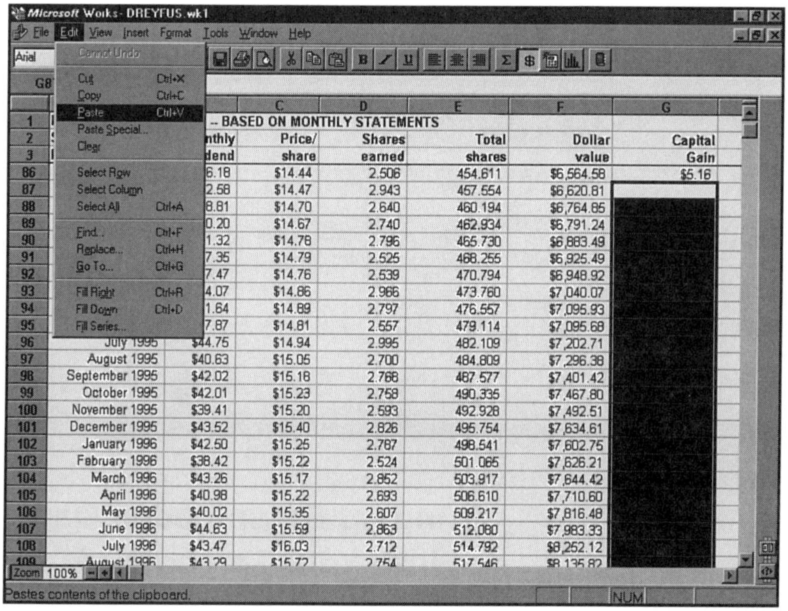

FIG. 2.5

Calculating capital gains is easier when you can copy a formula you entered once into a long range of cells.

fund rose from $50 to $54 over a year and paid a $1 dividend, the annual return is 10 percent or $5 divided by $50.

While you can trust Morningstar and other financial services on AOL to report accurate results, you also will want to add your own analysis when planning your personal strategy. For example, when comparing an investment you own to one that you're considering, you'll want to calculate the rate of return on your current investments. Now that you know how to build simple formulas in a spreadsheet, you'll find it's easy to do it yourself once you enter the total value of the account at the beginning and end of a year.

However, you also will want to carry your newfound knowledge to the science of evaluating new investment opportunities. While you're not likely to uncover any fraud, you'll be better equipped to chart your own future. For example, while Morningstar

uses January 1 as the date when it calculates annual return figures, you'd find a different return simply by using a different date for the calculation. Figure 2.6 demonstrates how a growing fund may produce dramatically different results simply by changing the date when you calculate the return.

Figure 2.6 shows an investment whose price rises dramatically between January 1, 1995 and January 1, 1996; an impressive 27.45 percent increase is posted during that period. But if you were comparing the results from June 1, 1995 to the following June 1, you'd find only a 4 percent gain. This is an over simplification, but if you download historical price results from AOL and try this same analysis, you'll find many investments whose outlook varies greatly depending on when you take the annual readings.

For example, if you are comparing a mutual fund with a stock, you'd want to go a little bit further than simply comparing January to January, as

FIG. 2.6

Comparing the rate of
return at two different
times of the year.

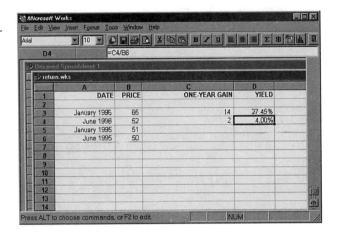

reported by Morningstar. You could download
quotes on both a stock and a fund from AOL's Historical Quotes and Graphs section (keyword: **quotes**)
and do your own analysis.

Analyzing
Downloaded Data

Now that you've developed the basic techniques
needed to crunch numbers on your own, you're
better equipped to download some of the reports
and databases available in AOL's Personal Finance
section.

The type of personal finance help you'll find on
America Online can be divided into two categories:
direct contact with others and detailed reports that
you can download. While some of the reports are
educational articles, many of the reports are financial
reports that you'll want to open with a spreadsheet.

There's just one last technical area to master: the
different types of data you'll encounter.

Bringing Downloaded Data
into Your Spreadsheet

Different spreadsheets store data in their own unique
file formats. For many years, this wreaked havoc on
anyone who wanted to share their numeric data with
someone using a different spreadsheet. Fortunately,
the situation is greatly improved. The programs now
do a good job of giving users access to other file
formats. So if you're using a recent version of Excel
or Lotus 1-2-3, you should be able to display financial reports you've downloaded from AOL as long as
the data was formatted as financial information.

The two most common spreadsheet formats are
WKS and XLS. WKS is the original Lotus 1-2-3
format, and it's read by every spreadsheet. The XLS
format is the original Excel format, and it can be read
by just about any spreadsheet released within the
past three years. Occasionally, you may come across
a newer version of the Microsoft Excel XLS format
that cannot be read by your software—for example,
a file that was written with one of the most recent
versions of Excel which is not compatible with
older versions of the product. (I said the situation

improved, I didn't say it was perfect.) Normally, you will have this problem only when sharing files with a friend or colleague, but you won't have this problem with data available for downloading from one of AOL's public areas.

You'll have fewer problems if you're able to match file formats with the best spreadsheet choice. Consult Table 2.2 for help in matching the file with the right spreadsheet.

Unfortunately, many of the financial tables available on AOL—company earnings reports and mutual fund performance reports, for example—can be downloaded only as text. Word processors can read text files without any problem, but in order to display the columns properly, you need to use a particular type of font known as a fixed-pitch font. Most fonts for Windows and the Mac are proportional fonts, meaning they give each character a proportionately different amount of space; a fixed-pitch font gives every character the same amount of space. When AOL displays a table on-screen, it uses a fixed-pitch font, and you'll need to use one in your word processor, as well, to re-create the columns of figures you see online.

But many of the online reports you'll want to download really belong in a spreadsheet, not a word processor. The process of converting these text tables into spreadsheet columns is fairly easy if you're using Lotus 1-2-3 or Microsoft Excel. Both products have a "parse" function which is able to break up imported text into spreadsheet columns. You often need to oversee the process, adjusting the spreadsheet's "guesses" on which bits of text belong in which column, but it goes quickly. On the other hand, Microsoft Works, HOT Spreadsheet, and others have no ability to handle this conversion. When you download a text report with numeric tables, you need to do a find-and-replace operation in an attempt to convert the extra spaces in the text file into tabs. It's a cumbersome and time-consuming operation. You'll find a description of how to perform this messy chore with Microsoft Works in the section "Formatting Downloaded Statements with Microsoft

> **"Download some of the reports and databases available in AOL's Personal Finance section."**

TABLE 2.2	The Spreadsheet File Formats You'll Encounter
File format	**Spreadsheets That Can Read It**
CSV	Comma-separate values in text format; Excel and Lotus 1-2-3 can usually translate correctly.
TXT	Text format if used for numeric data; columns are usually separated by tabs. Excel and Lotus 1-2-3 can usually translate properly.
WK1	Lotus 1-2-3 (2.1 and above), Excel
WKS	Lotus 1-2-3, Excel, Works, HOT Spreadsheet, Claris Works
XLS	Excel, HOT Spreadsheet, Lotus 1-2-3 for Windows

Works," in Chapter 3 in the discussion of company research.

Using the Charts You Download

In some areas of AOL, you can display data in a chart and then choose to either save the picture on your system as a CHF (chart) file, download the data in its original format, or save the chart to your clipboard. The CHF file is useful only if you want to have AOL display some of your old charts while you're connected—a very expensive way to display charts! If you want to see the chart again, the better technique is to save the data to your clipboard so you can view it in a graphics program on your hard disk, after you sign off. Once the chart is saved to the

clipboard, you will need to switch to a different program and paste the clipboard image into that program. Save the file to disk and you can view it anytime, edit it, or use it in combination with other data you download.

For example, in the Personal Finance area's Historical Quotes and Graphs section (Keyword: **historical quotes**) you can display the stock price for an equity over time. Figure 2.7 shows a stock chart with one of the options for saving the data.

When you use the clipboard option shown in figure 2.7 to save the data, you can import the saved text into a spreadsheet. Fortunately, the columns are separated by tabs so a spreadsheet can easily format it properly. You'll find detailed instructions in Chapter 3, "Downloading Historical Stock Prices," on the best way to use this area of AOL.

FIG. 2.7

When you have a choice, saving data in its original format is best.

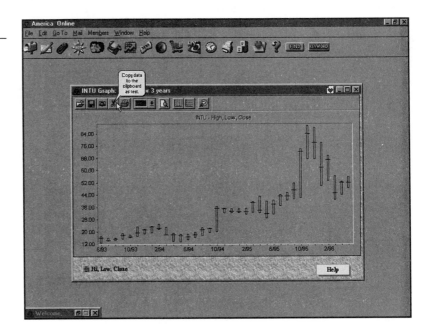

Organiz
Downloa

As you start to acquire int
put some effort into orga
downloading. When you :
loading a file, AOL's defau
in the AOL download dire
for an occasional file, but
load files there over time,
cluttered with all sorts of i
be able to find anything. I
information by topic or us
tem. If you don't have a hi
consider storing informatic
searching new mutual fund
when trying out new softwa
for recently downloaded sha
member that when you atter
spreadsheet or word processc
for it in this folder. If you're not careful, it's easy to
get in the habit of downloading information that
looks appealing, but you forget about later. It can
become an expensive habit.

When To Copy to the
Clipboard and When To Save

Occasionally, you'll come across some data that you
want to save, but it's not available for downloading.
It could be a message you're reading in a message
board, or an article displayed in a window. You can
store this data on your computer by highlighting the
text you want to save with your mouse and then
choosing Edit, Copy. The text is now stored on your
clipboard. You'll need to open an application on your
computer that you can use to store the data in a file.
If it's text, open a word processor; if it's numeric

n a spreadsheet. Then select Edit, Paste.
data is displayed, choose File, Save to retain
your system. You can't copy graphics from
ur system unless a download command
eneath them.

eping Your Goals
in Mind

word of caution. Millions of words and
re available on America Online to help you
finances.

e information you find online comes in
. The online world isn't properly set up to
ep analysis. That's why it's so important
arn how to take the data that's available
and apply your own judgment.

While online, you can search through company
reports, compare other people's investment strategies, and stay current on business news. It's easy to
become overwhelmed and distracted. The following
chapters are organized to help you find what you
need, and then make the best possible use of it.
Don't become caught up in the stock market just
because one of the message boards makes it sound
too appealing to pass up. And if you're considering
opening an online stock brokerage account, be sure
that you understand the risks you'll be taking.

Any financial planner with your interests in mind will
urge you to make sure you have an adequate financial cushion before you invest in the stock market.
Most analysts agree that you should have between
three and six months' living expenses saved in either
a savings account, certificate of deposit, money
market fund, or some other stable account. Only

then should you consider taking risks with your savings. Keep that in mind as you look at the new opportunities you'll find.

Don't be discouraged from taking advantage of the many sound personal finance opportunities just because there are so many or because they present risk. Start by creating an accurate assessment of how much you have saved already, look at your budget to see how much you can invest, and then closely follow the performance of every investment you make.

Remember: no one will be able to do as good a job at setting your financial priorities. Seek counsel from experts, but learn how to make your own decisions. Basic spreadsheets that you create can be one of your best tools in charting your own financial destiny.

3

Researching Stocks with Hard Facts

Look before you leap into new investments. America Online has everything you need to know—you just need to know where to look, and what to do with it once you find it.

Experts love to give stock tips and then follow it with the warning, "Be sure to thoroughly investigate a company before investing your money." That's great advice, but how do you do it? Libraries don't stock their shelves with the thousands of financial statements released by corporations. You can find a few corporate reports in your local library. But even if you do have access to a business-oriented library, it can take the better part of a day to find all the documents you need.

Whether you're investigating a company because you plan to buy its stock or bonds, or because you plan to buy a financial product such as a life insurance policy or mutual fund, your America Online subscription can help you find the essential details you need to know in minutes. Not only will you find basic corporate financial information, you'll also find earnings estimates prepared by major analysts. These earnings estimates are often a major influence on changes in stock prices, and they're normally available only to subscribers of expensive newsletters or favored customers of large stock brokers.

The first time you try to research a company through America Online (AOL), it may take extra time as you become familiar with the way data is organized. After you do it a few times, you'll be able to find all-important financial data in minutes. This chapter will help you understand what to look for and where to find it so you don't waste time while you're online.

There's a blizzard of information, so to help you find what you need, we'll take two approaches. We'll focus on finding information that will help you spot a healthy financial picture and spot trends that may affect the future stock price.

Brushing Up on Basics

Following a stock price isn't too difficult; all you do is compare an old price to the current price. But when you start to dig into financial statements and earnings estimates, your fiscal vocabulary may be taxed to a greater degree. You'll encounter acronyms like EPS, P/E, and ROE. (In case you're wondering, those stand for *earnings per share*, *price-earnings ratio*, and *return on equity*.) And you'll come across terms like *price-to-book ratio* and *market capitalization* that may seem clear but the exact meaning may be quite different than it seems. Don't give up just because the language seems foreign; it's all in English and can be understood. The AAII Investment Glossary explains it all.

AAII Investment Glossary

The American Association of Individual Investors (AAII) is dedicated to the proposition that the average person can match the returns posted by the best stock brokers, as long as you have the right information and are willing to work hard. AAII's section on America Online has a library of articles that explain many basic concepts—you gain an invaluable financial education here. But the most concise source of information is the Investment Glossary. Here you'll find clear explanations for the terms you'll encounter as you do your own research and read through reports posted in other parts of America Online.

The AAII glossary is divided into articles that cover broad categories—such as mutual fund, stock analysis, and trading terms—that are displayed on the main menu. Unfortunately, there's no way to search for a single term; you need to select one of these articles and then browse through the list of terms. But the process of opening a category and searching for a term doesn't take long, so even if you select the wrong category, it shouldn't take too long to backtrack.

Let's say you've seen the term "P/E" used and want a definition. Here's how to find it:

1. Connect to AOL and, from any menu, enter the keyword **AAII**. The opening menu for all of the services from American Association of Individual Investors will open.

2. Select The Reference Library. A list of the articles in this section will open.

3. Select Investment Glossary. A list of categories will appear, as shown in figure 3.1.

FIG. 3.1

You'll find an investment glossary in the AAII Reference Library.

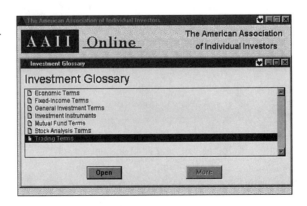

58

4. Select any category that seems to have the correct term. You'll see an article that's broken down by paragraph. Each paragraph defines a specific term. You can browse through the list to find the term, but there's a better way.

5. From the main AOL menu, select the Edit, Find in Top Window command. A dialog box opens.

6. Type in the term you want to find; for our example, type **P/E.** Since this term is usually typed in capital letters, select the Match Case option.

7. Select Find Next. If the term is in this article, it will be highlighted, as shown in figure 3.2. If the term is not in this document, a dialog box will report The text you entered was not found.

8. If the term is not found in this article, select Cancel to close the Find dialog box, and then close the current article. Open a different category and repeat Steps 5 through 7.

9. When you've found the correct term, you may want to print the article (select File, Print). To print only one definition, highlight the desired paragraph, and select Edit, Copy. Then switch to a word processor, paste the term into a new file, and print.

Wall Street Words, a Financial Dictionary

The AAII Investment Glossary is a good introductory resource, but one of its deficiencies is the lack of a search tool. You need to open one of the articles and scan through it yourself. Wall Street Words is a more advanced dictionary in two ways: the definitions are more sophisticated and a search feature will find the definitions you want. Wall Street Words gives more specific details on each term, so newcomers to investing may find the definitions are difficult to

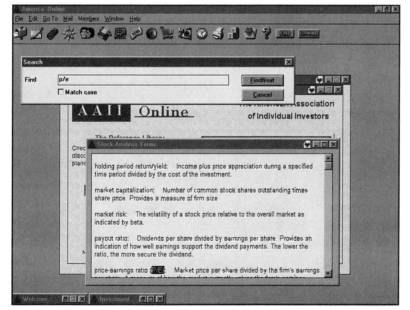

FIG. 3.2

Finding financial terms in the AAII Investment Glossary is much easier if you use AOL's Find in Top Window command.

understand. But if you want to learn both, first consult the AAII Investment Glossary and then try Wall Street Words.

To search the Wall Street Words Dictionary:

1. Connect to AOL and, from any menu, enter the keyword **wsw**. The Wall Street Words opening menu will appear.

2. When the menu opens, your insertion point is resting in the Enter Word(s) box. Type the term you're looking for.

3. The default setting for a search is Search Words Only, which means that Wall Street Words will look for only definitions of this word. The other option, Search Both Words & Full-Text Definitions, would search through every word in the dictionary to find every single time the word is mentioned. For example, a search on "P/E" with the default setting will find three definitions with the term, but "P/E" with Search Both Words & Full-Text Definitions would find ninety definitions that mention "P/E." So keep the default setting if you need help understanding a specific term; use the other setting when you want to expand your research into a broader category.

4. Click Look Up, and Wall Street Words will show a list of all the definitions that match your search criteria. Figure 3.3 shows the results of a search for "P/E" with the default setting.

5. Double-click the definition you want to read; a window will open with that definition. You can print a copy by selecting File, Print. Or you can copy it to the clipboard to use in a different program by selecting Edit, Select All and then Edit, Copy.

6. If the search finds more then 20 terms, only the first 20 terms are displayed. To see the others, you need to select More and then click the scroll bar. Only the next 20 terms will be displayed. If there are still more terms, you need to select More and then click the scroll bar again.

Ticker Symbols: A Stock Market Essential

Before you get very far into the world of investing, you'll want to master the art of the ticker symbol.

FIG. 3.3

Wall Street Words is a more detailed dictionary than the AAII Investment Glossary.

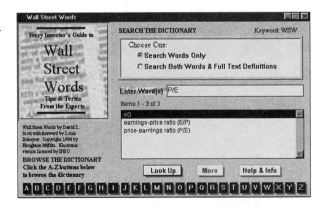

Every company stock and mutual fund that is publicly traded is identified by a unique code. Knowing this code can save a lot of trouble as you research companies and mutual funds. Every time you search for an organization, you may have to select among several similar-sounding names before you find the company or fund you're interested in.

▼ TIP

You can use AOL's portfolio to record the ticker symbols of stock you want to research but don't own. Create a portfolio called "Stocks to Watch" every time you look up a new symbol. Enter zero for the number of shares you own, and you can see the stock and its current price whenever you open the portfolio.

One reason for the confusion is that different companies use similar names. Another reason is that major corporations issue stock for different purposes. A company's common stock is the most popular, but new issues may appear, and they would receive a separate ticker symbol.

For example, if you decided to investigate Ford Motor Company, you might think it would be fairly easy to enter **ford** during a search. You'd find information on Ford Motor Company, all right—but you'd have to read through a list of 14 different listings to determine which one you want. If you want to follow Ford's common stock, you'll be able to hone right in on it if you use the ticker symbol F.

Here's how you can find a company's ticker symbol.

1. Enter the keyword **quotes**. The Quotes & Portfolio window opens.

2. Select the Lookup Symbol button, as shown in figure 3.4.

3. Type the name of the desired company and select Search by Company. A list of companies and their ticker symbols will appear.

4. In many cases, you need to read through the list to find the right company. If more than 20 companies are found, you'll need to select the More button to display the next 20 and then click the scroll bar to see the names.

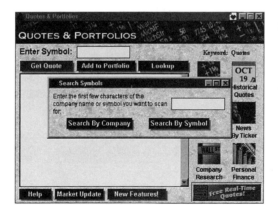

FIG. 3.4

You can't play the stock market without ticker symbols; you can find them in the Quotes & Portfolios section.

Finding Current Stock Prices

Once you've found the ticker symbol, you can see the current price of the stock or mutual fund. Select the Get Quote button to find the current price, EPS (earnings per share), P/E ratio, and statistics on current trading. If you want to follow the stock, click the Add to Portfolio button. Then, any time you're connected to America Online, you can see the price of the stock simply by clicking the Quotes & Portfolio button and then selecting Display Portfolio.

Recording a stock in a portfolio is a good way to track the stocks and mutual funds you're thinking about buying, but it's even more valuable if you already own shares. When you select the option Add to Portfolio, you will be able to record the number of shares you own and the price you paid for the shares. Then, whenever you select the Display Portfolio button, you'll see the current price of the issue, and you'll see a calculation of how well (or poorly) you're doing. Figure 3.5 shows a typical portfolio.

You can do a lot with the portfolio. In fact, there's so much you can do; Chapter 5, "Trading Stocks Online," is devoted to all of the techniques you can use.

Where To Ask Stupid Questions

They say there's no such thing as a stupid question. And that's a good thing, because the world would probably sink under the weight of them all—if they did exist. Everyone has questions: some are basic and some are sophisticated: When it comes to investing your money, the most important thing you can do is make sure you find good answers to all of your questions. Ignorance is your greatest enemy, and your "stupid" questions are part of your brain's defense strategy.

FIG. 3.5

The Display Portfolio option will track prices of shares for stocks and mutual funds, and it will also calculate how much you've earned (or lost).

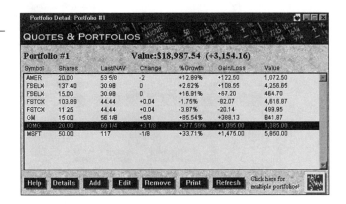

AOL has plenty of places to ask questions. The trick is to find the right place to post the question. As long as you post your question in the right place, no one will take offense, no matter how stupid the question would seem in the wrong place. You don't want to ask questions like "What's a stock?" in a forum where people are comparing their strategies for technical analysis of commodities futures.

One of the best places to ask stupid—uh, let's just say, "basic" questions, is the Help for Beginners section of the Investors' Network. To find it, type the keyword **investors network.** You'll see a list of services, as shown in figure 3.6.

Most of the choices are message forums devoted to discussions of a specific topic for experienced investors. Select the Help for Beginners option, and you'll find hundreds of messages from people who are just learning the ropes, or who know quite a bit but have come across something new that they don't understand. For detailed instructions on the techniques

you use to participate in a message board, refer to the section, "Finding Information in a Message Board" in Chapter 1.

Keep in mind that there's no guarantee your question will be answered or that the answer will be correct. Moderators are on hand to help make sure people don't abuse the bulletin boards, but they are not able to verify the accuracy of every message. Treat the responses you'd receive here with the same caution you'd give to any information you receive from a stranger.

> "Treat the responses you'd receive here with the same caution you'd give to any information you receive from a stranger."

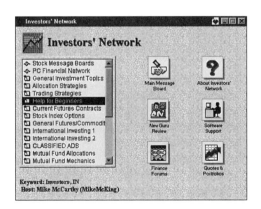

FIG. 3.6

Investors' Network has a number of services, including downloadable software, but it's mainly a collection of message forums.

 RESOURCES

Investors' Network is not the only forum that welcomes beginners. Here are a few more.

- AAII is a fairly serious place for small investors but you can get a good amount of help in the message board titled Investing Basics. Keyword: **aaii.**

- **Worth Online** is a section run by *Worth* magazine. Some of its message boards are for advanced investors, but you can ask anything in the Investor 101 section. Keyword: **worth.**

- **Real Life** is devoted to the financial issues faced by ordinary people. The Personal Finance and Investment Planning sections are good places to learn about financial markets. Keyword: **real life.**

Eavesdropping on the Experts

One of the great advantages to the message boards on AOL is that while they're tailored to specific interests, anyone can read the posted exchanges. If you're inquisitive and are able to mind your manners, you can learn a great deal by cyber-eavesdropping in message boards designed for professional investors and self-made millionaires. It's perfectly legal. Just select one of the message boards where sophisticated investors rub elbows, and read through the messages.

Just one warning: if you do feel the need to intrude on one of these discussions, respect the culture of the environment. Don't ask dumb questions; one reason these message boards are set up is so that knowledgeable people can have an undisturbed setting.

You may find an opportunity to post a question or two, if you're discrete. For example, when someone posts a vague recommendation for a particular stock, it's perfectly appropriate to ask for more information with a reply along the lines of "Do you have any specific reasons?"

RESOURCES

The following are some of the best places to eavesdrop on the experts:

- Keyword: **Investors Network**. You can select from dozens of boards on specific investment techniques.

- Keyword: **Motley Fool**. You can select from hundreds of boards devoted to the stocks of individual companies and to investment techniques.

- The newsgroup misc.invest.stocks on the Internet is a very busy forum for investors. To get there, use the keyword: **newsgroups** and add it to your list of subscribed newsgroups.

Finding Facts and Figures

Now that you know where to get help when you need it, you have the tools you need to do your own research on public companies. The following sections will guide you through the mountains of data available. To help make it easier to digest, I've organized the research process into three categories.

◆ Financial statements that detail the balance sheets published by companies.

◆ Historical performance charts that show changes in stock prices over time.

◆ Earnings estimates that report experts' opinions on the prospects for a company in the future.

Required Reading: Corporate Financial Statements

Reading through a company's financial statements may not be the most fun you'll ever have, but it's a prerequisite to any type of investment. You should consider financial statements required reading if you plan to buy a company's stock. This is where you'll see how much the company makes, how much of a profit or loss it reported, and how much the company is growing.

Finding a Financial Statement

The most complete source of financial statements on AOL is offered by Disclosure. You can reach their section from the Personal Finance menu, and you'll find links from several other places on AOL.

The following steps will guide you to a financial statement in the most direct way:

1. After you've connected to America Online, enter the keyword **financial statement**. You'll see the menu in figure 3.7.

2. Select either U.S. Financials or Int'l. Financials. A dialog box will open; type in the name of the company or ticker symbol, and click Search.

3. In most cases, your search will find several companies. Read through the list to find the desired company. If more than 20 companies are found, you'll need to click More and then the scroll bar to see the next 20 listings. When you've found the company, select it and a balance sheet for the company will open.

You may want to print the report by selecting File, Print, but you will definitely want to save the report of any company you're seriously evaluating. Select File, Save and select a folder and name that you'll remember. (Don't make the mistake of downloading a lot of valuable information and losing it all because you don't pay attention to the name and location you select. Many people do.)

FIG. 3.7

Disclosure's section on AOL provides financial statements on most publicly traded companies in the U.S. and overseas.

Analyzing a Financial Statement

Once the information is stored on your computer, you'll have the ability to use any software on your system to help you analyze it. If you simply want to read it over, you can open it with a word processor, but you need to make sure you're using a fixed pitch font or else the columnar figures will be in disarray.

If you want to perform your own analysis using a spreadsheet, you'll have to put in a little work before the data is in a form you can work with. The problem is that America Online stores the statements in a text format, and extra spaces are inserted between figures to form the neat columns you see on-screen, as shown in figure 3.8. These extra spaces need to be converted into columns or tabs by the software on your system.

Fixed-pitch fonts give an equal amount of space to each character, including blank spaces, the same way America Online does. So if you use a fixed-pitch font

(sometimes called a printer font) to display the text, it will be properly formatted in columns when you display it on-screen and print it. Line printer and Courier are the two most common fixed-pitch fonts. You can use the word processor to print copies of the statements, but you won't have analysis tools.

The power of advanced programs like recent versions of Lotus 1-2-3 and Microsoft Excel will pay off when you do this type of analysis; they provide tools that help you bring data into a spreadsheet format with little effort. When you open the text file you've downloaded, one of these spreadsheets will parse the numbers into the correct column format. You'll have the option of fine-tuning the process, but usually, you can sit back and let the spreadsheet do the work.

If you're using Microsoft Works, a shareware spreadsheet (such as HOT which is available for downloading from AOL), or an old version of Lotus 1-2-3 or Excel, you'll need to put in some extra work to format the data properly. The following sections will guide you through the process.

FIG. 3.8

Financial statements are formatted neatly for the screen, but unless you have an advanced spreadsheet, you'll have to convert the text to a more usable format.

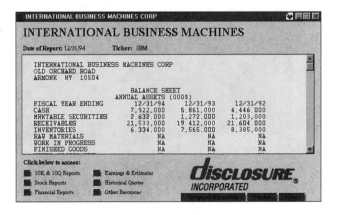

Formatting Downloaded Financial Statements with Older Spreadsheets

This example is based on Lotus 1-2-3 for Windows, Release 4, but the same basic technique applies to earlier versions of 1-2-3 and Microsoft Excel as well. (Microsoft Works, however, requires a different technique, which is explained in the following section, "Formatting Downloaded Statements with Microsoft Works.")

1. Open your spreadsheet and select File, Open to display the file you downloaded. Each row of the file will be displayed in column A, and as a result, none of the numbers will line up properly.

2. Select the cells where the figures need to be formatted into columns—this is normally only cells in column A—but do not select rows that display heading information. Normally, the first few rows of the statement display the address and phone number of the corporation; you do not want the spreadsheet to base its parsing conversion on these cells. Usually, the top row you select will include a header that identifies the date for the results that appear below.

3. Once you've highlighted a selection, choose Range, Parse. The Parse dialog box opens.

4. Select Create and the dialog box will make its best guess on how the cells should be formatted. An L should appear above the first character in cells that contain labels or text; a D should appear above the beginning of numeric data. The right angle brackets indicate that the cell continues until the next character and an asterisk indicates space between cells.

5. Edit the text in the Format Line box until L>> appears over the beginning of text and D>> appears above the first part of the cell that should contain numbers. This should be a bit to the left of the actual number in the top row and just to the right of the end of the previous column. Delete the asterisks and insert additional right angle > keys until the headings line up, as in figure 3.9.

6. Click OK and the rows will be parsed so that the numbers are in distinct columns. You may not be able to read it all since the width of the columns may be too narrow. Widen the columns by moving your pointer over the column header until it becomes a resizing icon, then click and drag the border to the right.

You may want to polish your spreadsheet by highlighting columns that contain dollars and formatting them as currency.

Formatting Downloaded Statements with Microsoft Works

The process of converting downloaded data so it can be viewed in the Microsoft Works spreadsheet is a fairly messy business. You need to use the Works word processor to convert the blank spaces to tabs and then open this edited version with the Works spreadsheet. You'll have to put in a fair amount of work to do the job as neatly as Excel and 1-2-3, but you can get adequate results in just a few minutes. And once you've learned the technique, you'll be able to convert future downloaded documents more quickly.

FIG. 3.9

When you convert
downloaded financial data
in earlier versions of Lotus
1-2-3, the spreadsheet will
do some of the work, but
you need to finish the job.

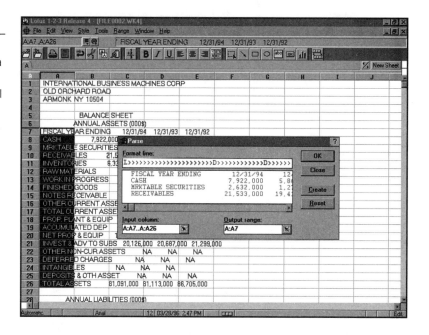

1. Open Microsoft Works.

2. Select the Works Tools tab and choose Word
   Processor.

3. Select File, Open and choose the file you saved.
   Works will ask which program you want to use.
   Select Word Processor.

4. With the file displayed, select Edit, Replace. The
   Replace dialog box opens.

5. Select the Find What entry box, and press the
   space bar four times. Press the Tab key to move
   your insertion point to the Replace With entry
   box. Click the Tab icon that appears just below
   (it looks like a big right arrow), as shown in
   figure 3.10.

6. Select the Replace All button, and Works will
   replace every occurrence of four spaces with
   a tab.

7. This is the messy part. You need to edit the file
   so that only one tab separates each number.
   Some of the rows will have several tabs between the numbers. Delete each of these extra
   tabs. You can leave the extra blank spaces
   alone.

8. Now you need to make sure the first column
   with the labels is wide enough. Select Format,
   Tabs. In the Format Tabs dialog box, enter **3"** in
   the Tab stop position and leave the Default Tab
   stops entry to 0.5". Choose OK and Works will
   adjust the columns.

9. When you have edited the file so that only one
   tab appears before each figure, select Edit,
   Select All. The entire document will be highlighted. Select Edit, Copy.

10. Select File, New and select Spreadsheet. A blank
    spreadsheet will open.

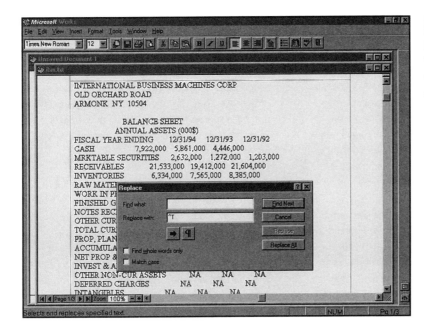

FIG. 3.10

Formatting statements for
Works requires both the
word processor and the
spreadsheet.

11. Move the cell pointer to the A1 cell (the top left cell) and select Edit, Paste. The financial statement will appear.

12. The numbers should be properly positioned into their own columns, but it will not be properly lined up because the labels in column A are truncated. Widen column A by moving your pointer to the column heading until it becomes a resizing icon; click and drag it to the right.

The above technique was created through much trial and error for U.S. Financial Statements in Disclosure. It can be adapted without too much effort to format other types of reports from Disclosure. The settings you may need to tinker with are in Step 5 where you may try different numbers of blank space, and in Step 8 where you can try a different tab width.

Understanding a Disclosure Financial Statement

Now that you have the data in a usable form, you can begin to devote your analytical ability to the company's performance instead of grappling with computer formats. The type of report we've downloaded from the Disclosure Financial Statement option combines three types of reports and shows results for the last three years. All of the results are in the file that we just downloaded and displayed in a spreadsheet.

The first groups of numbers is a balance sheet, a grand overview of the corporation's operations. The purpose of the balance sheet is to summarize assets, debts, and net worth. You can find some specific breakdowns in these categories. For example, under assets, the line "Prop, Plant & Equip" reports the value of the companies property, plants, and equipment. If it's a manufacturing concern, it will have sizable numbers in this column, but if it's a financial services organization, you wouldn't expect to see major assets in property and plants. Overall, the balance sheet says a lot about the company's financial health, but it doesn't really say a lot about it's potential for growth, which is what an investor wants to see.

You'll find indicators for growth in the next set of numbers, the income statement. These figures show how well the ongoing business operations of the company have been progressing. Key numbers are the Net Sales, at the top of the statement, and Net Income, near the bottom. You'll want to see that both of these figures have been growing in recent years. Any numbers that are in parentheses indicate a loss; while a loss in the past may not bother you,

you'll want to make sure you understand the company's strategy for turning the loss into a profit if the company has been showing a loss in income for the past year. Many relatively new companies that are considered to have great potential for long-term growth are likely to show losses under net income. But if the company does not show growth in Net Sales, it's hard to make an argument that this is a growth company.

Figure 3.11 shows the income statement for IBM after it was downloaded from Disclosure on AOL and formatted in Microsoft Works. To help clarify the trends, I created a graphic illustration of the company's performance by highlighting the Net Income row and selecting Tools, Create New Chart. The chart shows a healthy picture with IBM reporting a profit in the last year after two years of losses.

The final set of figures in the Disclosure financial statement is cash flow. Here you'll find details that

FIG. 3.11

Once a financial statement is properly formatted in a spreadsheet, you can display trends graphically, using the spreadsheet's chart command.

Chart based on figures in the Net Income row

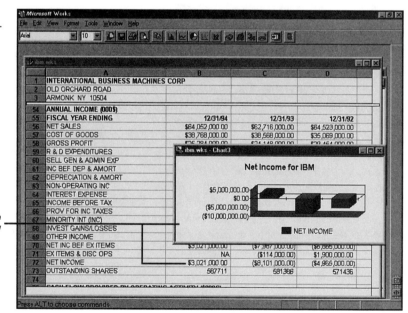

may uncover a weakness or confirm a healthy picture. For example, if the company is engaged in manufacturing, most of its cash flow should stem from operating activity rather than investing or financing activity.

One thing you will notice about the reports—especially if you use your spreadsheet to graph the numbers—is that the chronological order of the results moves from most recent to older results. This works well for reading the numbers, but may confuse you in a chart where you expect to see results show over time, from left to right. If you like, you can correct that by using your spreadsheet's Sort command. First, highlight the range to change, making sure the top number in each range is a year. Then select Tools, Sort, making sure that you are sorting by column, not row.

Historical Quotes: Tracking a Stock Over Time

Buy low and sell high, that's the idea. While it's impossible to accurately predict when a stock price will change, you will want to know the range where a stock has been trading before you buy it.

You can find the closing price for stock traded on the major exchanges since 1983 from AOL's Historical Quotes database. Select the keyword **historical quotes** to access this huge database. You'll see the window shown in figure 3.12.

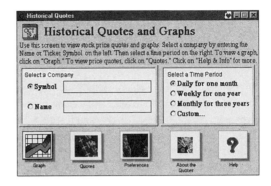

FIG. 3.12

The Historical Quotes window gives you easy access to stock price quotes and charts of price changes, but you'll save connect charges if you download the data.

You have an extraordinary amount of control over the reports that you can extract from this huge database. You can see stock prices at daily, weekly, or monthly frequencies. The default setting displays daily prices for the past month, weekly prices for the past year, or monthly prices for the past three years, but you can also choose your own time interval. No matter which time period you select, the reports show the high, low, and closing price for each period.

You can display the quotes in a chart while you're connected, which may be all you want to do when you're just casually looking at a company's performance. But if you are evaluating the company with the idea of investing, you'll want to download the data.

Downloading Historical Stock Prices

The Historical Quotes area has a well-designed interface that encourages you to relax and view as many prices as you want, using AOL's charting feature to make the data easier to digest. Of course, the meter is ticking all the time, so you'll save on connect charges if you learn how to download the data quickly and analyze your own spreadsheet while you're offline.

1. While you're connected to AOL, use the keyword **historical quotes** to begin the process of finding stock prices.

2. Select the Preferences button. A window opens, as shown in figure 3.13, where you can choose the file format AOL will use when you download data. If you're using a spreadsheet, select Comma-delimited; using this option, the data you download will be in a text format with commas in between columns. Just about any spreadsheet you can find will be able to properly read a comma-delimited file, which is also called a CSV, or comma-separated-value file. The other choices are to format data for the popular personal finances program, Quicken, or

in the MetaStock format used by a number of stock analysis programs. The graphing options in this window apply only to charts you display while online and will not affect the data you download. Downloaded data is always provided with the date, the high (or asking) price, the low (or bid) price, and the closing price for the day (or average if it's a longer period). Click OK to store your preferences.

3. After you've selected your preferences, you enter the ticker symbol or name of the stock on the main Historical Quotes and Graphs menu. You can also choose the period for the quotes. The default is the daily price for the last month. Select Custom if you want to see a specific period or want results that are older than three years.

4. Click the Quotes button. If you selected one of the standard time periods, the data will appear in a new window. But if you selected Custom Quotes, the window shown in figure 3.14 will open. Enter the frequency for the quotes (daily, weekly, or monthly) and then enter the dates in numeric format (for example, January 1, 1990 should be entered as **1/1/90**). You can specify any time period since 1983. Or, you can tell AOL to "count back" from today and provide data for a specific number of days, weeks, or months in the past.

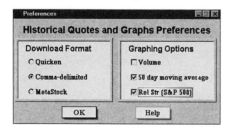

FIG. 3.13

The best option for downloading data if you use a spreadsheet is comma-delimited.

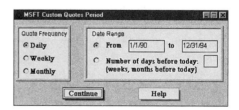

FIG. 3.14

You can specify the precise interval for historical quotes.

5. Select Continue and AOL will display a window with the prices for the period you selected, as shown in figure 3.15. (You may want to increase the size of the window by moving your mouse pointer over an edge and then dragging the window to a larger size.) Click Graph and you'll see a chart for these figures.

6. Click Download and you can begin the process of saving the data on your system. A dialog box will open, showing the name and directory AOL plans to use for the file. The name will be based on the ticker symbol of the stock, and the data format you selected. For example, if you selected Microsoft data and the comma-delimited format, the file would be saved as MSFT.CSV (Microsoft's ticker symbol is MSFT). You can edit the name of the file or choose a different directory. By default, AOL will download the file to the AOL download folder.

7. Stock price files are not very large, so normally they will download right away. But if AOL is very busy and the file is not ready for immediate downloading, you'll see a message asking if you'd like to download it later. When you begin the process of signing off from AOL, the Download Manager will ask if you want the file downloaded now. AOL will keep the file in its download queue until you give permission for the file to be downloaded.

The file you download will not have any headings so you may want to open the file with your spreadsheet and insert a new row at the top. If you've saved the file in a CSV format, here's how to identify the data in each column:

CSV column	Stock data
Column A	Ticker symbol
Column B	Date
Column C	Low price
Column D	High price
Column E	Closing or average price
Column F	Volume

Finally, you may want to delete the high, low, and volume columns. Unless you're performing a specific form of technical analysis, the closing or average prices are probably all you need.

Analyzing Historical Stock Prices

Once you've downloaded the file to your system, you can begin the process of studying it. Some experts warn that the average investor is never likely to be

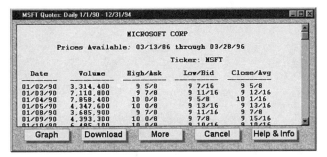

FIG. 3.15

You can choose a time period for historical stock prices but you'll always see the same type of data: high, low, and closing prices.

able to pinpoint the best time to buy or sell a stock, and you're not likely to uncover a magic pattern simply by looking at the numbers. But you may gain valuable perspective by comparing two stocks, or by comparing a stock to one of the leading stock market indicators, such as the Standard & Poors index of 500 stocks (the S&P 500).

To compare two stocks, you first need to download comparable figures, covering the exact same period and for the same interval. Then, you open one file in a spreadsheet and paste the second file into the same spreadsheet.

This technique could be used to compare how a stock was doing compared to a competitor in the industry. Let's say you were interested in a relatively small technology company, like the software company Intuit. You might want to see how it compared to a competitor who's also a giant in the same industry, Microsoft. Download data for both, and then display the results side by side.

1. Follow the steps in the previous section to download the data in a CSV format, including the process of stripping out the high, low, and volume columns.

2. Open the files in your spreadsheet, one after the other.

3. Select Window, Tile to display the files side by side. This will help you spot any differences in the two file formats.

4. Replace the label at the top of the closing price column with the name of each stock. Your screen will look like figure 3.16.

5. Select the column with prices for one of the stocks by clicking the column header. The entire column will be highlighted.

6. Select Edit, Copy. Move your cell pointer to the other spreadsheet and select the first cell in the empty column to the right of the prices (it should be labeled with the name of the

FIG. 3.16

Before you can compare the prices of two stocks, you need to make sure the data for each stock covers the same period.

company). If you've carefully followed the suggestions, that will be cell D1.

7. Select Edit, Paste. The closing price figures for the second stock will appear next to the first stock's.

8. Select File, Save As and enter a new name for this file. By saving this new spreadsheet to a new name, you'll retain the two original files just in case you want to do some other type of analysis on them.

With the two sets of prices in the same spreadsheet, you can now create a chart comparing the two. Figure 3.17 shows a chart created after following the above steps to build a new spreadsheet in Microsoft Works, and then tinkering with the charting options.

Looking at the two stock prices side by side may not answer the magic question, "Should I buy?" right away, but should help you understand the nature of the company you're considering for an investment.

The real value of this analysis is to reveal patterns. One thing that's clear is that Intuit's stock price (the lower line of the chart) is more volatile than Microsoft's. It's common for a small company, which has fewer shares on the market, to shift more dramatically than larger companies. Intuit's shares rose dramatically in October and November soon after it announced some new business alliances but dropped at the end of the year at a time when other technology stocks were also hurting. Microsoft, on the other hand, remained steady even though it shipped Windows 95 during this period. It should have been just as susceptible to the decline in technology stocks taking place at the time, but it held its ground.

Don't expect an analysis of historical prices to give you superhuman insight that will help you beat the market—after all, professional investors are poring over similar charts. But by looking at stock price charts, you'll at least gain perspective on how companies perform over time.

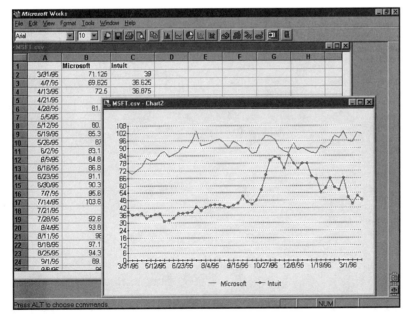

FIG. 3.17

Once the data for two different companies are displayed in the same spreadsheet, it's easy to create your own chart that shows changes in the stock prices, side by side.

Reading the Fine Print with EDGAR

Once you've mastered the art of analyzing financial statements and historical prices—if you still have any energy left—you may be ready to move on to the advanced level where usually, only professional investors dare to venture. It's a world populated with long stretches of boring reports, long columns of numbers, and little opportunity to see things graphed in colorful charts.

This world is ruled by the federal Securities and Exchange Commission (SEC) which protects investors by requiring that publicly traded corporations file detailed reports disclosing their activities. The reports must be made available to the public, and until recently, the reports were printed only on paper. Today, the reports are distributed electronically under

a program known as EDGAR (Electronic Data Gathering, Analysis and Retrieval).

You'll find these SEC filings on AOL by entering the keyword **EDGAR**. Be forewarned, the reports in EDGAR are not light reading. While you may be able to uncover a nugget of inspiration, to gain a perspective on the company, you'll need to do a lot of reading here. In Chapter 4, "Hot Stock Tips from Experts," you'll find out where you can get expert analyses from the reports. You can read the opinions of professional stock analysts, who are paid to read the filings and based their recommendations, in part, on what they've found in EDGAR. Don't pass up the opportunity to read the EDGAR report (see fig. 3.18); some investors consider it mandatory reading before investing in a stock. But don't expect to find a crystal ball that reveals the future here, either.

If you're ready to roll up your sleeves and dive in, you'll find the search methods are similar to those

FIG. 3.18

The EDGAR databases reveal minute details about every publicly traded corporations' financial maneuvers.

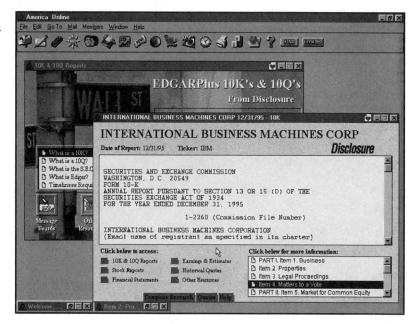

used in Disclosure's financial statements area. In fact, the EDGAR database and financial statements share some of the same menus. Figure 3.18 shows a report in the EDGAR database; you'll notice that the menus are similar to the menus seen in figures 3.7 and 3.8.

There are two basic reports:

- The *10-Q* is a quarterly financial report, and it must be filed within 45 days of the end of a fiscal quarter; some of the more important disclosures in these reports are reports on legal proceedings, and changes in stock ownership (including sales by management).

- The *10-K* are annual reports that include detailed financial statements, including three-year audited income and cash flow statements. One area of the 10-K you may want to look for are management explanations for their recent successes and failures.

Predicting the Future

Basing decisions on financial statements and historical data has some value—at least you're looking at certainties. But when investing, you're making a bet on the future. One way to help reduce the risk is to take a look at earnings estimates. Wall Street investors follow these estimates closely; major fluctuations in stock prices occur when a company reports its results that vary from the estimates.

Earnings estimates are prepared by professional analysts who base their opinions on a variety of sources, including EDGAR filings and discussions with managers at the corporations they track. In the past, you needed to be a client of a brokerage house or a

subscriber to an expensive newsletter to gain access to earnings estimates. AOL has something just as good: First Call earnings estimates.

Finding Earnings Estimates

First Call reports are based on surveys of analysts and reveal what Wall Street overall is estimating on earnings per share data. You'll find the reports by using the keyword: **first call**. First Call uses a similar interface to Disclosure. You search the earning estimate reports by company; you can use the company name or ticker symbol, but you'll find your reports faster if you use the ticker symbol.

Once you've selected a company, you'll see a report that shows earnings estimates for the next four fiscal quarters. Figure 3.19 shows a report for IBM.

Working with Earnings Estimate Reports

Working with the earnings estimate reports is very similar to working with Disclosure financial statements. You can print the reports (File, Print) or save the reports to your hard disk (File, Save). But once the reports are downloaded, you may need to put some work into the file format if you want to use them in a spreadsheet. Earnings estimate reports will be even more work to format in a spreadsheet since there is a variety of column formats used in the document. In general, you'll probably find less need to import these reports into a spreadsheet, anyway. For the most part, you'll be able to do most everything you need to do in a word processor. And they should display fine in a word processor, especially when you use a fixed pitch font.

FIG. 3.19

First Call's earnings estimate reports are based on a survey of professional stock analysts.

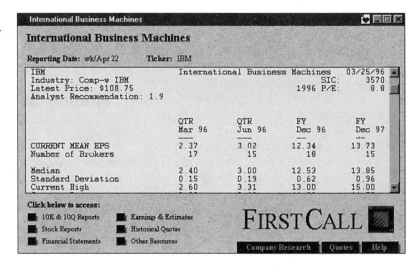

Staying on Top of the News

Active investors want to know when anything significant happens at a company they're watching. AOL's News Profiles makes that job easier. You can have news delivered on any company or industry you're following. Summaries of news reports will arrive in your mailbox soon after they're released.

Enter the keyword **news profile** and create a profile. You can enter a stock's ticker symbol or enter broader categories to track a specific industry. Be careful. Your mailbox will be overloaded with news reports if you use a category that has a lot of news, such as "computers" or "banking." Start by creating a news profile that's very narrow, covering just a few companies. And then you can expand when you feel you're able to digest the news you receive.

Having the Market Pulses Delivered to You

If you spend a lot of time online during the day when markets are open, you can track the markets without doing a thing. Chart-O-Matic will display a pulse of the market in a chart that you can keep active while you're online. The chart is updated every 15 minutes with the most recent updates (see fig. 3.20).

You can choose from over a dozen market indices, including the Dow Jones averages and the NASDAQ Composite. You can also display the price for any stock in the S&P 500.

You can display a live chart by entering the keyword **chartomatic** and selecting one of the indices from the list. A graph will appear immediately. To see a chart for one of the S&P 500 stocks, click the S&P 500 button on the Chart-O-Matic main menu.

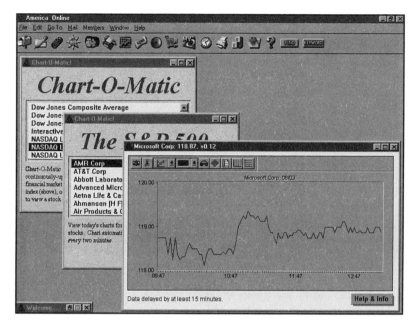

FIG. 3.20

You can see charts for the market averages and S&P stock prices updated constantly throughout the day with Chart-O-Matic.

You'll see a list of stocks; click any one of them and a chart will appear. You can display more than one chart at a time.

▼ **TIP**

To make the best use of Chart-O-Matic, you'll want to adjust the size of the chart window so you can display other services while you're online.

If you only want to use AOL as a live stock quote system, open several charts and select Window-Tile to see several graphs at once. You'll be only 15 minutes behind the expensive systems doing the same thing at Wall Street brokerage houses.

C H A P T E R

4

Hot Stock Tips from Experts

The stock market thrives on rumor. Everyone "in the know" has an opinion on what's going to be hot. And everyone who wants to make money is eager to know what these leading money managers really think. While you may be wary of "expert opinion" and prefer to make your own choices, the fact is, the opinions of experts have an impact on the market every day. The price of a stock can go up dramatically after one of these experts recommends it, or drop like a stone after a "sell" recommendation appears.

Even if you don't plan to buy a stock based on an expert's opinion, you will want to know what the experts are saying so you can keep an eye on the market's direction. The opinions of these experts can affect the value of your holdings because active investors buy based on their perception of how the market is moving. In the short run, a stock will rise if enough people buy it, even if the company is in dire financial straits, and companies with excellent long-term prospects can suffer if enough people turn against the stock.

Keeping abreast of the expert's recommendations will also help you track overall trends that affect entire sectors of the market. Stocks in a sector like technology or financial services are often caught in a trend affecting the entire sector, so even if a company has made an announcement that should push its stock price higher, the stock may not go up if the market consensus is against the stock's sector.

It's the great American dream—someone will slip you a stock tip that will make you rich. The reality is a little more complicated, but knowing what the experts are recommending can get you closer to your goals.

Separating the Experts from the Wannabes

The online community removes many barriers that we face in everyday life. Talking to people you'd never have a chance to meet in person is one of the great benefits. But you can also run into people who claim to be something they're not or who promise financial rewards they can't deliver. Fortunately, there are ways to tell the difference between someone who's genuinely knowledgeable and willing to share information and those who have another agenda.

> **"Be wary of the talk that goes on in message boards, chat rooms, and Internet newsgroups."**

The first rule is to be wary of the talk that goes on in message boards, chat rooms, and Internet newsgroups. In these public areas—especially when financial topics are discussed—self-promoters are free to peddle get-rich schemes and untested investments. Message boards where stock tips are traded can be abused by unscrupulous brokers who spread rumors in the hope of influencing the market. Even if a rumor is based on completely faulty assumptions, it may push a stock up or down.

■ NOTE

Refer to the section "Internet Newsgroups" in Chapter 1, "America Online: Filled with Facts, Opinions, and Opportunity," for further information on Internet newsgroups.

While America Online message boards are moderated and obvious phonies are often publicly rebuked if they're caught, even on the most carefully monitored message boards, an inappropriate message may appear for hours before a moderator challenges it. But America Online chat rooms and Internet newsgroups are usually not moderated; in these circles, no one can help you distinguish between the experts and the wanna-be experts other than your own common sense.

America Online (AOL) presents a number of features from responsible organizations that do proffer investment advice. There's one big difference between these experts and the pretenders: the experts are under contract with America Online to provide reputable information. The pretenders are anonymous; many pretenders have become famous figures on a message board. And, over time, the regular visitors learn to dismiss what they say. When you're new to a message board, pay attention not only to what people say, but to how others respond. It may seem like a crazy way to do business, but in some respects, it's a microcosm of the overall stock market. Some people posture, and others are straightforward, but both have an impact on the market.

Just remember that successful investing requires research, so you're never at risk simply from listening to the pitch of a get-rich-quick artist. You're only at risk if you don't do your homework and learn about the investment before you commit your hard-earned cash. Chapter 3, "Researching Stocks with Hard Facts," showed you the basic tools of investment research on AOL. This chapter will expose you to some of the strategies where you can apply those techniques.

Table 4.1 describes the professional stock investment advisors you may encounter on AOL.

TABLE 4.1   AOL's Professional Stock Investment Advisors

Advisor	Description
The Motley Fool	Run by two brothers who manage their own portfolio in public, and employ analysts to spot hot stocks. Also draws thousands of serious, small investors with strong opinions to the chat rooms and message boards.
Decision Point	Attempts to spot trends by applying technical analysis to market trends and to the performance of 152 of the largest companies.
Bizinsider	Herb Greenberg, a newspaper columnist who follows stocks and posts his own analysis of market trends.
First Call	Information service specializing in earnings estimates from analysts.
Top Advisors Corner	Daily columns on market trends from leading analysts and newsletter writers, including Charles B. Carlson.

Investing for Fun and Profit with The Motley Fool

If you're the type who thinks nothing is more boring than investment talk, then you owe it to yourself to visit The Motley Fool. The discussions here are wild, offbeat, and passionate. No one takes themselves very seriously, yet everyone here is devoted to the art of spotting good investments (and eager to welcome newcomers). Opinions are expressed strongly. Facts are delivered straight. And you never have any doubt about what people really think.

You can reach the Motley Fool area by using one of two keywords: **motley fool** or **fool**.

The Motley Fool is run by two brothers—Tom and David Gardner—who write some of the articles themselves and employ others to provide the rest of the material. All employees are identified by the initials "MF" at the beginning of their screen names. Within the Motley Fool area there are daily articles, stock recommendations, links to other places online, message boards, and chat rooms. There are so many services that The Motley Fool has its own index and a schedule of daily events. But finding your way around may be your chief obstacle to enjoying the place; the Fools admit that their Fooldom is disorganized. And finding your way requires constant attention. The screen in figure 4.1 shows the open Motley Fool menu on a typical day, but by the next day, its different features will appear on this menu.

At the heart of all these features is the Motley Fool Portfolio—a group of stocks that the Gardner brothers actually buy as their own investment. They explain the reasons why they're buying a stock and publicize their plans about a day in advance. Thousands of regular AOL subscribers follow their advice, making trades along with the Gardner's, or at least trying to learn something from their rationale. In addition to the main Motley Fool portfolio, one of their staff members manages "The Boring Portfolio" which takes fewer risks than the brothers' portfolio.

FIG. 4.1

The Motley Fool's main menu is always changing; there's so much in here—a daily calendar and index are needed to keep track of it all.

You can also follow several other stock-buying methods, mixed in with many discussions of individual stocks. In the Motley Fool message boards, thousands of people share tips on stocks.

The philosophy of The Motley Fool is to educate and entertain. The name comes from the line, "A fool, A fool! I met a fool in the forest, a motley fool," from Shakespeare's *As You Like It*. In the judgment of the Gardner brothers, a Shakespearean fool is the only person in the kingdom who would always tell the truth and yet managed to amuse the crowds. That's the goal for the forum and the people who work there. The "foolish" talk is actually a clever technique. By claiming to be nothing more than truthful jesters, Motley Fool staffers are freed from the restraint that forces more serious advisors to qualify each bit of advice with a warning. Other experts may dispute whether these Motley Fools always dispense wisdom (no expert is always right), but if you're looking for clear opinions from real investors, you won't be disappointed by a visit here.

"If you are looking for clear opinions from real investors, you won't be disappointed."

The Stocks They Buy

The Gardner brothers are unique. They didn't become experts by writing a best-selling book or earning a reputation on Wall Street. They earned their status by putting their own money on the line. The Motley Fool portfolio is a group of stocks that the Gardner brothers actually buy. They document their trades carefully in the many articles posted about the portfolio, even including the amount spent on broker's commissions in their calculations (see fig. 4.2).

When the brothers sell or buy a new stock, they give Motley Fool users advance notice, so they can plan their own trades. If you want to follow the portfolio closely and don't want to risk missing out on a trade, you can subscribe to a mailing list that will send portfolio announcements to your e-mail box (a small fee is charged for this service).

If you do plan to invest your own money, don't jump right in. You'll find that many of the stocks were bought months ago and are not necessarily good buys right now (the Gardner brothers may decide to sell them tomorrow). If you do invest your own

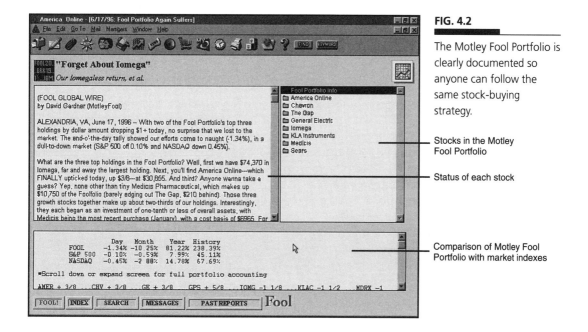

FIG. 4.2

The Motley Fool Portfolio is clearly documented so anyone can follow the same stock-buying strategy.

— Stocks in the Motley Fool Portfolio

— Status of each stock

— Comparison of Motley Fool Portfolio with market indexes

money, start by buying the next recommendation, rather than the older ones.

To really take advantage of the advice in The Motley Fool, you have to be willing to visit here regularly. At first, your visits will help you understand the philosophies that guide the trading. Later, after you've taken advice and bought some stock, you'll want to visit the message board of those stocks to see what people are saying about them now.

The philosophy behind the portfolio is to pursue high-growth prospects; as a result, there's a fair amount of risk, and the portfolio is subject to wild swings. The brothers have created a formula that expresses their overall investment approach; the stocks they buy for the portfolio are not necessarily the "winners" based on the formula, but you can expect that the stocks they select do well according to their formula, which they call the Fool Ratio.

Rather than wait for the brothers to buy a new stock for their portfolio, you may want to try applying the formula yourself.

The Fool Ratio: A Stock Picking Formula

The Fool Ratio compares a stock's current price-to-earnings multiple range with the company's growth rates. The Gardner brothers believe that market activity will always push a stock price to the same price-to-earnings multiple range found on other stocks, but many companies grow for years before the market is able to value them accurately. These are the stocks they recommend buying; if the company's underlying business is able to support the same rate of growth, you're likely to have a winner.

You can read a detailed explanation of the theory, including definitions of all the terms, by selecting choices from the menu. You can even download a calculator that will compute the ratio for stock prices you enter. You'll find it by using the keyword **fool** to display the main menu; select Index and look for Fool Ratio.

Beware, however, that just because a company's recent growth rate is favorable doesn't mean the company will continue to grow at the same rate. You need to learn about the company's market position to determine if the company is still on an upward path or if it's reached a peak. That's one reason why the Motley Fool message boards are so busy. Investors who own many of these growth stocks are hard at work looking for hints about the company's prospects from other investors.

The Boring Portfolio: A Modestly Aggressive Approach

Recognizing that many people don't want to take on the risks inherent in spotting high-growth stocks, the

Motley Fools also run a Boring Portfolio. In the same style as the main Motley Fool portfolio, all trades are carefully explained and activity in the portfolio is closely monitored daily. The manager of this portfolio looks for stable companies that are unlikely to encounter serious losses but have good growth potential. The portfolio manager credits legendary stock picker and best-selling author Peter Lynch as an inspiration.

The Daily Pitch: Stock Tips and a Quiz

Keeping true to the Motley Fool's goal of educating and entertaining, the Daily Pitch area combines stock-buying recommendations and a game. The Daily Pitch is a brief article that discusses a current business trend, speculates on the potential for growth of some of the major players in this sector, and then makes specific stock-buying recommendations. At the end of the article is a multiple-choice question where users are asked to pick a change in a stock price or market indicator. (For example, By how many points will the Dow Jones Industrial Average change tomorrow?) Winners earn free AOL connect time.

You can find the Daily Pitch by using the keyword **fool** to display the Motley Fool main menu; then, select Index and select Games from the list of choices.

Beating the Dow: The Classic and "Fool's" Versions

Following stock market trends is not only hard work, it requires constant vigilance. You can't take a long vacation without careful planning because market conditions can change dramatically in a short time. The market may be dragging your portfolio down while you're relaxing on a beach. A number of market strategies are designed to make you immune from short-term fluctuations, using historical patterns to pick stocks. They also require less work, since the strategy gives you the names of stocks to buy, rather than suggesting good options.

▼ T I P

Beware of short sellers who denigrate a stock, hoping to drive its price down. Investors who sell short borrow shares of a stock in the hope it will go down; they hope to buy it at a lower price to repay the loan, pocketing the difference between the two prices.

One popular strategy, the Dow Dividend Approach, requires less than an hour's time to get started and doesn't require any additional work for another year. The basic strategy is to rank the 30 stocks in the Dow Jones Industrial Average by their yield (that's the stock's annual dividend divided by the price of one share) and to buy an equal amount of the top 10. If you were investing $10,000, you'd buy $1,000 of each of these stocks. Hold all shares, and at the end of a full year, perform the calculation again. Sell any stock that has fallen out of the top 10, hold those still in the top 10, and buy the others with the proceeds of the sale—dividing up the proceeds equally among the new stocks. For example, if the portfolio was worth $10,100 at the end of a year, you'd invest $1,010 in each company on the list. Proponents of this strategy point to a 17 percent return, on average, over the last 25 years.

This strategy has attracted a legion of followers. It's been so popular that others have refined the theory.

Michael O'Higgins, in a best-selling book, *Beating the Dow*, shows how to improve the Dow Dividend return to 21 percent annually by buying only the five stocks with the lowest share price. But the Motley Fools have added a refinement on O'Higgins' version: they believe you can improve the return up to 25 percent by avoiding the one stock out of the five whose price is lowest. In the Motley Fool rendition, you eliminate the lowest price stock from the five selected by O'Higgins' method, dividing your investment evenly among the four stocks, except that you double up the amount you spend on the second-cheapest stock.

"No one can guarantee results but these strategies are relatively conservative."

Since the calculations must be done precisely if it's going to work (according to the theory, anyway), every day The Motley Fool publishes the current list of stocks that meet the criteria. The list shows the stocks that are recommended by all the three approaches: the original Dow Dividend 10 stocks, the "Beat the Dow" 5, and the Motley Fool 4 (see fig. 4.3).

You can find the list for today, along with detailed explanations of the theory including the formulas used in picking the stocks, by using the keyword **fool** to display the Motley Fool main menu; then, select Index and select Dow Dividend Approach.

No one can guarantee results but these strategies are relatively conservative. Your investments are limited to some of America's biggest companies, and you'll be earning income from the dividends these stocks

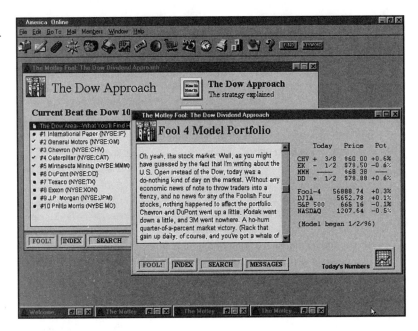

FIG. 4.3

The Motley Fool tracks the stocks recommended by the Dow Dividend approach and two variations; the list is updated every day.

pay. But reaping the full benefit requires that you wait a year before you sell and that you're willing to keep your money in this plan for many years. At the end of the year, you may not have achieved the 22 percent return (you may even post a loss after a year). It could take several years before your average return is in the range of 22 percent.

If you do follow the plan, you'll need to buy the stock through a broker. Motley Fool has nothing to do with the purchase of the stock; all The Motley Fool does is show you which stocks meet the criteria that day. If you buy the stocks, you need to record the date of your purchase, consult the Motley Fool's Dow Dividend Approach list exactly one year later, and switch your investment to these new stocks. You can't keep any of the money if you expect to achieve the 22 percent. (Chapter 5, "Trading Stocks Online," will guide you through the process of using AOL's online brokers).

Table 4.2 explains terms you are likely to encounter in the Motley Fool area of AOL.

Decision Point: Technical Analysis

If you're just looking for the best information on investments, you may enjoy going back and forth between the Motley Fool and Decision Point forum. However, you wouldn't ever want to be in the same room if partisans of these two approaches met: the sparks would fly. The Decision Point philosophy is, in many ways, the complete opposite of The Motley Fool and represents much of the conventional wisdom that Motley Fool staffers rail against.

TABLE 4.2   A Motley Fool Glossary

Term	Definition
Boring Portfolio	A group of stocks tracked daily; the Motley Fool staffer who selects the stocks aims to find growth opportunities among large corporations.
Daily Pitch	An article written by one of the senior staffers that recommends a handful of stocks and posts a quiz.
Dow Dividend Approach	A stock-picking technique based on the Motley Fool's refinement of the strategy in Michael O'Higgin's book, *Beating the Dow*.
Evening News	A column from the Motley Fool staff that summarizes market activity at the end of the day, paying attention to stocks recommended in recent editions of the Daily Pitch.
Fooldom	All of the services that can be found from AOL's Motley Fool main menu.
Fool Ratio	A formula for picking stocks that compares a company's growth rate with the stock's price-to-earnings multiple. The goal is to find a company with revenues growing faster than the stock price.
MF	These initials appear at the beginning of the screen name of a Motley Fools staffer; many offer a clue about the staffer's role. MF Edible is an analyst following the food services industry and MF Wings follows aviation.
Motley Fool Portfolio	A group of stocks recommended by the Motley Fool staff and tracked as a group.

Decision Point's focus is on technical analysis of market trends and data on 152 of the largest companies (only stocks listed in the Dow Jones Industrial Average, Dow Jones Transportation Average, Dow Jones Utility Average, and the S&P 100 Index). The approach is careful and methodical, shunning risky, growth stocks in favor of large corporations with long track records. The goal is to spot rising stocks by calculating market index lines and oscillators (a trend line derived from a formula, using marketing statistics as variables). The highlight of the Decision Point area is daily and weekly charts that illustrate a new finding from all that number crunching. You'll find Daily/Weekly Reports & Charts listed prominently on Decision Point's main menu (see fig. 4.4).

Delving into Serious Stock Analysis

The type of number crunching that goes into Decision Point's reports is typical of the analysis performed at large professional stock brokerage houses to predict market trends. So if you want to delve into serious stock analysis, this is the place. You can gain a quick perspective by viewing the charts that illustrate the trends. If you want to delve into technical analysis, you'll find explanation of the Decision Point formulas by selecting the Instructions/Definitions option on the menus, and you can download

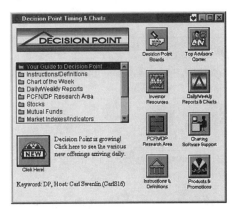

FIG. 4.4

Decision Point provides detailed technical analysis of the market and stocks of 152 of the largest corporations.

exhaustive spreadsheets that provide all the calculations in exacting detail. You can display the main Decision Point menu by using the keyword **dp**.

You'll find it hard to jump into Decision Point and follow the recommendations unless you've got a good grounding in the mathematical principles behind technical analysis. (If you do have such an education, you'll be interested to know that Decision Point follows John Bollinger's school of Rational Analysis).

Since Decision Point generates so many reports with its analyses, it's easy to become overwhelmed, sorting through daily charts, quick charts, reports, and spreadsheets. The following sections will help you get started with Decision Point's highlights. Once you've explored these, you'll know if you want to dig deeper.

Viewing Decision Point Quick Charts

Even if you don't know an oscillator from an ostrich, you may want to make Decision Point's Daily Charts part of your online routine. Once you take a few minutes to understand the basic theories, you'll find the charts offer a good perspective on overall market trends and often highlight good stocks to buy. A single chart out of the hundreds created during the daily analysis is singled out to demonstrate a clear trend.

1. Connect to AOL and use the keyword **dp** to enter the Decision Point area.

2. Select Daily/Weekly Reports from the list of services. A dialog box will open with more choices.

3. Select Daily Quick Charts. A window similar to the one in figure 4.5 opens.

4. The main chart in this window displays one of the most interesting charts from the Decision Point's database. The other charts can be selected from the list that appears to the left of the main chart.

5. If you want to see the numbers behind the charts, double-click the chart (this works with the chart that appears in the main window, or with any other chart you select from the list). A window opens with a list of reports.

6. Select the Daily Market/Signal Summary for today's date; a window will display the chart. Some charts overlap two different trend lines on the same chart, as in figure 4.5.

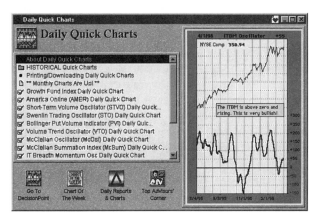

FIG. 4.5

Decision Point's Daily Quick Charts menu highlights one of the market indicators that reveal a trend.

7. With the report open, you can save it to your system by selecting File, Save.

The top of a Decision Point report usually includes tips on the best way to view the report. The Daily Market/Signal Summary reports (which provide the numbers behind the Daily Quick Charts) are best viewed in a word processor with a fixed-pitch font, such as Courier (on a PC) or Monaco (on a Mac).

A good way to determine if this philosophy is for you is to look at charts from recent weeks. If you believe they've accurately determined a trend—or at least expressed a trend that you can see—you'll be sold. Otherwise, you may feel it's over your head. To see older charts, from the main Decision Point menu, select the listing for Stocks, Mutual Funds, or Market Index/Indicators. The menu will display the current chart and a list of earlier charts. Scroll down the list and click the start for a particular day and see if the trend in the chart matches your own experience.

Spotting Companies Whose Prospects Have Changed

One of an investors' best friends is a tip that the market may be changing its opinion on a stock. If you're willing to do a little digging, you'll find a list of such stocks in the First Call area. In Chapter 3, "Researching Stocks with Hard Facts," you learned how to check First Call's database of earnings estimates to evaluate a company's overall prospects. But First Call also creates lists that spotlight some of the more interesting changes in earning estimates.

1. To find the reports, use the keyword **first call**. The First Call opening menu will appear.

2. From the main menu, select The Buzz on Wall St. A list of reports will open (see fig. 4.6).

Some of these reports list stocks that are planning to split (that is, lower the prices of shares and issue additional shares to every shareholder). A split usually occurs in a stock that has been rising steadily. Some investors see it as a sign of upward momentum; others dismiss stock splits as an attempt by the company to hype itself.

Look further down the list and you'll find more interesting reports. The reports that begin with the words, "Is It a Trend?," contain lists of stocks that are likely to be the focus of active trading because at least one financial analyst has recently changed an earnings estimate. If it's a positive revision (better earnings than expected), the stock price is likely to go up; if it's a downward revision, the stock is likely to suffer.

For example, select the report "Is It a Trend? Positive Revisions for Underfollowed Companies," and you'll

see a list of small stocks that were recently upgraded (see fig. 4.7).

Unfortunately, you can't print or save this report to disk. You need to read it online (and you may want to take notes). If you really want to capture the information, you may want to use a screen capture program; see the section "Keeping What You Find" in Chapter 1 for directions on how to obtain a screen capture program. However, you can do more research on one of the stocks with little effort. Here's how you can quickly display a chart for this company's stock, while passing by a roster of other financial resources you can use to research the companies on the list.

1. Select one of the stocks on the list and click the Open button. The First Call Earnings Estimate

FIG. 4.6

Reports in the First Call database show companies that analysts recently upgraded or downgraded.

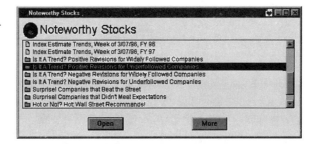

FIG. 4.7

First Call's spotlight on small stocks with upgraded earnings estimates is a good place to spot a winner.

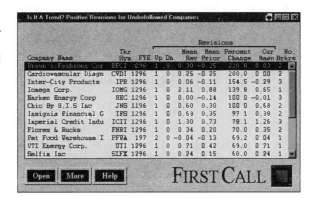

report will open. Make a note of the stock's ticker symbol (it appears at the top of the report).

2. Select the Company Research button. The Company Research window opens.

3. Then select the Historical Stock Quotes button. The Historical Stock Quotes window opens.

4. Type in the stock ticker symbol and select any other options. For this type of analysis, the graph option "Weekly for One Year" works best. Select the Graph button, and a chart will open. Your screen will look like figure 4.8.

In most cases, you'll find the stock has started to rise within the past few days. It's a safe bet that the favorable earnings reports affected the change. Of course, there's no guarantee that the stock will continue to rise, but you may find other positive indicators if you keep digging.

Talking to Other Investors

You'll find plenty of tips in the AOL message boards and chat rooms. Some are from experts but most are from other investors. Don't rush out and buy a stock just because someone in a chat room recommended it. As mentioned earlier, public discussion areas are often visited by professional stock traders who are hoping to influence public opinion. So view everything you read in a public discussion with scrutiny. Participating in chat rooms can be valuable for a couple of reasons:

◆ You can take the pulse of the market.

◆ You can get a different perspective on an investment.

◆ The value of chat rooms is that they are filled with other people who are following the markets.

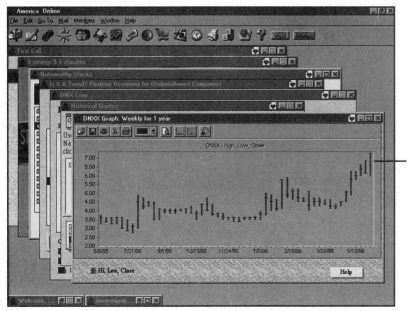

FIG. 4.8

With a few clicks, you can move from the earnings revision report to a chart of the stock's price history.

Stock rose after a positive earnings revision

Message Boards Where the Subject Is Stocks

Message boards are great for asking questions. Whether you're puzzling over a new term you heard, or you're trying to decide whether to sell a stock, you have nothing to lose by asking a question. Your level of success in getting good information in return can be attributed to two factors: asking the question in the right board and phrasing the question properly.

▼ T I P

Don't just take one person's word for it. If you read something about an investment in one message board, go to the message boards in a different area and see what people there think about the idea.

Finding the right message board is really a two-part process. You probably have the time to keep up-to-date on only one or two message boards on a regular basis, and so you'll seek out a place where the general discussion suits your everyday interests. But that may not be the best place to ask every question you have. On occasion, you'll need to seek out a board that attracts a different type of person. For example, a small investor who owns a few growth-oriented stocks may usually read the message boards in the Motley Fool where those stocks are the main topic of conversation. But if you become interested in technical analysis and want to learn more, those boards are unlikely to be fertile ground; you'll want to take your question to a board in the Decision Point section.

Phrasing a question properly is easy; too many people phrase a question badly by saying too much. Don't try to unravel the mysteries of the universe.

Ask just one question, not 10. Keep it simple and to the point. And check back every day or so to read any responses. While your message will be seen by others who visit the board within minutes of when you post it, it could be many days before someone responds (if at all).

When you first investigate an investment area's message boards (see Table 4.3), you'll need to select a folder to explore. These folders are organized by category. For example, in the Motley Fool message boards, you'll find "Talk with the Editors," "The Dow Area," and dozens more. Once you open the folder, you'll see a list of all recent messages, identified by the subject, date it was posted, and the screen name of the person who wrote the message (see fig. 4.9). Read through the list of messages to find any that interest you, or select the Post Another Message button to ask a question. (In Chapter 1, the section "Finding Information in a Message Board" provides detailed steps on using message boards.)

Chat Rooms Where the Subject Is Stocks

AOL has hundreds of individual chat rooms devoted to all sorts of topics, but only a handful are devoted to the stock market and mutual funds. So when you join a chat room on investing, you'll make good use of your time online; the discussion will be completely focused on investing. You won't need to "say" a thing. Just read comments from others, and you'll get a feeling for what other investors are thinking (see fig. 4.10).

For active traders, chat rooms have an advantage over message boards. When the market changes in the middle of the day, you'll be able to talk about what's happening right now. So during major stock

FIG. 4.9

Message boards are organized by category; after you select a category folder, you'll see the individual messages.

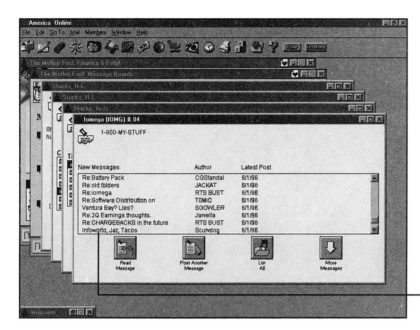

Subject of each message

TABLE 4.3	Message Boards Where Investors Swap Tips
Message Board	**Description**
AAII	A good place for beginners. Much of the investment talk focuses on long-range planning rather than stock tips. Keyword **aaii**
Decision Point Boards	The talk generally bogs down into arcane comparisons of technical analysis techniques, but the main theme is forecasting market trends so you may find interesting posts here. Keyword: **dp**
Investor's Network	Similar to AAII. For stock tips, look for the New Guru review; you'll find message boards run by financial planners and newsletter editors. You can also find message boards devoted to a specific stock. Keyword: **in**
Motley Fool	The most popular place for investors. There are dozens of individual boards. In the alphabetical listing by company, individual stocks are closely tracked by people who own shares and analyze every bit of news about the stock. Keyword: **fool**
Nightly Business Report	Discussions are based on segments of the PBS TV series; look for the alphabetical listing of companies to find talk about an individual stock. Keyword: **nbr**

FIG. 4.10

Investment-oriented chat rooms can be a good place to take the pulse of the market.

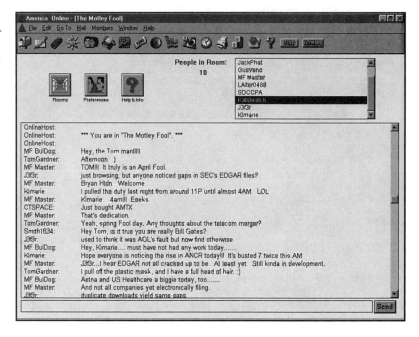

market changes, you'll find investment-oriented chat rooms become very busy. Aside from these exceptions, chat rooms are busiest during the evening hours.

Here are some tips for getting the most from the investment chat rooms:

◆ Be patient. Even in a busy chat room, you need to wait two or three minutes to get a feel for the discussion. At first, the comments won't make any sense, but after a few minutes, you'll be able to pick up the flavor of the chat room and the current topic.

◆ Hop around. If the topic in one room doesn't interest you, try another.

◆ Check up on people. Everyone's name is listed when they enter a room. If someone has an interesting point of view, look up his or her Member Profile. Select his or her name from the

People in Room list, and double-click. A menu opens; select Get Info to find his or her personal bio.

◆ Go private. If someone says something that intrigues you but it's ignored by the rest of the conversation, send an instant message to the person who made the comment. Find his or her name in the People in Room list, double click, and select the option Message. You can then type a message in this box; if you click the Send button, it will be seen only by the person you selected. If they choose to respond to you with an instant message, you'll be the only one to see the response.

Checking the Facts, Fast

The purpose of participating in investment-oriented chat rooms is to learn about the stocks other people are considering and the reasons they're looking at them. People who check into a room regularly tend to follow certain stocks and exchange the latest news on each. Because many of the participants are familiar with the stocks, they refer to their ticker symbols very casually. As a newcomer, you're likely to come across the ticker symbols of many new stocks. Rather than slow down the conversation by asking others to identify each stock, you'll want to look at one of AOL's business databases, such as the Stock Quotes, Company Research, or Morningstar Stock Reports database while you're logged into the chat room. While the first two are essential tools for researching a stock (as explained in Chapter 3), the Morningstar Stock Reports, which is a snapshot on a company, works well in this application by combining some stock price information with a few lines from the company balance sheets.

You'll be able to check out the stock without leaving the room and losing track of the conversation. Once you know the name of the stock and something about its business, you'll be in a much better position to ask questions than if you were totally ignorant of the company.

Running a Fact Check While You're in a Chat Room

The following steps will demonstrate how to open an AOL research database while you're participating in a chat room. This example uses the Morning Stock Report Database for fact checking with the Motley Fool chat room, but you can use the same technique with other databases and chat rooms.

1. Connect to AOL and type the keyword **company research**. The Company Research main window opens.

2. Select the Stock Reports icon. The main menu for Stock Reports from Morningstar opens.

3. Now that the Stock Reports database is ready for use, you can switch gears and enter the chat room. Type the keyword **motley fool**. The Motley Fool main menu opens.

4. Select the Chat option. A main chat window opens.

5. Select whichever chat room seems most interesting. The chat display opens.

Both windows will remain active. You can participate in the chat until you come across a company you want to research. Select Window-Stock Reports to display the Morningstar main menu. You can perform a search, and read up on the company without disconnecting from the chat room. Then, when you're done reading, you can switch back to the chat room by selecting the Window menu again. If you're logged into the Motley Fool chat room, select Motley Fool from the window menu. You can even keep your eye on the chat room chatter if you rearrange your windows; you can resize the chat window by dragging its borders, but you cannot resize the Stock Reports windows. Figure 4.11 shows how your screen would look during such a session.

▼ **T I P**

Most AOL chats about stocks and investing take place in the evening hours. During the day, most of the chat rooms are devoted to socializing, not business.

You can continue switching between the chat room and the Stock Report window as you come across other companies you want to investigate.

FIG. 4.11

You can read about a company mentioned in a chat room by opening one of the databases in Company Research. Use the Window menu to switch between the two.

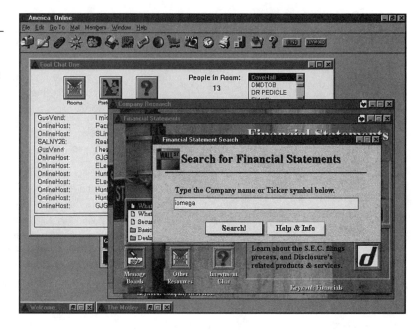

5

Trading Stocks Online

AOL's online trading ser-

vices can save you money

over traditional brokers

and give you complete

control over your invest-

ments, day or night.

Now that you know how to research stocks and consult the experts for the latest market-wise opinions, you've got the skills you need to be an independent investor. The online brokerage services on America Online (AOL) are available to execute your trades day or night, seven days a week. Setting up an online account and making those trades is simple, once you understand the basic terms. Do make sure you understand the risks and the need to conduct proper research before you invest! Before you begin to trade, you'll need to choose between the three brokers who are available through America Online.

PCFN (Personal Computer Financial Network) is the more popular service, and it's easier to find since PCFN appears on the AOL main menus. A second service, TradePlus, provides fewer features but offers lower prices and gives you a choice of two brokers (Quick & Reilly or E*Trade). TradePlus is almost invisible on AOL, but you'll learn how to find it later in this chapter.

Online Trading Basics

Before you put your hard-earned money at risk, do yourself a favor and make certain that you're familiar with the basic terminology used in online trading. If you have any questions about the basics of stock trading, look through the list of articles in the American Association of Individual Investors (AAII) section on AOL. There's a library that has complete explanations for every aspect of stock trading (keyword **AAII**, select Reference Library).

You'll also find research on stockbrokers, showing how they compare using current prices and services. Figure 5.1 shows the main screen for AAII.

Online trades are executed within minutes or seconds of when you place an order, so you have little room for error. If you make a mistake while trading, you may be able to have it corrected by calling the brokerage service on the telephone and waiting to speak to a customer service representative, but there's no guarantee he or she will be able to reverse the trade.

Because online trading is performed using ordinary menus, placing a trade online will seem as familiar as searching for information from an AOL menu option. But since the stakes are a little higher when you select Place Order from a menu than when you're browsing for information, you'll want to make sure you understand the turf before you get started.

Feel free to explore the menus for PCFN and TradePlus. You can't do any harm; until you open a brokerage account, you won't be able to place any trades.

How Online Trading Works

There are many online brokers, aside from those on America Online. Some of the larger securities traders, like Charles Schwab and Fidelity Investments, sell their own software that allows their customers to connect directly to their own trading computers. A few online brokers are making plans to provide trades over the Internet. So don't feel you need to use AOL for your trades; shop around to make sure you're getting the best service and prices for your trades.

America Online gives you access to three brokers—PCFN, Quick & Reilly, and E*Trade—but America Online has no direct involvement in the trades. In fact, these three brokers are also accessible through other online services, such as CompuServe and Prodigy, and have thousands of customers who place their orders by phone.

The software you see when you're using an online broker connects into an automated trading system.

FIG. 5.1

The AAII library is filled with good reports on brokers that can answer most of your questions on buying stock.

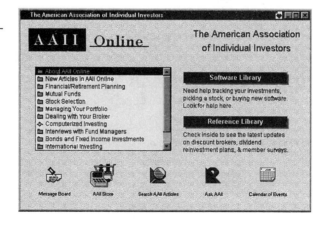

It's not like the old days when every purchase or sale of a stock was made by a stockbroker, waving a piece of paper and shouting on the floor of a stock exchange. Today, most stock transactions are conducted by computer systems, even those placed by brokers who receive all of their orders during telephone conversations. In fact, when you use an online broker, you're doing essentially the same work that a stockbroker does after a customer places an order on the phone.

If you're concerned about the security of the online trading systems, don't be. While the Internet is not yet secure enough to provide a safe environment for online trading, no problems have surfaced from the more secure networks used by AOL for online trading. That doesn't mean you'll never have a problem. Online trading systems may occasionally lose an order or fail to execute a trade correctly, just as a broker who takes orders on the phone can make a mistake. But many investors feel online brokers are more dependable since they don't become overwhelmed with phone calls when the market is busy, and you've got a better chance of reaching the system when you need it.

Discount vs. Full-Service Brokers

One thing you will not get from an online broker is advice. Many professional stockbrokers help their customers choose the stocks they buy during those phone calls, so when you execute your own trades online, you're relying only on your judgment and the information you learned after reading Chapters 3 and 4. Brokers that proffer advice are known as full-service brokers. They'll spend time with you to help you formulate a strategy and will call you with tips when they see opportunities that fit in with your investment strategy.

Critics charge that most stockbrokers are merely sales agents, pushing you toward the purchase of any stock in order to collect a commission. With hard work and discipline, you should be able to do just as well or better than if you consulted with a full-service broker.

▼ **T I P**

Before choosing an online broker from the three that are offered on AOL, try both PCFN and either E*Trade or Quick & Reilly. There's a big difference between the graphic menu system that PCFN uses and the barebones structure offered by E*Trade and Quick & Reilly.

For many investors, the reason to use an online broker is that it's far less expensive. The online brokers offered by AOL are discount brokers: they don't offer advice, and they keep their prices low. A personal stockbroker will invariably charge you more than a discount broker. Prices vary widely, but a full-service broker may charge over $100 a trade; AOL's online brokers charge between $20 and $50 for a typical trade. For the latest price comparisons, look in the AAII Reference Library and open the Dealing with Brokers folder. You'll find an article that looks at brokers' prices (see fig. 5.2).

FIG. 5.2

When shopping for a broker, read through the price comparisons in AAII's Reference Library.

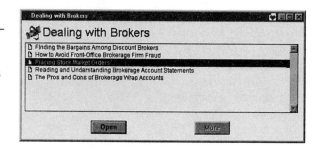

The Mechanics of a Stock Trade

The stock markets are designed to give every trader an opportunity to set the value of stocks. Every time you buy a stock, you're placing a bid for shares. Only if the seller is willing to take your bid will you complete a purchase.

All stock prices are established by computer trading systems at the major exchanges (New York Stock Exchange, NASDAQ, American Exchange). During the course of an ordinary day, the price of a stock is likely to change hundreds or thousands of times as new bids are made. Part of your broker's job is to make sure you'll be given the opportunity to buy shares at the actual going rate within seconds. One way that brokers compete against each other is by boasting that they execute trades faster than the other guy. Online brokers have an advantage here since you don't have to rely on your broker to enter the order in the computer system; you're doing that yourself.

When a trade is ordered—no matter who initiates the trade—a broker's computer contacts the computers at a stock exchange (including regional exchanges in major cities) and enters the bid or sell request. A good broker will have a system that completes this process quickly. A broker who has a high-

volume business can help you execute trades faster because the markets trade in lots of 100 shares. When the average individual buys 10 or 20 shares, their orders are grouped with other odd lots.

Almost all stock transactions take place solely on computer, with paper records only printed after the fact to help customers track their holdings. So don't expect to receive a gold-plated paper certificates for your collection; they're a thing of the past. Most online brokers do mail statements that document transactions and holdings on a regular basis, but you can view a statement of your stock holdings and their current value at any time from the online menus. (The section "The Safety of Bonds," in Chapter 7 will show you some techniques for downloading this data and managing your portfolio with a spreadsheet.)

Basic Stock Trading Techniques

No matter which broker you use, you'll need to choose from the following options when you trade. You'll see these choices presented on the menus that you'll use to execute trades and manage your brokerage account.

◆ *Buy order*. You ask your broker to buy stock; the broker submits a bid to a stock exchange.

◆ *Sell order*. You ask your broker to sell stock that you own; the broker submits an offer to the stock exchange.

◆ *Ask or offer price*. What the price shares now cost, or what you will pay to buy a stock right now.

◆ *Bid price*. The price others have bid for the stock; if you're selling, this is the amount you can get right now.

◆ *Market order*. An instruction to your broker to trade as soon as possible at whatever price your broker can get. If you're selling, you'll pay the ask (or offer) price; if you're buying, you'll receive the bid price. Even if you check the offer and bid price just before you issue a market order, you may pay more than the current offer (or receive less than the bid price) because market conditions change quickly. This is especially true when placing a market order while the market is closed. If there is strong demand for the stock, the price may be higher by the time your broker is able to conclude the purchase, and you'll have to pay whatever price your broker can get. The advantage of a market order is its certainty: you are sure you'll buy the shares as soon as possible.

◆ *Limit order*. You select a target price, and your broker will execute the trade only if the stock can be traded at that price. If the broker is not able to trade at the price, your order will remain unfilled. Limit orders work best with trades on the NYSE and AMEX exchanges, where limit orders are centrally posted. The NASDAQ exchange does not have such a facility, and it's up to your broker to make an effort to trade at the limit price.

▼ **TIP**

A good technique for buying a stock at the best price while increasing your chance of trading quickly is to issue a limit order in between the current ask and bid price. For example, if a stock is offered at 50.5, and the bid is 50, you'd place a limit order of 50.25 which means you're bidding slightly more than others have, so you have a very good chance of paying less than you would in a market order (since stocks are traded in one-eighths of a share, you can do this only if there's a spread of a quarter point or more between the bid and ask prices). And unless you're trading in significant volumes of 100 shares or higher, you can't expect to get the best price. Orders below 100 shares are known as odd lots and must be grouped in with other small orders before they are executed. A sell order with a limit can be effective if you fear a stock may drop, and you want to sell before you incur a big loss.

◆ *Good till canceled (GTC)*. This instruction tells the broker to keep your limit order in effect until you change your mind. If the market does not offer the price you've selected, the order will remain in effect. You can cancel it at any time, but the broker will keep trying until you can get your price. Brokers usually set limits on the duration of a GTC order; PCFN will cancel it after 90 days.

◆ *Day order*. Your market order will remain in effect just for one day's trading.

◆ *Stop order*. An instruction to your broker to cancel an order that has not yet been executed.

Choosing Your Broker

There are differences among brokers. The main difference is the prices you'll pay. While brokers do boast about the services they offer, there's really not a big difference among the services offered by online brokers.

Exact prices are subject to change, but in general, PCFN is most expensive, Quick & Reilly is in the middle, and E*Trade is the least expensive. In AOL's AAII section (keyword: **AAII**), you should be able to find reports comparing the current prices of the different brokers; look in the reference library.

If you currently have a brokerage account and want to switch, you can move your portfolio to one of AOL's brokers by completing a form available from the AOL broker's online menus. Transferring a stock brokerage account from one broker to another is fairly common; it's not like breaking up with a lover. You don't have to call your old broker and explain your decision. Your new broker will notify the older broker.

PCFN: Service and Discount Prices

PCFN (or Personal Computer Financial Network) is run by the brokerage firm Donaldson, Lufkin & Jenrette Securities. PCFN's prices are a bit higher than those offered by many discount brokers but are still lower than full-service brokers. You might call PCFN a premium discount broker; it offers a few services not usually provided by discount brokers, but it doesn't provide the personal consultations and

portfolio advice that full-service brokers offer. You'll find PCFN on the Personal Finance menu, or you can enter the keyword **pcfn** (see fig. 5.3).

Financial Services

The extra financial services you receive with a PCFN account are essentially ways to manage the assets in your account that are not tied up in equities. A PCFN account gives you the following:

- ◆ You can switch funds between mutual funds, CDs, precious metals (gold, silver, or platinum), and money market funds.

- ◆ PCFN will provide *sweeps*, automatically transferring the proceeds of your transactions into a money market fund so you can draw interest on your cash between trades. When you choose to invest, PCFN draws the amount from the money market fund.

FIG. 5.3

PCFN offers a range of asset management services that lets you easily move money between stocks and money market funds; you can even withdraw cash from an ATM.

◆ You can write checks against the money market funds.

◆ You can withdraw cash from the money market fund from ATMs in the MasterCard and Cirrus network.

If a significant portion of your assets are invested in stocks, this type of asset management account may be appealing. You will spend more for each trade, but you can consolidate all of your assets here and eliminate separate bank accounts for checking, savings, and money market funds. If you want to be prepared to pounce on an opportunity, it may pay off. You can quickly move funds from your savings account into a stock, or sell a stock and draw cash in hours.

Most small investors won't want to pay for this extra convenience, but they may be attracted to PCFN's well-designed interface. Unlike the spartan TradePlus menus, PCFN menus do a good job of guiding you through transactions, helping to reassure you that you're accomplishing what you intend to. Every menu choice is clearly explained, and you can step back through the menus in the middle of a trade if you need to change an option. That's in sharp contrast to the interface provided by Quick & Reilly and E*Trade, where you need to type a number every time you want to do something. And, if you're not paying close attention, it's easy to lose track of where you are.

Placing an Order with PCFN

If you take advantage of PCFN's offer to try a sample trade, it may convince you that the extra cost is worth paying. When you are ready to trade, PCFN will let you do it right away. Just complete the online form, and unless one of your entries flags you as a bad credit risk, you'll be given the authority to begin trading (the TradePlus system is slower; you'll have to wait a few days for clearance). Of course, you'll need to pony up the cash for any trades you make, or they'll be canceled.

> **"If a significant portion of your assets are invested in stocks, this type of asset management account may be appealing."**

After you open an account, you'll receive e-mail with your new account number and password. Be sure to print or save this message since you'll need the password to access your new account. The first time you use the account, you'll be asked to change the password PCFN assigns with a password of your own choice.

When you access your account, you can choose from research databases, account management, and trading options from the Alerts! menu, as shown in figure 5.4. If any trades or other messages about your account have been sent to you from PCFN, you'll see them here.

When you're ready to begin a trade, here's how you place an order:

1. Access your PCFN account; you'll see PCFN Alerts!, as shown in figure 5.4.

2. Select Trading. A menu of trading choices open. You can choose to trade stocks, options, or mutual funds. You can review the commission prices or practice trading. Two choices exist for trading stocks: EZTrade and Express Trade. There's no difference in the type of order you can create between the two options. EZTrade guides you through the process with simpler

FIG. 5.4

All of PCFN's menus are organized around clearly labeled buttons, so it's easy to navigate through the online trading system.

menus; Express Trade lets you complete the trade more quickly from a single menu. The first time you trade, you'll want to select EZTrade so you can be sure you're completing the form correctly.

3. The first EZTrade screen asks you to choose to Buy or Sell. Make your choice and click Next.

4. The next screen asks you to enter the ticker symbol or the name of the company. Enter either one and select Next.

5. The next screen shows a current quote for the stock, with bid and ask prices. The menu also prompts you for the quantity of shares. Enter a number and select Next.

6. Note that the next screen will show your order being completed in the lower right corner, as shown in figure 5.5. On this menu, you need to choose between a Market or Limit order. Once you do, select Next.

7. If you choose Market, PCFN will show you a summary of your trade and ask you to confirm it before the order is placed. If you choose Limit, you will be asked to enter your limit price and to choose between a day or GTC order. Once you do, select Next. You'll see a summary that PCFN will ask you to confirm before placing the order.

After you submit an order, PCFN will notify you on the Alerts! menu as soon as the trade is executed. If it was a market order and the markets are open, you'll see the notification within seconds. If you placed a limit order, you'll only see a notification after the trade was placed; you'll also be notified when a day order expires without being executed.

Once you've gone through the EZTrade menus, you may want to use the Express Trade option. As you can see in figure 5.6, the menu choices are essentially the same. The only difference is that you select all options from the same menu.

No matter which one you choose, after you start trading you'll be able to track your portfolio from the Accounts menu. Here you can check balances in your accounts, check the status of orders that have not yet been executed, and review the history of your trading.

You'll also find that PCFN provides buttons that access many of the other financial resources on America Online, including the Motley Fool, Decision Point, and Company Research. Regular traders who want to quickly get in and out of America Online may find that the PCFN menus provide the best way to use all of the available financial resources.

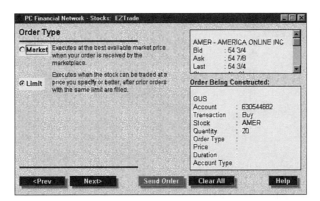

FIG. 5.5

As you complete an order with PCFN EZTrade, you see a current quote for the stock with the ask and bid prices.

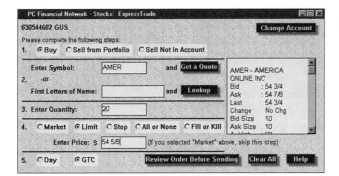

FIG. 5.6

PCFN's Express Trade gives you the same amount of information as EZTrade, but it cuts down on the number of menus you use to place an order.

TradePlus: The Gateway to E*Trade and Quick & Reilly

TradePlus is a service that provides the interface for several brokers and is available through a number of online services. For example, the TradePlus system available on CompuServe is identical to the one available on AOL. When you connect to TradePlus, at first you'll see some AOL menus that provide information about using TradePlus, as shown in figure 5.7. But if you select Enter TradePlus Gateway, you'll

be switched over to a different computer system, and rather than seeing the familiar, user-friendly AOL menus, you'll see mainframe-style read-outs.

This interface requires you to type in the correct numbers in order to accomplish anything (Want to see your portfolio? Type **311**). So, be prepared to spend extra time figuring out the menu structure if you choose a TradePlus broker.

On America Online, you can use TradePlus to trade with either E*Trade or Quick & Reilly. (TradePlus is actually owned by E*Trade, but there's no difference in the way TradePlus works with either broker.)

FIG. 5.7

The only services TradePlus offers from AOL menus is information about the trading gateway; once you connect to the gateway, you leave AOL menus behind and see only TradePlus menus.

▼ **TIP**

Before you enter a buy order with one of the brokers in the TradePlus system, check the stock price by using the AOL keyword quotes. PCFN lets you check a price while you're trading; TradePlus does not.

So in choosing a broker on AOL, you actually have two choices: first, you choose between PCFN and TradePlus. And if you choose TradePlus, you have a choice of either Quick & Reilly or E*Trade.

Quick & Reilly: A Discount Broker Online and on the Phone

Quick & Reilly is not primarily an online broker. Most of the company's customers conduct business over the phone. Like other discount brokers, Quick &

Reilly's customers don't get advice or sales pitches from the customer service representatives, but Quick & Reilly's prices are lower than full-service brokers.

With a Quick & Reilly account, you'll be able to keep your extra cash in a money-market fund, or choose a mutual fund. You can't perform all of these services from the online menus; for some, you'll need to call Quick & Reilly and speak to a customer service representative.

If you open an account with Quick & Reilly, you will be able to place trades either by speaking to customer service or through the TradePlus system.

E*Trade: The Ultimate Discount

If you're looking to save, E*Trade is likely to be your best bet. Studies by AAII (available in AAII's Reference Library section), found that E*Trade is among the least expensive brokers available anywhere—online or by phone. While most brokers vary their rates based on the number of shares traded or your use of specific options (such as limit orders), E*Trade charges one low price, no matter how many shares and how you trade.

E*Trade provides its services only through online services, so you won't have the customer service options available from PCFN or Quick & Reilly. But E*Trade offers some of the services they promote, including sweeping funds into money markets. E*Trade is a relative newcomer in the world of stockbrokers, but it's growing fast. While broker's prices are always changing, it's likely that E*Trade will remain a low-cost trader since the company was created solely to provide online trading.

Placing an Order with TradePlus

Don't look for TradePlus on the Personal Finance menus. Like a hidden treasure, Trade*Plus is buried deep inside AOL. You can connect to the TradePlus area only by using the keyword **tradeplus.** When TradePlus starts, the first menu choice provides a choice of reading information about TradePlus or accessing the service directly.

Before you begin trading with TradePlus, select the option How to Use Trade Plus. You'll find help screens that explain the menu choices. Print these out by selecting File, Print and set them aside for when you're actually connected to the TradePlus gateway.

You'll navigate through TradePlus more easily once you understand the overall structure. The menus are organized by a decimal system although not all

numbers are used (I guess they figured it would be easier to add services as they go along). Refer to figure 5.8 to understand the system:

◆ 10—19 are price-quote selections, allowing you to review current stock, commodity, and futures prices before you trade.

◆ 20—29 are menus for buying stocks or options. Specific choices allow you to choose between a market and a limit order and choose the length of a limit order (day or good till canceled).

◆ 30—39 are portfolio management tools. You can review the value of any stocks you own, or setup a dummy portfolio so you can monitor stocks that have perked your interest.

◆ 40—49 is the records choices. Here you can review the history of your trades, helping you to track capital gains.

◆ 50—59 is the information menu. You can look up a company's ticker symbol or send a message to TradePlus.

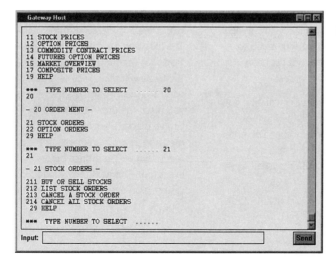

FIG. 5.8

TradePlus organizes its menus by decimal number. Everything between 10 and 19 is related to price quotes.

At first, you'll need to read through each menu and type the correct number to manage your account. But, as you begin to memorize the numbers for each activity, the process of placing an order in TradePlus becomes easier. The following steps explain how you'd place an order to buy 10 shares of America Online (AMER) at the market price. Figure 5.9 shows a typical trade; you may want to refer to the screen as you follow these steps:

1. Open TradePlus by connecting to AOL and entering the keyword **tradeplus**.

2. Select Enter TradePlus Gateway from the menu. The display changes to a terminal emulation mode. For best viewing, you'll want to maximize this screen by double-clicking the Maximize button in the upper right corner of the window.

3. You'll be prompted for your user name and password; these are different from the AOL screen name and password. After you enter a valid password, you can proceed.

4. Enter **211** to go directly to the Buy or Sell Stocks menu. You'll be asked to choose a New Order (N), Change a Former Order (C), or If Nothing Done (I) order; this last option allows you to change a limit order that has not yet been executed. Select N for a new order.

5. You'll be prompted for the stock symbol; if you don't know the symbol, you'll need to look it up before you can place an order. When you enter a valid stock symbol, TradePlus displays the current bid and ask price, and asks whether you want to Buy or Sell.

6. Enter **B** for buy; you'll be prompted for the number of shares. Type in the number.

7. The menus will prompt you for Your Limit or Market (M) order. To enter an order at market price, type **M**. If you want to enter a Limit order, enter the price you want.

8. Trade*Plus will prompt you for the length of the order: either (G)TC for Good Till Canceled, or (D)ay for a single day order.

9. You'll be asked to select the payment method: (C) for Check, (M) for Money Market account, or (F) for Funds in account.

10. You have a choice of choosing whether the stock certificates are transferred to you or to the broker.

11. Finally, you'll be asked to supply your password. If you enter a valid password, TradePlus will display a summary of the trade so you can confirm the details before the order is placed.

When a trade is executed, TradePlus sends you a message to report the number of shares you bought, the price, and the amount you'll be charged. You won't see this message from your AOL e-mail box. The message can be read only from within the TradePlus account. If you've placed a market order, the trade will take place very quickly, and you may want to check your messages a few seconds after you place the order. Enter **513** to read messages. If you've placed a limit order, it will take longer for the message to arrive (remember, the market has to be ready to meet your price before a limit order can be executed). The next time you log into the TradePlus system, you'll be notified if there are any new messages.

```
*** TYPE NUMBER TO SELECT  ...... 211
- 211 BUY OR SELL STOCKS -
- Portfolio: QS3853-D001 203-27816-15 -
- Type CTRL/C to Escape -
  (N)ew Order, (C)hange Former Order
  or (I)f Nothing Done Order...
> Order Type: (N,C,I) ...... N
> Stock Symbol ............. AMER
  AMERICA ONLINE INC
  *: Comtex Newsgrid story (GO NEWS)
  Delayed Price is.... 54 13/16
    Bid..  54 3/4     Size ..  1,000
    Ask..  55         Size ..  1,000
> (B)uy or (S)ell .......... B
> Number of Shares ......... 20
> Price:Your Limit or (M)kt. 54 7/8
> (G)TC or (D)ay Order ..... G
  (C)heck, (M)oney Fund,
  (F)unds in Acct
> Payment Method (C,M,F).... C
> Deliver Certificate: (Y,N) N
> Password .................
```

FIG. 5.9

Placing a stock order in TradePlus.

Trying Before Trading

Both TradePlus and PCFN often give you the opportunity of setting up a game or practice account. You can learn the ropes, going through the motions of buying a stock, watching its price fluctuate, feeling your blood pressure surge and then selling it—all without spending a penny. The games are not always running, but if you don't find them, check back in a few days and they may have returned.

These accounts use the same menus and track stocks at their actual market price, so it's a good way for a beginner to become familiar with the technique of trading online before putting money at risk.

▼ **TIP**

After you receive confirmation that your buy order has gone through, record the purchase in the portfolio. You can also keep a separate portfolio just for the market orders you've issued.

On PCFN, look for the practice account choice on the Accounts menu. When you open the practice account, you'll find that PCFN, like a rich uncle, has already built a sizable portfolio for you. You can examine the portfolio and sell it all off as you buy new stocks.

On TradePlus, you select Game Account. Here you start from scratch but there's a side benefit; TradePlus runs contests, so you can compete against other players for prizes.

One bit of advice: This is your chance to indulge your fantasies. Don't just buy 10 shares of IBM and hold it; buy 500 shares and throw in another 100 shares of some risky growth stock that you heard about on a Motley Fool message board. You can experience the thrills, chills, and spills of a big-time investor without quitting your day job.

6

Shopping for Mutual Funds

With over 6,000 mutual funds on the market, selecting a fund can be a daunting task. Fortunately, America Online has tools up to the challenge.

Mutual funds have become an important component of many people's retirement and savings plans for good reasons. A mutual fund can give you far better results than savings bank accounts, CDs, and money market funds, since the funds invest directly in stocks and bonds. For many individuals, a mutual fund can produce the same, or better, long-term results as individual stocks—without the risk and without requiring the careful attention that stock traders need to devote to their portfolio.

A mutual fund is watched by a team of professionals, under the daily supervision of a professional money manager who has access to leading economic forecasts and analysts' reports. You may have the skill to do a better job than a mutual fund manager, but unless you have the time and energy to devote to the job, you'll probably do better in a mutual fund.

Choosing a mutual fund is not as demanding a job as picking stocks. Even the most active mutual fund investor would have little reason to make a switch between funds more than once a month. As a result, America Online (AOL) has fewer services available for mutual funds than it has for stocks. Yet, there's no shortage of information. You'll find America Online has all the data you need to be a successful mutual fund investor.

Mutual Fund Basics

A mutual fund is a way of sharing the risks and rewards of investing. Since a fund starts with a pool of assets, it has the ability to invest in a great

number of individual opportunities. In the normal course of events, every investment has good and bad days, but since a mutual fund has its risks spread out, the fund's overall performance is less volatile than any of the individual investments.

Mutual funds have become so popular that they're now available for just about any type of investment. In fact, there are now more mutual funds than individual stocks. Most funds are limited to a specific type of investment, such as a type of stock or bond, but there are even funds that move their investments between stocks and bonds.

As a result, it's possible to find a fund that matches just about any investment philosophy, from extremely risk-averse government bond funds to highly volatile aggressive growth funds. But it's also very easy to become overwhelmed by all the choices. You may feel like a kid in a candy store; they all look good. Before you invest in any mutual fund, be sure you are aware of how volatile the fund's performance will be. Table 6.1 shows a summary of some of the most popular mutual fund categories.

Creating Your Own Mutual Fund Strategy

You can make your choice easier if you start by considering the amount of risk you're willing to accept.

TABLE 6.1   Major Mutual Fund Categories

Type	Volatility	Investments
Aggressive growth	High	Companies with strong growth potential, especially small and new companies
Asset allocation	Moderate	Stocks, bonds, and money market funds, at the discretion of the fund manager
Balanced	Moderate	Mixture of stocks and corporate bonds
Corporate bond	Low	Fixed-income securities issued by corporations
Equity income	Low	Stocks that pay regular dividends
Foreign stock	High	Equities traded on overseas exchanges; sometimes limited to a specific region
Government bond	Low	U.S. Treasury securities
Growth	Moderate	Stocks with growth potential but not high risk
Growth and income	Moderate	Mixture of stocks with growth potential and dividend income
Municipal bond	Low	Bonds issued by cities
Sector	High	Stocks of companies in a specific industry, such as travel or technology

First, keep it in perspective; the level of risk is not the same type of one-in-a-million shot you have with a lottery ticket. If you invest with a licensed mutual fund company, you're not likely to lose any money, as long as you're able to invest the money long enough to endure normal market ups and downs. (Concerned about a fund's reliability? Make sure you can find it in the Morningstar ratings discussed later in this chapter in the section "Morningstar Mutual Fund Ratings." If the fund is not there, be wary.)

A mutual fund with high risk may drop ten percent or more during a down cycle, but it stands to recoup all of those losses and post a gain when the market rebounds. So if you want to grab the higher rewards of the volatile categories—like sector and aggressive growth funds—it's important that you invest only money that you will not need for several years. (A down cycle may last many months.) If you may need the money on short notice, invest in a mutual fund with low volatility, such as bond and income funds. Remember that even funds with low volatility are subject to ups and downs, so you don't want to put all of your savings in a mutual fund.

The general rule is that you should keep enough cash in a savings or money market fund to equal about three to six months living expenses. Everything else should be invested in vehicles that have stronger growth potential. You'll want to keep between ten and twenty percent of your investments in a low-risk fund so it will be readily available in case of an emergency. The remainder should be invested at the highest level of risk you and your nerves can stand.

For the individual, there's less risk in a mutual fund since the fund is managed by professionals who are supervised and reviewed. But you still face the risk of the public markets; if your fund owns bonds and the overall price of bonds drops, your fund will fall along with the market. Nothing guarantees your invest-ment—mutual funds are not insured the way savings bank accounts are insured by the government—but mutual funds are regulated by the government.

Understanding Mutual Funds

When you invest in a mutual fund, you're buying a share of the total assets managed by the fund. Invest $1,000 in a fund whose share price is $10, and you'll own 100 shares. The price of each share is known as the NAV (Net Asset Value), which is calculated by dividing the assets of the fund by the number of shares outstanding. The NAV rises and falls, based on the market value of its holdings. At the end of each day that the markets are open, every fund re-calculates its NAV to reflect changes to the value of the shares owned by the fund.

Most mutual funds also pay dividends to dis-tribute any gains that result from trading stocks and earnings paid by the fund's investments—some pay monthly, others pay annually. You have a choice of receiving your dividends by check or re-investing them; if you choose to re-invest, your account will be credited with more shares every time a dividend is issued.

"You should keep enough cash in a savings or money market fund to equal about three to six months living expenses."

The performance of a fund can be evaluated two ways. You can look at the changes in the NAV and look at the total return, which is a calculation of how much you would have earned if you owned the fund during a specific time period. Total return calculates how much an investment would have changed, including changes in the price of the shares and the value of any dividends paid by the fund.

You can find a fund's NAV record from AOL's Historical Quotes database (keyword: **historical quotes**), but you won't find any information there on the dividends paid to shareholders. For that information, you'll need to consult the Morningstar databases.

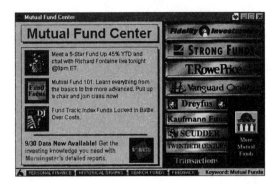

FIG. 6.1

The Mutual Fund Center highlights all services related to mutual funds on AOL.

Surveying the Mutual Fund Scene

The roster of services for mutual fund buyers is always changing at AOL. New mutual fund companies may add or leave the service at any time, and the research tools are subject to change.

The best way to survey the mutual fund services is to visit the Mutual Fund Center. You can choose the Mutual Fund Center listing on AOL's Personal Finance menu or use the keyword **mfc** (see fig. 6.1).

Many of the references are to services provided by some of the larger mutual fund companies, like Fidelity Investments, Dreyfus, and Vanguard. The services these companies provide on AOL is mainly useful to find descriptions of the company's offerings and contact information for getting more information on a particular fund. You may learn a bit about the company's investment strategies, but you won't find the hard facts and figures you'll need to plan your investments here. These sites are mainly extended commercials for the mutual fund companies.

After you've made a decision to buy or investigate a fund, come back to the Mutual Fund Center to find out how to sign up.

Before you make a mutual fund decision, you'll want competitive information from an impartial source that shows how all of the funds are doing. Click the FundWorks button or enter the keyword **fundworks**. You'll find a variety of services for mutual fund buyers (see fig. 6.2).

Many of the services listed in the Mutual Fund Resource Center do not specialize in mutual fund information. Some of the links are to general business sites (such as Market News and Stock Quotes) that a mutual fund investor might use on occasion. Others are to the sites of magazines that occasionally run articles about mutual funds (for example, articles in *Consumer Reports* and *Business Week* that report on mutual fund issues). If you're new to the concept of mutual funds, you may want to read some of these magazine articles for perspective.

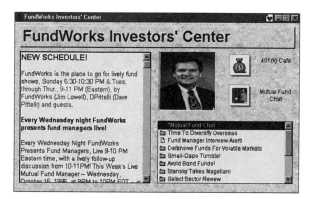

FIG. 6.2

The Mutual Fund Resource
Center brings together a
variety of information
about funds.

Choosing a Mutual Fund Category

A general education in mutual funds starts with the concept of fund categories or investment objectives. You could spend days reading all the books and magazine articles on the topic, but you can get the basic information you need from FundWorks on AOL.

You'll find FundWorks listed on the Mutual Fund Resource Center menu, or you can jump there from anywhere on AOL by using the keyword **fundworks**. The editors of FundWorks regularly schedule online chats where you can post your questions directly to one of the FundWorks experts. But you may find you'll get the information you need from the articles that are posted here, which can be read anytime. You'll find an explanation of the risks and strategies of different funds if you select Guide to Fund Categories from the FundWorks scrolling menu. A dialog box will open with a list of articles explaining the different fund categories (see fig. 6.3).

The articles won't tell you which fund to buy, but they will help you formulate your own strategy. For example, they'll suggest how much of your investment portfolio should be devoted to a particular fund category. Look for the series of articles titled "Creating a Model Portfolio" for some thoughts on how to select the best funds to meet your own goals.

Remember that you should begin to shop for a fund only after you've decided on a basic approach to investing. You can print all of the articles in the FundWorks library, so don't rush through. Print everything that seems interesting and then read it over later to either formulate a mutual fund strategy or fine-tune your current plan.

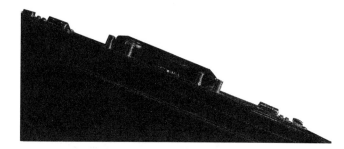

FIG. 6.3

FundWorks publishes articles that explain the basic concepts of mutual fund categories and can help you formulate your own fund strategy.

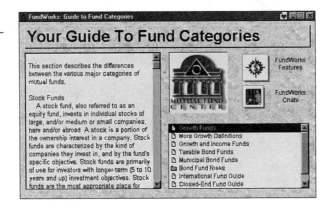

Morningstar Mutual Fund Ratings

When you're serious about comparing mutual funds and you're ready to get down to bare facts and figures, your best choice is Morningstar.

Every industry has organizations that set the standards. In the mutual funds industry, Morningstar is a leader in tracking performance. Before America Online made Morningstar reports available to all subscribers, you would have had to be a subscriber to one of Morningstar's newsletters to see the complete reports (although you may have read an excerpt while reading a popular business magazine like *Money* or *Business Week*, since they often base mutual fund articles on Morningstar research).

Morningstar compiles hard facts and figures on over 6,800 mutual funds on AOL. Select the Morningstar option from the Mutual Fund Resource Center or type the keyword **morningstar** to see an overview of the site. If you access Morningstar from the Mutual Fund Resource Center, you see the opening menu shown in figure 6.4. If you type the keyword **morningstar**, you'll be asked to choose between

stock information and mutual funds before you see the menu in figure 6.4.

Mutual fund owners will want to come here often; click the Heart icon in the upper right corner, and AOL will add this menu to your list of favorite places.

You can find a report for every fund that shows total return during several periods and an overview of the fund's investment strategy. You can see these reports by searching directly for the fund by name, or you can see lists that group the funds according to two different criteria:

◆ Rankings of the best funds in each category, using total return as the measure.

◆ Ratings, based on Morningstar's five-star system.

You'll want to take a look at both rankings as you shop for a fund. Don't use just one criterion when selecting an investment. After all, these measurements look at past performance; you'll be betting on the future, so you'll want to dig a little further and see how well each fund did during several time periods, not just one period.

FIG. 6.4

Morningstar has reports on over 6,800 mutual funds with ratings that show how well each fund is doing.

Understanding the Morningstar System

A few general principles apply to using Morningstar reports. Whenever you select a list, only the first 20 entries will be displayed at first. To see others, you need to select the More button. For example, if you open a list of all Aggressive Growth mutual funds, you'll need to click the More button many times before you can view the funds at the bottom of the list.

Any time you're not sure of a term you see on a Morningstar display, select the Guide ? button. A list of mutual fund terms will open; click any term to see a detailed explanation.

Morningstar's criteria for ranking funds—the system used in creating the list of Top-Performing Funds—is quite simple. It calculates the total return for every fund it follows and reports the results over four periods:

◆ 3-month return

◆ 1-year return

◆ 3-year return

◆ 5-year return

Remember that a return includes change in NAV (or share price) and dividends that are paid to shareholders. In calculating total return, Morningstar assumes shares were purchased at the beginning of the period and dividends were re-invested. Because funds pay dividends at different times, a fund that has recently paid dividends will do better in a 3-month or 1-year comparison. Investors planning for the long-term may want to completely ignore 3-month returns in favor of longer horizons; however, those 3-month results will interest the current owner of a fund, curious to see how well the fund has been doing lately.

In contrast to the rankings, Morningstar's rating system is anything but simple. Every fund is judged on a five-point system (with five stars the highest) that evaluates how well the fund's returns have matched the level of risk inherent in the fund's strategy. After assigning a value on this scale (which is not published), Morningstar ranks all funds and plots the score on a bell curve. The 10 percent that earn the best scores receive the highest rating; 22.5 percent receive four stars; 33.5 percent receive three

"In the mutual funds industry, Morningstar is a leader in tracking performance."

stars, 22.5 percent receive two stars, and the lowest-scoring 10 percent receive one star.

Morningstar warns against using its rating system as the primary criteria in building a portfolio, since high-risk funds often do poorly and the system tends to reward funds that match expectations, rather than those that exceed expectations. For example, if a fund followed a low-risk strategy that historically returned 6 or 7 percent, and it is now returning 7 percent, the fund will have a high rating. But if a fund's strategy suggests it should be earning 10 percent and it is now returning 9 percent, it will have a low ranking, even though it is returning more profit than the first fund. The ratings are revised monthly.

When selecting a fund, keep in mind that no single fund is always at the top of the ratings. Some advisors believe that mutual fund performance is cyclical and the best strategy is to buy today's low-performing funds so you can take advantage of the inevitable upswing.

The Top Funds in Each Category

Now that you know the ground rules, a good way to shop for funds is to start at the top. Even if you don't buy one of the top funds, you can see the best returns being posted by funds. Morningstar's

Top-Performing Funds are organized by investment objectives. When you've settled on a category of funds that you want to explore, this section is a good place to help you find the high achievers, and it's a good way to compare the results among the categories. For example, during a period when the stock market is down, you'll find that the top-rated funds in high-risk categories (such as aggressive growth funds) post very low returns or even a loss; to some people, that's scary but to others, that's a signal to buy.

The following steps will guide you through the process of finding the top-performing funds ranked over different time periods.

1. Select Top-Performing Funds and you'll see a menu listing the investment objectives, as shown in figure 6.5.

2. Choose a category. You'll see a window asking you to select the period for the ranking (either three months, one year, three years, or five years).

3. After you've chosen a time period, Morningstar displays the list. To see more information about a fund, double-click its name.

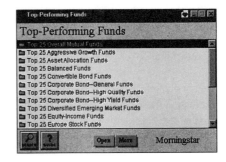

FIG. 6.5

Morningstar organizes its Top-Performing Funds by investment objective.

When you're serious about investing in a specific category, be sure to look through all four time periods. One fund is unlikely to be the winner in all periods, but you may find a few funds that show up in more than one of these rankings.

You'll find that in high-risk categories, the total return may be radically different across the four periods. For example, a loss over three months could turn into a big gain over five years. But in low-risk categories, like bond funds, the total return will be fairly consistent in all of the time periods.

The Top Funds by Star Rating

Morningstar's star ratings aren't as important in selecting a fund as long-term performance, but the star ratings may reassure you that a fund is well-managed right now. For example, a fund may have shown up in the top 25 list for 5-year returns but didn't show up lately. A good star rating in the most recent reports should reassure you that the fund is in good shape today.

Don't pass on a fund just because it's rated a 3 or 4. As long as the fund has shown consistent returns over a long period and it matches your investment objective, you shouldn't be discouraged. On the other hand, if you find a fund has only 1 or 2 stars, and its return is relatively low, you may want to keep shopping.

To read through the entire list of funds, listed alphabetically, select Detailed Fund Reports from the Morningstar Mutual Funds main menu and then select Grouped by Star Rating. You'll then be asked to select one of the 5-star groupings, as shown in figure 6.6.

FIG. 6.6

Morningstar lets you search for funds according to the star ratings assigned each month.

Searching strictly by star rating is probably not the best way to find a good fund. The list of funds within each star is so long it will wear you out—several thousand funds are on some of the lists.

However, one reason you may want to read through the ratings this way is that you can easily compare the ratings within a mutual fund company, since the star ratings appear alphabetically. Many investors (myself included) like to stay with one mutual fund company; you can see all of your funds on the same statement, and you can switch among funds with a single phone call. Once you've settled on a mutual fund company, you'll find yourself drawn to comparing the funds you own against others offered by the same company.

Looking at a Fund's Objective

One of the smarter ways to shop for a new fund is to focus your search on investment objectives. First, decide on the level of risk you are able to stomach and then shop for a fund. As outlined in Table 6.1, a fund's objective will have a big impact on the level of risk you assume and the type of earnings you can hope to gain.

Morningstar groups funds by investment objective under the option Detailed Fund Reports. Choose the option Grouped by Investment Objective, and you'll see a list of the categories, shown in figure 6.7.

You'll also want to consult the list of the 25 Top-Performing Funds in the category, but the alphabetical listings under Detailed Fund Reports can help you gain perspective. For example, the difference between making the list of top 25 funds and being left off the list could be only a fraction of a percentage point. You may come across funds that did very well

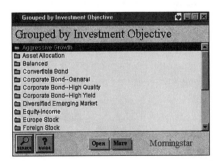

FIG. 6.7

You can review all the funds within any mutual fund investment objective from Morningstar's option Detailed Fund Reports.

in all the time periods but didn't do well enough in any one period to make the list; that fund could be the better choice for you.

Comparing Funds

Comparing funds is much easier if you save the lists that interest you, so you can analyze them in a spreadsheet. You can save any of the lists available under top 25 funds.

Printing or Downloading a List of Funds

Any time you find a list of top-performing funds you'd like to keep, click the first entry, PRINT LIST. A new window opens, displaying the list in a form that AOL can download (see fig. 6.8).

You can print this new window with the File, Print command, or save it to your hard disk with the File, Save command.

The file will be saved in text format, so you can open it with any word processor. The file will be much easier to read in a word processor if you use a fixed-pitch font, such as Courier; the tables will line up neatly, making comparisons easy.

The information will be even easier to analyze in a spreadsheet. Importing this text data into a spreadsheet will take seconds if you own a spreadsheet like Lotus 1-2-3 or Microsoft Excel. These high-powered programs can parse tabular data into individual cells because they're able to translate the extra blank space between figures into columns. After the file is

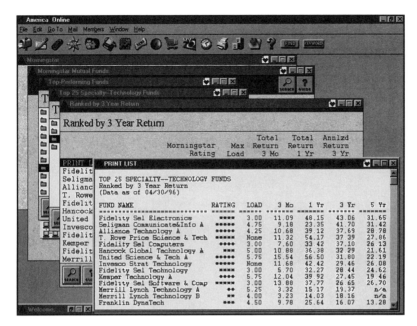

FIG. 6.8

You can download Morningstar tables comparing the top 25 funds in any category.

downloaded, you can open it in the spreadsheet, and the spreadsheet will guide you through the process of formatting the figures correctly.

Comparing Funds with Microsoft Works

The process of importing text into older spread-sheets, or Microsoft Works, will take a little more work. You'll start in the Works word processor, con-verting blank spaces to tabs, and then open this edited version with the Works spreadsheet. After you've downloaded the file, here's how to proceed:

1. Open Microsoft Works.

2. Select the Works Tools tab and choose Word Processor.

3. Select File, Open and choose the file you saved. Works will ask which program you want to use. Select Word Processor.

4. When the file is displayed, move your insertion point just to the line where the report headers are entered; click a few spaces to the left of the word "RATING."

5. Select Edit, Replace. The Replace dialog box opens.

6. Select the Find What entry box, and press the space bar three times in this text box. Press Tab to move your insertion point to the Replace With entry box. Click the Tab icon that appears just below (it looks like a big right arrow), as shown in figure 6.9.

7. Select the Replace button and Works will re-place the blank spaces with a tab.

FIG. 6.9

Converting a Morningstar list to a spreadsheet format for Microsoft Works is time-consuming, but worth the trouble.

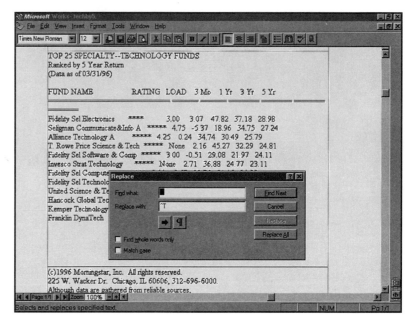

8. Select Find Next and, if this is the beginning of a new column, select Replace. If the spaces do not represent a new column, select Find Next instead.

9. Repeat Step 8 until you reach the end of the report.

10. You can check your work by moving your insertion point through the document with the right-arrow key. The insertion point should jump every time you pass over a tab; a tab should separate each figure, and there should be only one tab between figures.

11. Highlight the table you've created and select Edit, Copy to copy the table to the clipboard.

12. Select File, New, Spreadsheet.

13. Select Edit, Paste to insert the table in the spreadsheet.

The secret to doing this right is to pay close attention during Steps 8 and 9. An easy mistake is to insert an extra tab in the Fund Name column. You should be able to correct some mistakes by cutting and pasting after you insert the data in the spreadsheet.

Charting Your Future in Funds

Once you have downloaded the performance data on funds and stored it in a spreadsheet, you can analyze or chart the results. You may want to combine different types of funds, or build a spreadsheet with all of the funds you own.

One advantage of having the data in a spreadsheet is that you can focus your attention on only the funds you really want to explore. Figure 6.10 shows one example of how the list of performance data that was downloaded in figure 6.8 (and massaged in Microsoft Works) could be charted in a spreadsheet.

In this figure, Microsoft Works is used, but any spreadsheet with charting tools can build a chart from the Morningstar performance data.

Detailed Reports on Funds

So far, you've seen Morningstar's comparison reports, showing just a few performance results on each fund. More extensive reports are available on each fund. You can find the report by looking through the rankings, the list of star ratings, or using

the Search button to look for an individual fund. The same style report is available for every fund, as shown in figure 6.11.

Every Morningstar fund report includes the same information on each fund:

◆ Morningstar star rating

◆ Level of risk, as determined by Morningstar, and the beta (a measure of a fund's volatility; a beta of 1.20 indicates the fund fluctuates 20 percent more than the S&P500, while a beta of .80 means it fluctuates 20 percent less.)

◆ NAV or share price, as of the end of last month

◆ Size of the fund in billions of dollars

◆ Description of the fund's strategy

◆ Annual return showing the total earnings (including reinvested dividends) dating from

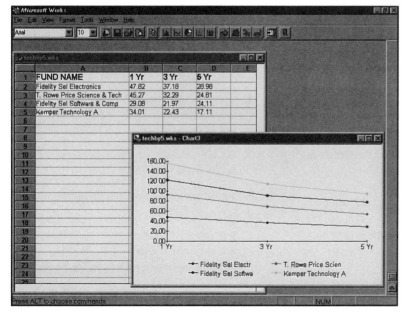

FIG. 6.10

Once you've saved Morningstar mutual fund performance numbers, you can display the numbers in a spreadsheet chart.

FIG. 6.11

Every Morningstar mutual fund report includes the most essential information you need to evaluate a fund.

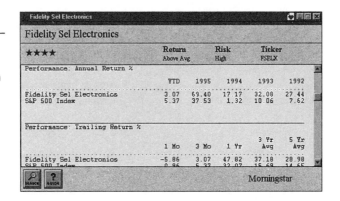

Fidelity Sel Electronics					
★★★★	Return Above Avg	Risk High	Ticker FSELX		

Performance: Annual Return %

	YTD	1995	1994	1993	1992
Fidelity Sel Electronics	3.07	69.40	17.17	32.08	27.44
S&P 500 Index	5.37	37.53	1.32	10.06	7.62

Performance: Trailing Return %

	1 Mo	3 Mo	1 Yr	3 Yr Avg	5 Yr Avg
Fidelity Sel Electronics	-5.86	3.07	47.82	37.18	28.98
S&P 500 Index	0.96	5.37	32.07	15.69	14.65

Morningstar

January 1 to December 31 for each of the last four years; current year's return spans from January 1 to the end of last month

♦ Trailing returns showing total earnings (including reinvested dividends) over five different periods; these cumulative returns are averaged to give an indication of annual returns. These are the most common benchmarks for comparing performance.

♦ A list of the top holdings, including the amount held

♦ Statistics on the fund's holdings (such as the price/earnings ratio)

♦ Information on fees, such as the load (the commission charged on purchases of new shares) and the mutual fund's management fee

♦ Contact information (address and phone number)

This report is a treasure chest of valuable information. You'll want to print out or save a copy of the report for every stock you're considering and every stock you own.

Unfortunately, this detailed report is not easy to work with after you downloaded it. The reports are a mixture of text and figures. Since the figures are not formatted with tabs or any other delimiter, you can't simply import them into a spreadsheet and do your own comparisons with other funds. You can buy CD-ROMs with the information (order information is available from the Morningstar Marketplace section on AOL). With a little bit of work, you can begin to build a spreadsheet that compares the total return for different funds.

The following steps may seem like a lot of work, and for the first report, it will be a hassle. But after you've gotten a feel for the process, it won't take any time at all.

1. Open the Morningstar Mutual Fund menu (keyword: **morningstar**) and select a fund from one of the lists.

2. Double-click a fund name and a report will open (as shown in fig. 6.11).

3. Save the report by selecting File, Save.

4. Open the file with a word processor, delete the text and any figures you don't need for your analysis (such as expense fees). You may want to delete everything except the Trailing Returns.

5. Use your word processor's Find command to replace all spaces with tabs. Make sure only tabs

separate columns but only one tab appears between each column of figures.

6. Highlight the table and select Edit, Copy.

7. Open your spreadsheet program and select Edit, Paste. The table will be inserted into the spreadsheet. If you were careful in Step 5, each column heading and figure will appear in its own cell.

8. Review the spreadsheet to be sure the numbers and headings are properly lined up. If not, repeat Steps 4 through 7.

You can use this technique to build a spreadsheet with records of every spreadsheet you own or are considering for investment. After you create the first spreadsheet, you can use it in Step 7 to receive new data. Just be careful you don't insert new figures into an outdated spreadsheet. Morningstar updates the lists every month, so you'll need to update all of the figures any time you add new funds to your spreadsheet.

7

Shopping for Interest Rates

U.S. Treasury securities and bank accounts promise safe, predictable returns. And with a little online shopping, you can increase your returns.

CDs and Treasury securities may not be the most exciting investments you can find. You won't find frenetic message boards where everyone is trading tips on where to find the hottest CD rates, and you won't need to spend hours researching the return on the latest government T-bill offering. The appeal of CDs (certificates of deposit) and U.S. Treasury bills is security. You know how much of a return your money will bring. You may not stand to gain as much as you would with a soaring stock or mutual fund, but on the other hand, you don't risk losing even a fraction of your investment.

While you won't need to spend long hours doing research on these relatively stable investments, your America Online (AOL) account can help you maximize your return if you're willing to spend a few minutes before you buy your next CD, or treasury bill. You'll be able to buy the best rates for CDs. And if you've been buying Treasury securities through a broker or with mutual funds, you can start to buy your own securities. You'll find everything you need to know online.

Treasury Securities

Government securities are one of the most popular investments for conservative savers. No one has ever lost a penny in these financial transactions because they are backed by guarantees of the U.S. Treasury. Unless the U.S. government topples, you'll get your money and earn the interest

promised at the time you buy the bond (and if the U.S. government falls, don't expect the stock market to be a safe haven). Paying back treasury obligations is, by law, one of the government's first priorities.

And because the interest rates paid on these bonds are set at public auctions, they usually pay the highest interest rates currently available for a fixed investment. The drawback is that you need to invest a sizable amount to gain the full benefit and you need to spend some time learning about the different options before you buy. But if you do put in the effort to educate yourself, you can save broker's fees by buying the bonds yourself, directly from the U.S. government. Everything you need to know is available on AOL. The U.S. Treasury Department, through its Bureau of Public Debt, maintains a section on AOL (keyword: **treasury securities**) as shown in figure 7.1.

While the Treasury Department is savvy enough to dispense information through AOL, it has not entered the information age with both feet: you cannot buy securities or access your treasury account online—at least not yet. You need to write a letter that includes detailed information about you and your bank in order to open an account (all disbursements are deposited directly to a bank account).

The U.S. Treasury Securities section on AOL gives you the definitions and details you need to know in managing your own portfolio of government securities. The only drawback is that the section is written in government legalese. Experienced bond buyers will have no trouble, but everyone else may benefit from reading a primer.

Understanding T-Bills, Notes, and Bonds

When you buy a treasury security, you're lending money to the U.S. Government Treasury. Rather than negotiate individual loans with millions of investors, the government created three programs for selling securities: bills, notes, and bonds. Each has its own terms for minimum investment and the length of the investment, outlined in Table 7.1.

Treasury bonds are the least expensive—you can start with a bond for as little as $1,000—and they often

FIG. 7.1

You can learn everything you need to know to buy your own U.S. Treasury securities online.

131

TABLE 7.1   U.S. Treasury Securities

Security	Term	Min. Investment	Interest Interval
Bonds	30 years	$1,000	Every 6 mos.
Notes	2, 3, 4, 5, 7, or 10 years	$5,000	Every 6 mos.
Bills	3 mos., 6 mos., or 1 year	$10,000	At purchase

carry the highest interest rates but they don't mature for 30 years. That's a long time to wait for your money, no matter how good the interest rate offered.

Treasury notes and bills (also called T-bills) are the more popular investment options. Each is offered in a choice of maturity terms. Treasury notes require a minimum investment of $5,000 and can be bought for a maturity as short as 2 years or as long as 10 years (see Table 7.1 for the range of terms). Treasury bills require a minimum of $10,000 and mature in less than one year.

There are also differences in the way the interest is paid. When you buy a bill, you receive your interest payment immediately. You send the government a check for the full amount (let's say $10,000) and a few days later, the government deposits in your bank account the interest you'll earn (on a 6 percent bill, you'd receive a check for $600). At the maturity date, the government deposits a second amount, for the face value of your T-bill. Treasury notes and bonds pay interest at 6-month intervals; when the security reaches maturity, you receive a payment for the face value of your investment.

The interest on any of these investments is subject to federal income tax, but exempt from state and local income taxes.

The programs are so carefully structured that a secondary market has grown up around these securities, increasing their appeal. If you decide to cash out of your investment before the maturity, you can trade the bonds on a regulated open market and receive the going rate.

Buying and Selling Treasury Securities

Hundreds of brokers will buy the bonds for you, but you can deal directly with the government and save on brokers' fees and commission. It will require a little more work to deal with the government than if you use a broker, but not too much more. You can learn how to take part by reading through the articles available on AOL; click the Bank Vault icon on the Treasury Securities main window to see a list of articles that explain the process, as shown in figure 7.2.

Select the Becoming a TREASURY DIRECT Customer option and you'll find several articles that explain how you can buy securities and have the yield deposited in your bank account. There's more information here than you can absorb in a single session online so you should either print or save each article to your hard disk.

FIG. 7.2

The Treasury Direct system allows you to buy treasury securities directly from the government, bypassing brokers.

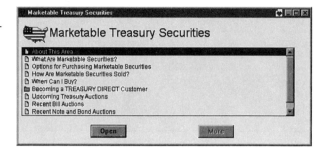

Current Treasury Rates To View and Download

Reading through the hundreds of rules and guidelines may make the process seem more difficult than the reality: you buy a security, you earn interest. Before you spend too much time mastering the intricacies of the government bureaucracy that surrounds the offerings, be sure to look at the current rates to get an idea of whether this is your idea of a good investment.

The treasury establishes rates at public auctions that are held every few days, and it publishes a list of the rates established for each security on AOL.

> "Treasury notes and bills (also called T-bills) are the more popular investment options."

Here's how to find the most recent list of rates:

1. Log on to AOL and enter the keyword **treasury securities**. The main menu for U.S. Treasury Securities will open.

2. Select the Bank Vault icon that's labeled You Can Buy United States Treasury Bill, Notes and Bonds. A list of articles will open.

3. To see the list of T-bills, select Recent Bill Auctions. To see a list of note and bond offerings, select Recent Note and Bond Auctions. A screen similar to figure 7.3 will open.

4. You can print a copy by selecting File, Print or store a copy on your system by selecting File, Save.

If you save the file to your system, it is stored in text format. The best way to view it is to open a word processor and select a fixed-pitch font, such as Courier. Because the columns in this file are formatted using blank spaces, not tabs, proportional fonts will not display the columns properly.

The file can be opened in a spreadsheet, but it will need to be parsed from the text columns into spreadsheet columns. Microsoft Excel and Lotus 1-2-3 can perform this translation for you; if you're using Microsoft Works, you'll need to convert the blank spaces between columns into tabs. First, open the file in a word processor and use the Find, Replace command to change blank spaces to tabs. Then, paste the table into a spreadsheet. For a detailed explanation of the basic technique, refer to the section, "Formatting Downloaded Statements with Microsoft Works" in Chapter 3.

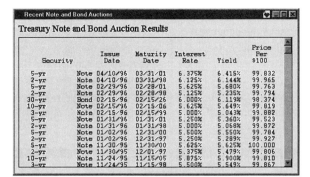

FIG. 7.3

The latest rates for treasury securities are posted within a few days of the auction.

Details About Each Treasury Issue

The list of recent prices and interest rates is valuable information, but it's only part of the story. It doesn't tell you if all of the securities sold or if the issue is callable (that is, could the government pay off the issue before the maturity date).

If you're serious about following treasury securities, you'll want to follow up on auctions that piqued your interest for all of the details. You can find them in a Gopher site on the Internet.

Gopher sites can be reached in two ways from AOL's Internet connection: you can select the Gopher menu or the World Wide Web browser from AOL's Internet Connection area. No matter which choice you make, the end result is the same. Gopher sites are displayed in the Web browser.

When you reach the site, you will see a menu showing folders with the Gopher directory; each folder represents a group of files reporting the specific details about a treasury auction. The files are in text format and show only the specific details about that particular auction. Here's how you'd find the file on a recent treasury note auction:

1. Connect to AOL and select Internet Connection from the main menu.

2. Select World Wide Web browser; the Web browser opens. (If you prefer to take the Gopher route, select Gopher; you'll see an opening Gopher menu; click Quick Go and the Web browser opens).

3. In the Web browser's Location box, type

   gopher://una.hh.lib.umich.edu/11/ebb/treasury

   and press Enter. The opening menu will appear, as shown in figure 7.4.

4. To see the most recent issues, select Latest Treasury Auction Results. You'll see a list of the different auctions.

5. Select any auction that interests you. A text file will open with all of the details available about that auction.

6. To review a different auction, select the Back button on the Web browser. You'll return to the list of recent auctions, and you can select a different one.

The information here can help anyone who's serious about following treasury securities on his or her own.

For example, you'll find the range of bids and the amount of the issue that actually sold (the difference between the amount tendered and accepted); see figure 7.5.

If you mail in a bid for a treasury issue, you'll probably want to check this site frequently. You should be able to find the specific details of an issue before you receive your notification by mail. You'll also probably want to save the file to your hard disk for any issue you own. You can save the file by using the File, Save command; the file will be saved in HTML format, a type of file used by the World Wide Web that is essentially text. The same rules apply to this file as

FIG. 7.4

You can find details about treasury auctions at an Internet Gopher site.

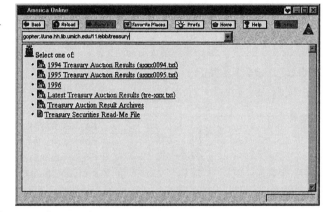

FIG. 7.5

You can find out how many shares of a treasury auction were sold and how many remain available from the Internet.

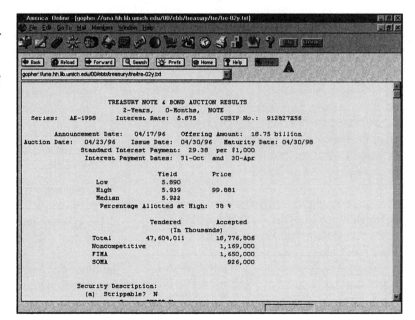

was explained earlier in the section "Current Treasury Rates To View and Download." You'll be able to open it in a word processor or spreadsheet, but any numbers displayed as columns will need to be parsed before the spreadsheet will display them properly.

Tracking Savings Bonds

Savings bonds are the slow lane of personal finance. But for many people, that's a perfectly good way to travel through life. Started by the U.S. government as a way to fund World War II, today's savings bonds are used mainly as a gift to children or offered through a corporate savings plan. You won't get rich quick with savings bonds, but you'll be earning a decent interest rate and have the same security as owners of the more expensive treasury securities while putting up a lot less cash.

Even though they're very simple financial instruments, a lot of mystery surrounds savings bonds because the rules governing how and when they earn interest have changed over the years. And while a bond has a face value, the amount you receive when you cash it in depends on the rules governing its maturity. Bonds are identified as part of a Series, and each Series has a unique maturity. For example, Series HH bonds were issued between 1959 and 1979, and they have a maturity of 30 years. Series E bonds, issued before 1965 have a 40-year life, while Series E bonds issued after 1965 mature in 30 years.

Today, bonds earn 85 percent of the average rate established for five-year Treasury securities (the government publishes the new rate every year on May 1 and November 1). When you buy a bond, you pay half the face value and can cash in the bond any time after a short holding period of about six months. The exact amount you'll earn depends on when you decide to cash it in. Until recently, you'd need to be trained as an actuary and an accountant to have a hope of calculating the value of your savings bonds.

Fortunately, a site on the World Wide Web will calculate the value of the current bonds. You'll need to run AOL's Web browser and enter the following address

http://www.execpc.com/~mmrsoft/

At this Web site, you enter details about bonds you own, select the Calculate button and you'll see the current value of the bond (see fig. 7.6).

The saving bond calculator at this site is actually a demo for EEBond for Windows, a shareware program that can do more than just determine the current value of a single bond.

FIG. 7.6

A Web site run by MMR Software can calculate the current value of saving bonds.

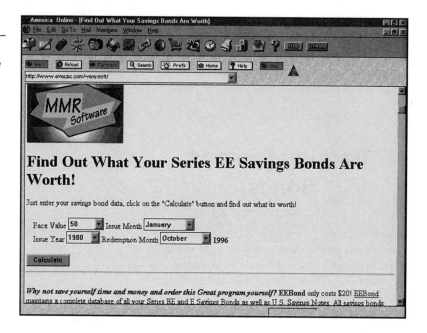

Working with EEBond

EEBond for Windows will keep track of the value for a large number of savings bonds, showing you the total value of your savings bond portfolio and the value of each individual bond. The program keeps a database of savings bonds, using the information you enter about each bond's issue date and its face value. The program is then able to determine the current value of the bond by using tables distributed by the government. These tables are updated twice a year and contain the exact value for every savings bond.

While you may be able to estimate the value of a bond if you know the rules governing the redemption rates, you can only determine the precise value by consulting these tables. In order to see the most accurate current prices, you need to purchase the latest update to the software. Since the software is

distributed as shareware, you are able to use it for 30 days without paying; after that, you'll need to pay a $20 registration fee.

You can download a copy of EEBond for Windows from the Internet by using the keyword

http://www.execpc.com/~mmrsoft/

The file you download is a zipped or compressed file that you need to unzip. After you download and unzip the file, run Setup from the Windows Run command to install the program.

Once you've installed the program, you'll want to gather your savings bonds together and enter them in the program:

1. Open EEBond for Windows. The Bond Records window will open (after you use the program once, you'll be asked to select the file you want to work on before you see the Bond Records window).

2. Select the button New to enter a new bond. Enter information about your bonds, beginning with the serial number. After you complete an entry, press Tab to move to the next entry.

3. For the bond Type, Face Value, Month (of issue), and Year (of issue), you can select the value from a drop-down menu.

4. As soon as you have entered the Type, Face Value, Month, and Year, the current value of this bond is displayed in the Turn In box (see fig. 7.7).

5. When you've finished entering information about the bond, select the Add button. The first time you add a bond to the EEBond database, you'll be prompted for a name for the file. If you plan to track only one portfolio of bonds, you can keep all of your bonds in the same file. But if you plan to track bonds for several people—perhaps two different children—then close the first file after you've finished entering bonds by selecting Done, File, Close. Then, select File, New to start the second file.

After you've stored records for a few savings bonds, you can review details about each by opening the database for that portfolio and using the arrow keys to display each record in the database.

You will also be able to view reports showing the total value of all the bonds, the amount of interest earned by each bond, and the maturity date for each bond. To display a report, you select Reports and choose from one of the options. Figure 7.8 shows a report sorted by issue date.

> "EEBond helps you calculate the value of bonds and explains the rules that govern bonds."

EEBond is a great resource for anyone with more than a few bonds. Not only does it help you calculate the value of bonds, it also includes a lot of explanation about the rules that govern bonds. And you can print the reports or export them to Quicken files.

Searching for the Best Savings Rates

Years ago, it was common to use the same bank for all banking needs, but that's all in the past. The deregulation of banking laws has made banks more competitive. You'll find that one bank has the best deal on checking accounts, but others have better rates on the accounts that pay the highest interest, certificates of deposit (CDs).

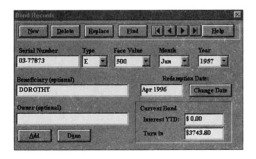

FIG. 7.7

EEBond can calculate the value of a single savings bond and keep track of all the bonds you own.

FIG. 7.8

EEBond reports show current value of each bond, the amount of interest earned, and the total value of all the bonds recorded in the database.

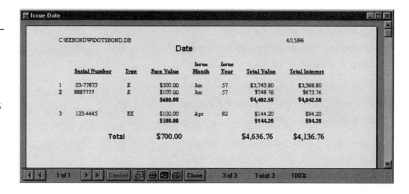

Tracking down the best rates being offered on CDs can be a full-time job. Some banks advertise their rates in newspapers but others don't. And while it makes good sense to use a local bank for your checking account, you don't need to be limited to a local bank when shopping for a CD. You can open the account with a call to an 800 number, send your check by mail, and shop for the best rate using the Internet.

There are two ways to shop for the best bank rates with America Online. Bank Rate Monitor publishes surveys showing the best rates. And Bank CD-Rate Scanner will connect you with a bank offering competitive rates.

Bank Rank Monitor: A Nationwide Hunt for Interest

Before signing up for a new CD, you'll want to always remember to check the rates at Bank Rate Monitor's Infobank, a Web site devoted to publishing information about banks and the services they offer. Bank Rank Monitor compiles the current rates offered by hundreds of banks and creates lists showing the best rates both nationally and by region.

The lists are organized by the types of accounts, and each list shows the bank, the interest rate offered, and the bank's phone number. Here's how you'd find the best nationally available rates:

1. Connect to AOL and enter the keyword

    http://www.bankrate.com

    The browser will connect to the Bank Monitor site and display the opening page, shown in figure 7.9.

2. Select the Savings button at the top of the page. A page with information about savings banks opens.

3. Select the option Nationwide deposit rates. A list of different types of accounts opens, ranging from money market accounts to five-year CDs.

4. Select the type of account you're interested in opening. A list of banks offering the highest rates for this type of account will open (see fig. 7.10).

5. You can print a copy of this list by selecting File, Print, or you can save a copy to your hard disk by selecting File, Save. The file will be stored in HTML, a text format that can be read when opened with any word processor.

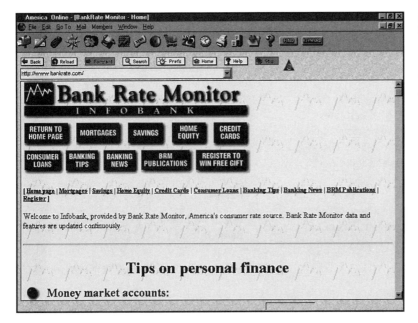

FIG. 7.9

Bank Rate Monitor publishes the best rates for CDs on a national basis and by region.

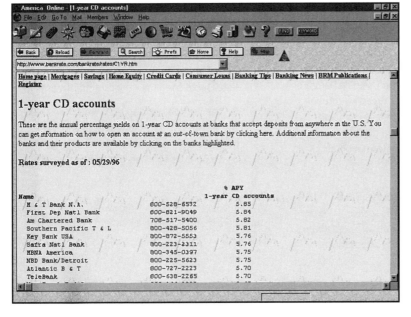

FIG. 7.10

When Bank Rank Monitor displays the banks that offer the best interest rates, it displays only the phone number for each bank.

Some banks are highlighted to indicate a link has been established between the listing here and the bank's Web site. You can learn more information about the bank by clicking these links.

If you prefer to do business with a local bank, you can view the Bank Rate Monitor list of best rates available in your area. Follow the steps above but in Step 4, select Local Deposit Rates instead of Nationwide Deposit Rates. A list of cities and states will open.

While you're searching through the lists, you'll only notice links to other good resources about banking services, including tips on how to protect yourself and your credit rating.

Bank-CD Rate Scanner Does the Shopping for You

While it's not as comprehensive as Bank Rate Monitor, Bank-CD Rate Scanner does require less work. When you log into this Web site, you can view a list of some top CD rates but you don't see the names of banks offering the rate. Instead of reading through lists of banks, you need to complete a form and submit it to the Web site. Within a day or two, you'll receive an e-mail message with information about the bank account.

As you might imagine, there's a catch. Bank-CD Rate Scanner isn't doing this as a public service. The company has a marketing arrangement with some banks, and you'll receive information only about those

banks. And since the system does not include as many banks as Bank Rate Monitor's survey, you won't always find the best rates available. In my experience, the rates available through Bank-CD Rate Scanner were a few percentage points lower than those available through Bank Rate Monitor. However, they were still higher than the rates offered by many banks.

To try the service, follow these steps:

1. Connect to AOL and enter the keyword

   http://vanbc.wimsey.com/~emandel/ BankCD.html

   The main Bank-CD Rate Scanner page will open (see fig. 7.11).

2. Select the option List of Top CD Rates in the USA which appears near the bottom of the screen. The display that opens will show the best rates being offered by banks included in the current survey (see fig. 7.12).

3. If you're interested in pursuing an account with one of the service's banks, select the link CD-Rate Quote form near the bottom of this page.

4. On the form that is displayed, you need to enter the type of account that interests you, your name, and e-mail address. Be sure to select only an account being offered, or you will not receive a quote.

Within a day or two, you'll receive an e-mail message with details about the banks offering this type of account.

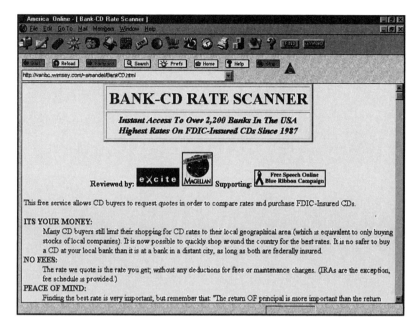

FIG. 7.11

Bank-CD Rate Scanner is a service that sends you bank quotes by e-mail.

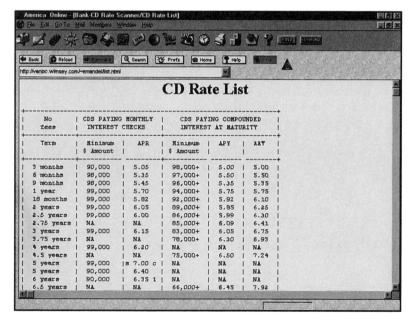

FIG. 7.12

The list of rates displayed by Bank-CD Rate Scanner does not include the names of banks; you need to request a quote by e-mail.

8

Tracking Your Online Investments

No matter how smart you are in investing your money, you'll never reach your full potential as an investor without good records. Whether you're learning from your past or preparing your income tax returns, a good portfolio tracking system can save you time and money.

America Online (AOL) will keep records for you on every stock and mutual fund you own. You can see the most recent share price for each investment, and if you put in just a few minutes of work, your portfolio will calculate the total value of your holdings, updating the amounts as the markets change. You can track different investments in separate portfolios to suit your personal goals. For example, you might track your children's college fund in one portfolio and your retirement savings in a separate portfolio. You can even use the portfolio to keep you up-to-date on an investment that you don't own, but want to follow.

With a little forethought, you'll be able to use these records to create a permanent record of your earnings that will be needed for tax filings. This chapter will show you how.

Building Your Personal Portfolio

The Personal Portfolio feature will record the number of shares you own in any stock or mutual fund, and show you the current value of the holdings based on the most recent market prices. It even goes one step

Making your investments grow is hard work, but the job's not done until you've finished the paperwork. Fortunately, your AOL account has some tools to speed you through the job.

further: If you enter the original purchase price for this investment, AOL will display your profit or loss every time you check in.

For anyone with a few investments, this service alone can justify the cost of a subscription to AOL. You can buy this type of stock-tracking service from several Web sites on the Internet, but you will be charged a monthly subscription (the typical cost is about $10 a month) just to have quotes delivered to your e-mail account, and that's over and above the cost of accessing the Internet.

Setting up your portfolio will take just a few minutes, and it can be updated easily. Best of all, you can download the reports and create your own spreadsheet analysis. The rest of this chapter will guide you through the process of making the most of this valuable resource.

Finding and Saving Your Ticker Symbols

The first step in adding a stock or mutual fund to your portfolio is to look up a current quote. You'll need to know the ticker symbol but if you don't have it already, it's easy enough to find. Once you know a ticker symbol, you can display the quote and add it to your portfolio.

Before you begin to build your online portfolio, you may want to dig out records that will show how many shares you own of each investment and the original purchase price for those shares. It's not necessary to have this information when you start the portfolio—you can enter zero for the number of shares you own or you can estimate the size of your

original investment. But the benefit of being able to track your total holdings is worth the few minutes it will take to dig out your records. You'll want to do it eventually, so you may as well get off on the right foot and create an accurate snapshot of your investments when you start working with the portfolio feature.

The following steps will guide you through the process of creating an online portfolio for stocks and mutual funds. If you know the ticker symbol of the stock or mutual fund, skip ahead to Step 5:

1. Connect to AOL and enter the keyword **quotes**. The Quotes & Portfolios window will open.

2. To find a ticker symbol, select the Lookup button. The Search Symbols dialog box will open. Enter the name of the company you want to track, as shown in figure 8.1. If you already know the ticker symbol, enter it directly in the Quotes & Portfolio window and jump ahead to Step 5.

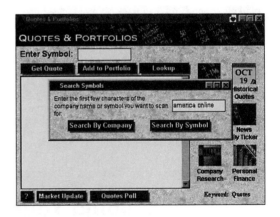

FIG. 8.1

The first step in building a portfolio is to get a ticker symbol.

3. Select the Search By Company button. A window will display the name of the company and its ticker symbol; if other companies have similar names, you'll see a list of companies that come closest to matching the name you entered.

4. Select the company you want to track and click the Get Quote button. A window will display the most recent price information on the stock, as shown in figure 8.2.

5. Select the Add to Portfolio button. A window opens with the question, "Add to which portfolio?" When you start your first portfolio, AOL uses the name Portfolio #1. You can change the name later, so click OK to add the investment to your Portfolio #1.

6. A window will open prompting you for the Number of Shares you own and the original Purchase Price. For the number of shares, you can enter partial shares as either fractions or decimals (for example, .25 or 1/4). For purchase price, be sure to enter the price per share (not the total cost of buying the stock). When you've entered both numbers, choose OK. (If you don't own any shares but want to track the stock or fund, leave the spaces blank.) A window opens to confirm that the stock or fund was added to your portfolio.

FIG. 8.2

Displaying the latest stock quote is part of the process in adding a stock to your portfolio.

7. Now you can view your portfolio. On the Quotes & Portfolios menu, select the Portfolio button. The Portfolio Summary window will open. Select Portfolio #1 to see the investment you've recorded.

Understanding the Portfolio Display

The portfolio will display the most recent price for the stock or mutual fund every time you open it under the heading Last/NAV. (Last refers to the most recent price that a stock traded at; NAV refers to the last Net Asset Value reported by a mutual fund.)

During the course of a day when the markets are open, the price in this column will change every 15 minutes with the most current market prices if the investment is a stock. Mutual fund NAVs do not change throughout the day; a new NAV appears at the end of each day's trading and remains the same until the next NAV is posted. (Mutual Fund prices are updated on trading days every night soon after the markets close.) After hours, on weekends, and on

holidays, the portfolio will display the last closing price for each issue. Figure 8.3 shows a sample portfolio.

The number displayed in the Change column is different for stocks and mutual funds. For stocks, the Change column shows how much the stock price changed since the last price update. During a trading day, the Change column is updated every 15 minutes. But after the markets close, the column shows the Change during the last two days of trading.

For mutual funds, the Change column always shows the difference between the current NAV and the previous NAV. There's one exception—between the time when the markets close and the latest NAV arrives, the Change column displays a 0. When the new price is available, the Change column is updated.

When you first add a stock to a portfolio, the value in the Change column is 0; but the next time AOL updates prices, the correct value will be entered.

If you enter the number of shares you own and the original purchase price, the portfolio updates the value of your holdings every time you display it, using the (last trade price or current NAV) current price. This number, the Value, is at the far right of each holding; just to the left of the Value is the Gain/Loss column, which shows your profit or loss.

At the top of the Portfolio window, you'll see both the total value of all shares, and the total amount of your earnings or losses.

Whether you're using the portfolio to track prospective investments or to monitor stocks and funds that you own, you'll probably find yourself checking the portfolio frequently. You'll come across portfolio buttons in a number of places on AOL; many investment-oriented resources, such as the Motley Fool, Decision Point, and the main Personal Finance menu display a Quotes & Portfolios button. But a faster way to view it is to use the keyword **portfolio**. Better yet, add it to your list of Personal Favorites. When the portfolio is open, click the Heart icon that appears in the upper right corner of the Portfolio window, and AOL will add a Portfolio icon to your list of personal favorites.

FIG. 8.3

The AOL portfolio will show you the most recent price for an investment, and it will calculate the value of your holdings.

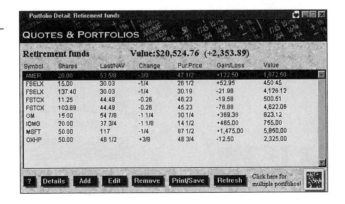

▼ T I P

If the portfolio has been displayed on your system for a while, new price updates may have been posted. To make sure you're seeing the most recent prices, click the Refresh button.

Organizing Your Investments To Reflect Your Goals

If you own more than three or four investments, you'll want to create more than one portfolio. You don't want to have a different portfolio for each holding since it would be cumbersome. But you should create portfolios that reflect your own philosophy. For example, you don't need to review the mutual funds that are earmarked for your child's education as often as you check the price of stocks you're considering as a possible investment. And if you're investing your retirement savings in a group of mutual funds, you may prefer to have a portfolio that can show the total amount set aside for this purpose, rather than mingling these investments with stocks you plan to own for a short period. Figure 8.4 shows one way to organize different portfolios.

▼ T I P

Put some time into planning how you want to organize your portfolio before you record many investments. You can't easily move an investment from one portfolio to another but you can rename portfolios. So even if you're not sure what to call each portfolio, create a separate portfolio before you record all of your investments.

To create a portfolio:

1. Use the keyword **portfolio** to display the Portfolio Summary window, as shown in figure 8.4.

2. Select Create Portfolio. A dialog box will ask for the name of the portfolio. You can enter any combination of letters or numbers up to 23 characters. Choose OK and the name will be added to the list of portfolios displayed in the summary.

3. Repeat Step 2 until you've created as many individual portfolios as you think you may need. You don't need to add investments now, so plan ahead. It's easier to create the new portfolio before you're ready to record individual items, so add as many as you think may be useful.

4. Now you're ready to record individual investments in the portfolios. If you know the ticker symbol of the investment, from the Portfolio Summary screen, select Add Item. If you need to look up the ticker symbol, enter the keyword **quotes** and select the Lookup button. Once you've found the correct symbol, select Get Quote and then Add to Portfolio.

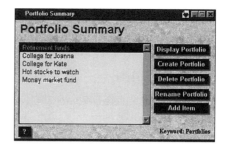

FIG. 8.4

Separate portfolios can help you organize your investment goals.

You can change the name of a portfolio whenever you feel the need with the Rename button on the Portfolio Summary window. In the current version of AOL's software, the only way to move an investment from one portfolio to another is to use the Add Item command, entering the information in one portfolio, and then deleting it from the other portfolio.

Adjusting Your Portfolio for Stock Splits and Dividends

The portfolio does a great job of delivering the latest prices and performing basic arithmetic. Once the portfolio updates the current price, it multiplies the price by the number of shares you've recorded to calculate the value and your gain (or loss). But there are times when the portfolio will become inaccurate because the number of shares you own changes.

You'll need to change your portfolio when any of the following occur:

◆ You buy or sell shares

◆ You receive shares of a mutual fund as dividends

◆ A stock you own splits

◆ You discover you entered the wrong value for the purchase price or number of shares owned

You can easily change the number of shares you own. In order to correct an entry in the portfolio, highlight the entry and select the Edit button. You can change the number of shares you own or the

purchase price of the investment. If you made an error in the ticker symbol of the entry, you'll need to delete the current entry and add a new one.

In some cases, when you acquire new shares—either through a stock split, mutual fund dividend, or a purchase—you may want to account for the new shares with a new entry, and keep the old one. The following sections look at some of these situations.

Adjusting Stock Prices After a Split

When a stock splits, you receive additional shares in a stock, and the stock's price is lowered. The value of your holdings doesn't change in a stock split, but if you don't adjust the portfolio listing for the stock, it will not be accurate.

In most cases, when a stock splits, the number of shares you own is doubled (other splits, such as a three-for-two split or a three-for-one split occur, too, but a two-for-one split is most common). The stock price will be displayed accurately in the portfolio after a split, showing the new, lower price for the stock, but the number of shares you own is not changed automatically. As a result, the portfolio will display a value less than you own. The day after a stock split, you may be shocked to see the drop in the price. The portfolio will calculate your holdings with the original number of shares while using the newer, lower price.

For example, if you owned 10 shares of a stock that split two-for-one when it traded at 100, you'd now own 20 shares of the stock with a value of 50; the value of your holdings didn't change. It was $1,000 before and $1,000 after the split. But the portfolio will display the value of your holdings at $500, using the original number of shares (10) and the new price ($50).

You have a choice of two ways to fix this problem. You can change the original listing, entering double the number of shares you own for the initial purchase and half the price. This technique essentially fudges your record, but it will display an accurate view of your initial investment and current holdings, so you'll see a correct display for the value of your holdings and the gain (or loss). To make this change, display your portfolio, select the stock that split, and click the Edit button. A window will open with the number of shares and purchase price. Enter the current number of shares you own after the split (for example, double the original number); change the purchase price to half the original price. Figure 8.5 shows a stock changed to reflect a split; originally, the purchase was 10 shares at a price of $40 per share; but after the split, the entry was changed to 20 shares purchased at $20.

The second method is to leave the original entry as is and add a second entry, showing the additional shares you received in the split at a price of zero.

After all, you didn't buy the shares; they were a dividend. Figure 8.6 shows how the portfolio entry looks after using this technique, using the same holdings and split used in figure 8.5.

To add the shares in this technique, display the portfolio and click the Add button. Enter the same number of shares recorded already for this investment, and enter zero for the purchase price (assuming it's a two-for-one split; if it's a three-for-two split, enter a number equal to half the original number of shares for this new transaction).

I prefer the first technique since it consolidates the holdings in one listing and you can see exactly what you now own in the stock. But because it introduces an inaccuracy into your records by changing your original purchase order, it works best if you keep your permanent records elsewhere, such as in Quicken's portfolio manager.

The second method will appeal to people who want their online records to be their main source of investment records, since it more accurately records what happened.

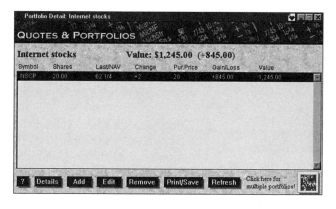

FIG. 8.5

This stock was adjusted for a stock split by changing the number of shares purchased originally.

FIG. 8.6

You can also record a split with two separate entries, using zero as the purchase price for the shares received in a split.

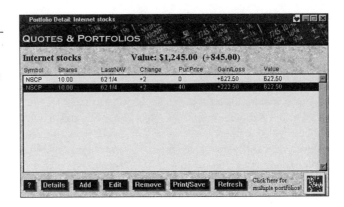

Updating Mutual Fund Records with Shares Earned

Mutual fund owners don't have to worry about splits, but every time a new statement arrives reporting earnings from dividends and capital gains, you'll need to adjust your AOL portfolio. You have a choice of two record-keeping methods.

In the first method, you edit the original entry to record the current number of shares owned after the dividend but leave the purchase price unchanged. The advantage of this method is that you will see a single number showing the current value of your holdings in the fund. But it gives an incorrect amount for your loss or gain, since the shares were purchased at separate prices.

The second method is more accurate. You leave the original record of your purchase as is and add a new entry every time you receive dividends. This method shows the correct amount for the total value of all your holdings and the correct amount for your gains (or losses). A drawback is that it divides the holdings in a fund over several lines, so you cannot see a

complete gain/loss number for the fund. One line tracks change to the initial investment, and another line tracks the changes to the dividends. Figure 8.7 shows a fund tracked with separate entries in the portfolio.

This method will be appealing if you don't use a portfolio management program, like Quicken or a spreadsheet, to record each transaction in your mutual fund account. The reality is that you need to break down and calculate the value of each transaction anyway. When you sell your shares in the fund, your tax return must itemize the capital gain for all the shares you own, including earnings, so you'll have to show the original price and selling price for each share. The best solution is to use a spreadsheet or Quicken to track each transaction, but if you don't, you will definitely want to use this method to track each mutual fund transaction separately.

If you own just a few mutual funds, you may want to create a separate portfolio for each fund. You can accurately track the dividends at the correct NAV every time you receive new shares, and the total gain/loss for the portfolio will reflect an accurate total for your holdings in that fund.

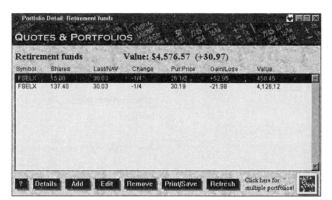

FIG. 8.7

The most accurate way to track a mutual fund is to add new entries in the portfolio whenever you receive dividends.

Saving Your Portfolio

You'll want to regularly save your portfolio, either to a disk or on a printout, so you can have a copy of your records when you're not online. Making those copies is easy—whenever the portfolio is displayed, select the Print/Save button. A window will open asking you to confirm the downloaded folder and the name of the file. You can get more from the downloaded file if you put in a little bit of planning.

You should be prepared to name the file and assign it to a folder before you start the download. If you want to update the portfolio on your hard disk frequently, you will want to reserve a special folder for that purpose alone. Normally, downloaded files are stored in the AOL download folder, but you can create a new folder anywhere and select this folder before the download process begins. The best location is a folder that you use for other financial records or a folder that will be easy to find from your word processor or spreadsheet (for example, the folder that opens by default when you open the spreadsheet).

For most people, the portfolio name should include the date that the file was saved. While Windows users can find the date that a file was saved by using

the Windows Explorer (in Windows 95) or File Manager (in Windows 3.1), you'll find it's easier to organize your records if the date is in the file name.

While you can choose any name for the first part of the file name, the second part should be determined by the software you'll use with the file. The file you download is in text format but if you name it with a prefix that your spreadsheet will understand, you can save a step and have the spreadsheet open it directly. If you use Microsoft Works, the suffix should be WKS; if you use Microsoft Excel, use XLS. You'll find it's easier to work with the file if your system knows the correct data format.

It will be much easier to find your portfolio files if you store them in the same folder. And if you download your portfolio frequently, you'll want to use a naming convention that will force your system to sort the files. By using a numeric date format, files will always be displayed in chronological order. For example, store a file created on January 1, 1997 as

    010197.WKS

Be sure to use a zero as a placeholder before numbers below 10; otherwise, the months 10, 11, and 12 will appear before months numbered 1 through 9.

Building a Spreadsheet with Your Portfolio

Once you have a system for naming the portfolio file, you will want to save it fairly often by selecting the Save Portfolio button that appears on the Portfolio display. Do it often so that you'll be able to check a recent portfolio without needing to log on to America Online.

With the number in a file on your hard disk, you can easily display it in a spreadsheet to extract more information or to print reports that will be more helpful than the simple printout that you get while online.

Fortunately, when you save the portfolio to your hard disk, it is stored in a format that's easy to read with any word processor or spreadsheet. The problems Microsoft Works and other spreadsheets have with text files do not emerge with the portfolio file since the file is stored as a text file with tab-delimited columns. You can open the file directly with any spreadsheet program.

If you track investments in different portfolios, you'll need to download each portfolio separately, and then combine them into a single spreadsheet to see a complete summary of your investments.

Finding the AOL Money Guide Template

You can build your own spreadsheet that calculates the total value of your portfolio, but it's easier to

download and use a template I've written. You can insert your own portfolio into this spreadsheet with very little work. The spreadsheet will do the rest. To download the spreadsheet, use the keyword

http://www.mcp.com/que/desktop_os/ money

You'll find the Web home page for this book with directions to the most recent version of the file. Different versions of the file are available for Lotus 1-2-3, Microsoft Works, and Microsoft Excel. Download the file and store it in the same directory where you will store copies of your portfolio. The next section will explain the spreadsheet so you'll understand what to do with it after you download it, and help you either build your own from scratch, or adapt it with your own special touches.

The Structure of the Portfolio Spreadsheet

In creating a spreadsheet that uses the AOL portfolio, it makes sense to place the formulas at the very top since there's no way of predicting how many rows you'll have in your portfolio. You'll want easy access to the totals that the formulas display.

The AOL Money Guide Portman spreadsheet begins with a label and formula in the first row to calculate the total value of the portfolio. In cell A1, you'll find a label and in the next cell, B1, a formula that totals up the value of each holding. When the most recent portfolio is downloaded and then pasted just below these cells, the formula in cell B1 will calculate a total for the value of each holding. This formula is SUM, and it will add up all of the cells specified. In figure 8.8, you can see that the SUM formula includes the cells G5 to G100.

The range of G5 to G100 is used in the formula since that's where the value for each holding is stored when the AOL portfolio is downloaded and pasted into a spreadsheet. The first few rows (G1 through G4) are needed to display labels for the headings; cell G100 was chosen arbitrarily as the end of the range. It's a high enough value that it should allow for a large number of holdings, but any number can be used as long as it will include all rows in the portfolio.

The next step is to enter a formula that will calculate the value of the original investment in each holding. While AOL stores the original number of shares and purchase price, it does not display the initial cost. You need to add a formula to find the amount for your initial cost or Original Value in order to calculate the amount of gains or losses. The most logical place to add this formula is in column H, just to the right

of the Value column. The formula entered in this row, as shown in figure 8.9, multiplies the quantity of shares (row B) times the purchase price (the value in row E).

In figure 8.9, notice that the cells in column H near the bottom of the screen (H13 and H14) display $0; that's because the formula was inserted into all of the cells in column H down to row 100. This is a result of using a copy-and-paste technique to duplicate a formula, rather than typing it over and over. The cell was typed just once—at the top of the column in cell H5—then it was copied and pasted into cells H6 to H100. Our spreadsheet is now flexible enough to accept a portfolio that reaches cell 100; that may seem like a lot, but if you're tracking dividends for mutual funds, a portfolio of just a few investments can stretch to many rows.

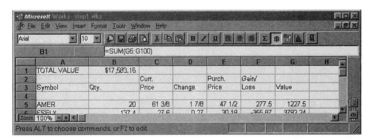

FIG. 8.8

The first step in building a portfolio manager spreadsheet is to use a SUM formula to add the value of each individual holding.

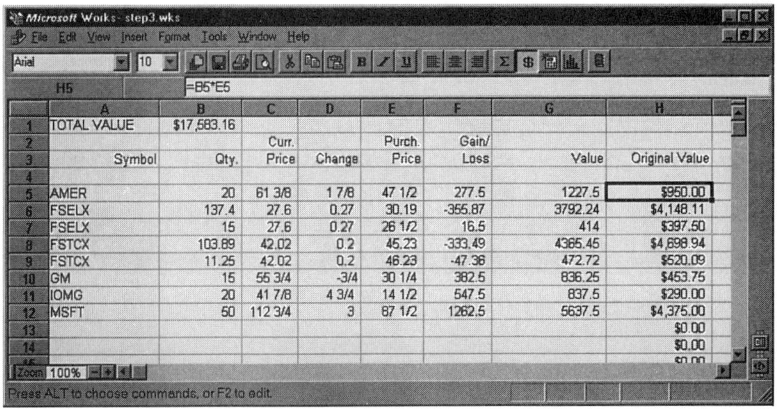

FIG. 8.9

In column H, under Original Value, the spreadsheet calculates the original investment made in each stock and mutual fund.

Next, enter a formula that will calculate a total for the original value of all investments and another formula that will calculate the gains (or losses). You'll want to see this formula at the top, so two rows are inserted just below the Total Value formula and the formulas are entered in cells B2 and B3, as shown in figure 8.10.

The original value is found with a SUM formula that adds the cells in the row you just created—column H. Now that you've found the total amount invested, you can calculate the gain (or loss). The formula in cell B3 does that by subtracting Original Value from Total Value (B1–B2). If the value of the investments has dropped, the amount in this cell will be a negative number.

Adding an Analytical Touch

Now that you've seen the basic operation of this portfolio management spreadsheet, you can extract information that can help you make decisions. For example, in building a diversified portfolio, you'll need to consider how much of your investments are already devoted to each holding. It's easy to find the answer by adding a formula that divides the amount of one investment by the total value of the entire portfolio.

To do that, I created a new row, which I labeled "Percent of Total." The formula in the first cell is

$$=G7/\$B\$1$$

This formula divides the value in G7 by the total portfolio. The dollar signs ($) are used in the formula to indicate that the reference to cell B1 is absolute: when the formula is copied, the reference to cell B1 will not change. That makes it possible to enter the formula just once, then copy it and paste it into every cell from I8 to I100.

Figure 8.11 shows this formula in action. The percentage that each investment represents has been calculated and a chart was created, showing how the total investments are broken down in a pie chart.

FIG. 8.10

In cell B2, the formula for Original Value totals the amounts originally invested. Cell B3 calculates the difference between the original investment and the current value.

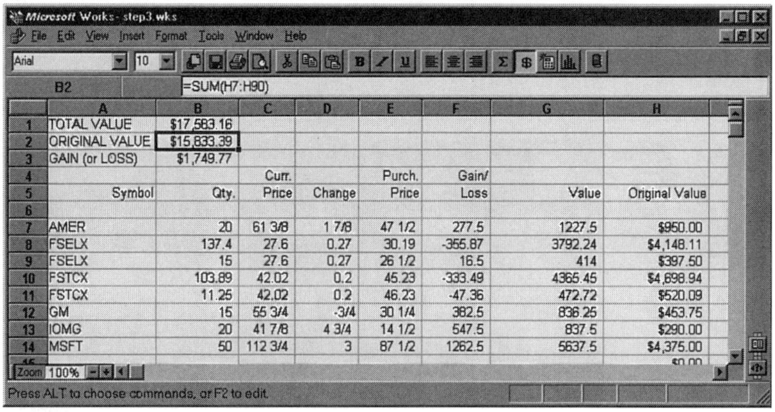

	A	B	C	D	E	F	G	H
1	TOTAL VALUE	$17,583.16						
2	ORIGINAL VALUE	$15,833.39						
3	GAIN (or LOSS)	$1,749.77						
4			Curr.			Purch.	Gain/	
5	Symbol	Qty.	Price	Change		Price	Loss	Value	Original Value
6								
7	AMER	20	61 3/8	1 7/8		47 1/2	277.5	1227.5	$950.00
8	FSELX	137.4	27.6	0.27		30.19	-355.87	3792.24	$4,148.11
9	FSELX	15	27.6	0.27		26 1/2	16.5	414	$397.50
10	FSTCX	103.89	42.02	0.2		45.23	-333.49	4365.45	$4,698.94
11	FSTCX	11.25	42.02	0 2		46.23	-47.36	472.72	$520.09
12	GM	15	55 3/4	-3/4		30 1/4	382.5	836.25	$453.75
13	IOMG	20	41 7/8	4 3/4		14 1/2	547.5	837.5	$290.00
14	MSFT	50	112 3/4	3		87 1/2	1262.5	5637.5	$4,375.00

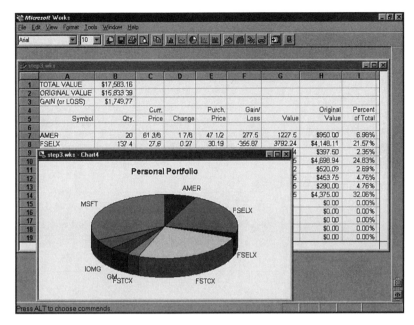

FIG. 8.11

Simple analysis: the percent for each investment is calculated, with a pie chart showing the big picture for this portfolio.

Building a portfolio manager on a solid footing will pay off over the long run since you can do the type of analysis that interests you without too much effort. For example, you may be curious about how changes in the value of each holding have changed the amount of your diversification. If your foreign stock mutual fund has grown while your domestic investments have stagnated, you may find that you have allowed the percentage of your portfolio devoted to overseas investing to become larger than you planned.

To compare the two amounts, enter a new formula that calculates the percentage that each investment originally represented in your portfolio. The formula you enter in cell J7 is

=H7/B2

You can then copy this cell and paste it into the rows below.

Using the Downloaded Portfolio Management Spreadsheet

You don't need to enter any of these formulas if you download the spreadsheet from America Online. They're already stored in the spreadsheet.

You will need to paste the data you download from America Online but that should take about 15 seconds:

1. After you've downloaded the spreadsheet, connect to AOL and display the portfolio you want to analyze.

2. Select the Print/Save button. A dialog box will open, asking you to enter a name and select a folder. Enter a file name and folder that you're

using to organize your portfolio data. Choose OK and AOL will download the data and store it.

3. Disconnect from AOL.

4. Run your spreadsheet program and select File, Open to display the file you just downloaded; if you're using Works, you'll be asked whether the file should be opened in a spreadsheet or word processor. Select Spreadsheet.

5. If you have been using the portfolio to track a fund or stock that you do not own, delete this row.

6. Place your cell pointer in the cell where the name of the first investment is stored, hold down the left mouse button, and drag the mouse to the last value of the last investment, as shown in figure 8.12. Select Edit, Copy.

7. Select File, Open to display the Portman worksheet you downloaded from AOL.

8. When the file opens, place your cell pointer in the cell labeled, PASTE NEW PORTFOLIO HERE (cell A7) and select Edit, Paste. Your portfolio data will be inserted, and the totals will be calculated by the formulas already entered.

9. Select File, Save As to store this file using the date as part of the file name.

▼ TIP

Be sure you do not save this file as Portman, since you'll want to use the original spreadsheet each time you download new portfolio data.

FIG. 8.12

Select the cells to copy into the Portman worksheet.

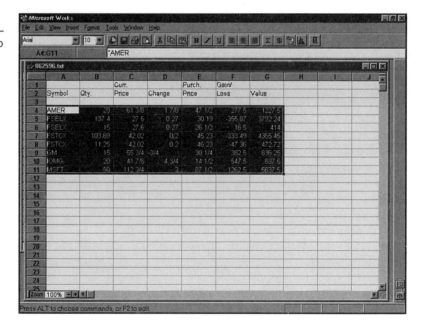

C   H   A   P   T   E   R

9

Protecting Yourself and Your Credit

No financial plan is complete without a defensive strategy. Careful investing will help to make your money grow, but you also need to ensure that you'll be able to borrow money when you need it and to guard against losses. Your America Online (AOL) account can help you with both tasks.

A good credit rating is essential for major goals, like buying a home and or funding your children's education, but a poor credit history can eat away at your financial progress. You won't be able to take advantage of credit cards or borrow money for home improvements or a new car.

Insurance is also a necessity. Property insurance protects the investment you have in your home, car, and possessions, and life insurance protects your loved ones after you're gone. But shopping for insurance is not easy. Aggressive insurance agents promise to save you money, and well-established agents try to sell you insurance you may not need.

Fortunately, information available with your AOL account can help you protect your family and your assets. And using a spreadsheet that you can download from AOL, you'll be able to compare the quotes you find.

Cash Across the Net

Before you begin to take stock of your defensive strategy, make sure you're equipped to deal with the swarm of con artists operating in the online world.

Protecting your assets is an age-old struggle, but in today's information age, there are new challenges and opportunities. In this chapter, you'll learn how to keep your credit cards and your credit history secure.

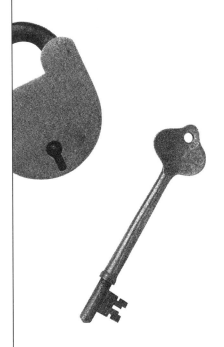

As more of the world goes online, offers to buy merchandise and services are being made directly to consumers from the Internet. While some day you should be able to buy virtually anything online, today the offers are limited to relatively small items.

On America Online, you can safely buy books, computer products, and small items at the America Online store (see fig. 9.1). These transactions are secure since your connection to AOL does not travel through a public network to reach AOL; it travels through a controlled network designed for secure transactions. And if there is a problem with the merchandise, you know you can always call AOL's 24-hour toll-free service line and talk to a representative.

When you use AOL's Web browser to visit sites on the Internet, you'll find a much wider range of products. But outside AOL, you need to be more careful when shopping.

The problem is that transactions conducted across the Internet are not secure; any information sent to an Internet Web site can be captured by a snoop. That means a credit card number can be intercepted in the middle of a transaction. Several security plans are in development to encrypt credit card transactions,

but it will take time for them to be debugged and to become widely accepted.

Also, on the Internet, it's easy for a fly-by-night operator to set up a Web site and offer incredible—too good to be believed—offers. No large company is there to back up the claims or guarantee satisfaction. Only your own common sense can protect you when you're shopping on the Web.

Risks Worth Taking

As a consumer, you can take small risks. The risk of having your credit card number stolen through the Internet is no greater than if a waiter, sales clerk, or telephone operator who handled a transaction for you attempted to steal the number. Moreover, if your credit card number is stolen and your account is charged for merchandise you did not buy, you are protected by federal laws that limit your liability. You have the right to challenge any fraudulent charges that appear on your statement. And since charges that could be made with an online scam will have been processed without your signature, you're on very safe ground.

FIG. 9.1

Your credit card is safe when you shop within the America Online Marketplace because the communications network is not open to the public.

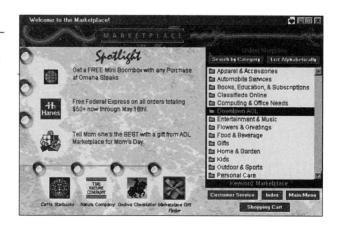

158

The real reason why few companies accept credit cards on the Internet is that the seller will be liable if there's a problem, not the consumer. The threat of an online vendor being scammed with a phony credit card number is far greater than the threat to a consumer shopping through the Internet.

So as a consumer, you may want to buy products across the Internet by posting your credit card number at a Web site as long as you're careful about the supplier. A few businesses have decided that the risk is low, and they are starting to sell merchandise this way. The key question to a consumer is whether you trust the company making the offer to deliver the product. Ordering merchandise from a Web site is similar to ordering by phone. If you're buying from a large company that you trust, you have no reason to worry. But because it's easy to set up a Web site and promise to deliver merchandise, you should always be wary of doing business with a company you do not know.

As always, the best advice is, if the offer sounds too good to be true, it probably is.

Paying as You Go on the Web

A growing trend on the Web is for sites to have a subscription charge or a per-visit fee for delivering specialized information. Some of these sites control access with a PIN (personal identification number) you receive when you call an 800 number and charge the subscription fee to your phone number. But other sites use one of the online payment systems. Two legitimate, online payment systems— WebCharge and First Virtual—are currently available on the Web (more are, no doubt, on the way).

WebCharge operates like an online cash account. When you open your account, a fixed amount is charged to your credit card account, and you have this amount available for spending. Usually, you'll pick from a list of fixed amounts, such as $20 or $40. Once you complete this transaction, you receive a code number that you enter at any Web site that uses WebCharge. When you buy a service, you enter the code, and credits are deducted from your WebCharge account. After you've used up all of your credits, you'll need to return to the WebCharge site and purchase more credits. Figure 9.2 shows the WebCharge Web site.

> "The Key question is whether you trust the company making the offer to deliver the product."

First Virtual is like a middleman for paying Web sites. The First Virtual (or FV) system is a way to buy with your credit card that spares you from the need to send your credit card number to each site you visit. When you open a First Virtual account, your credit card information is stored in First Virtual's computers, and you receive a First Virtual personal identification number.

Any time you choose to buy something at a Web site, you submit the PIN. Within a few hours, First Virtual will send you an e-mail message asking you to confirm the purchase. Your credit card account will be charged only if you send a positive reply to this message. You pay a small service charge (about $2) to open the account, but you don't pay any additional charges to complete individual purchases. Figure 9.3 shows the First Virtual Web site.

FIG. 9.2

When you set up a
WebCharge account, a
charge is made to your
credit card account.

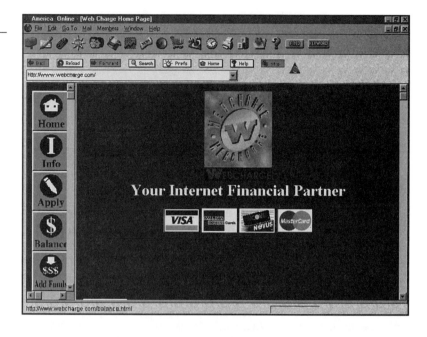

FIG. 9.3

First Virtual will always ask
you to confirm a charge
before it is billed to your
credit card account.

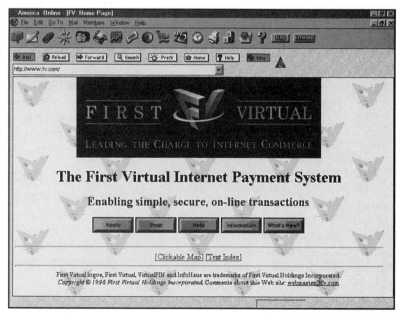

The Future of Online Payment

The systems already in place are designed for making small purchases of a few dollars at a time. But a number of systems are in the works that will allow you to buy just about anything from a Web site—from a pair of shoes to a car. The two systems with the most potential are eCash and CyberCash. These systems are being designed as totally secure, and as a result, they will probably require you to download a special software program that will be activated any time you need to pay. These programs encrypt the transaction (that is, they convert the characters and numbers to code that cannot be understood without a unique key generated by the software program). If you're interested in learning more about each system, visit their Web sites (see Table 9.1 for the URL).

Protecting Your Credit

Banks, credit card companies, and lenders have been traveling on the super-highway before most of us even knew it existed. Every day, financial institutions share information about all of us. They share information about what we buy, what we earn but most importantly, they share information about what we owe. All of this information is used to generate credit reports that help lenders decide whether to loan money.

Anyone who's ever been denied a credit card or turned down for a loan is paying the penalty for having received a bad report credit. The first step in salvaging your credit rating is to settle your outstanding bills, either by paying them in full or negotiating with the creditor. But after you've cleared up delinquent charges, it can take years to overcome the effects of a bad credit report.

Your AOL account can help you improve your credit rating by supplying the information you'll need to repair the damage.

Real Life Advice on Climbing Out of Debt

You can't begin to fix a credit problem without facing up to the hard work of paying old debts or negotiating a settlement for debts that you don't believe are fair. Lawyers can help but for many situations, they're an unnecessary expense. Simple, straightforward talk with the people you owe is the first step, and it may lead to a quick resolution.

TABLE 9.1 Electronic Payment Systems for the Web	
Service	Web Site
CyberCash	http://www.cybercash.com
eCash	http://www.digicash.com
FirstVirtual	http://www.fv.com
WebCharge	http://www.webcharge.com

Unfortunately, settling a problem debt may take more effort. If you and a creditor disagree on how much you owe, there are a few steps you need to take in order to protect your rights and a few creative ideas that others have successfully used to settle disputed bills amicably. Talking to other people who've been through similar problems can save you from the expense of hiring a lawyer. One place to find people who have experiences to share is AOL's Real Life forum; you'll find hundreds of people who are willing to talk about their problems and solutions (see fig. 9.4).

The Real Life forum was established to give ordinary people a chance to learn and share information on everyday financial challenges. Here you'll find a message board specifically devoted to credit problems. There's a lot of material in the Real Life area, but the following steps will help you find the discussions of credit problems very quickly:

1. Log on to AOL and use the keyword **real life**.

2. Select Message Boards. A list of categories opens.

3. Select Personal Finance. A list of topics opens.

4. Select Managing Credit & Debt. A list of subjects opens, such as Debt Collection, Using Credit Cards, or Been Bankrupt?

5. Select a subject, and a list of postings from other AOL members opens.

Read through the list of articles until you find one that sounds interesting. At first, you'll want to read through the comments others have made and see if a discussion covers a topic that's relevant to you. Be sure to read through all of the messages. Some messages will raise a question, and others will provide an answer; more than one person may have answered a question so try to be patient and read

FIG. 9.4

The Real Life forum is a good place to learn techniques that have helped others resolve their credit problems.

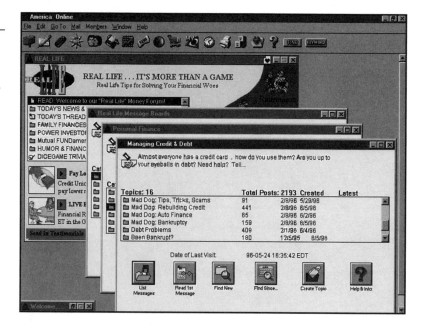

through all of the messages on any topic that interests you.

After you become familiar with the current discussions, go ahead and post your own question. Feel free to just post your own experience, even if you don't have a question. Others may be able to lend a (virtual) shoulder or share a similar experience.

Working your way through a credit problem will require stamina and real effort. But it is worth the effort.

Learning Your Own Credit History

Some people know they have a credit problem because they're unable to pay their debts. But others think everything's fine and believe all their bills are paid—until they run into a problem obtaining a loan or credit card. The problem may actually be an error that was recorded in your account by a company you dealt with and then reported to a credit reporting bureau.

If you have any problems in obtaining credit, you should obtain a copy of your credit report. Equifax, Trans Union, and TRW are the leading credit reporting bureaus. These companies maintain files on consumers' credit histories and sell the reports to corporations that extend credit. Equifax and TRW maintain sites on the Web (at the current time, Trans Union does not). If there is a problem with your credit, it almost certainly is detailed in a report created by one or all three. You have the right to see the reports they've prepared on you, and once you have the report, you can begin the process of correcting any errors by talking directly to them.

It's a good idea to obtain a copy of your credit report, even if you're not experiencing problems, to ensure that it contains only accurate information. A bad credit report may not cause you problems today, but if you decide to buy a new home or car, the problem could delay a loan and ultimately, sour the deal.

Credit histories are carefully protected to ensure against any invasion of your privacy, so none of the companies will let you order or view your credit report online. TRW will send you a copy of your personal credit history for free. Equifax and Trans Union charge small fees (less than $10) if you are not having credit problems, but they will send you a free copy if you were recently denied credit. Each of the three companies requires that you supply very specific information that will help ensure you're authorized to receive the report (such as a recent bill).

You can get background information on the reports and learn how to formally request a copy at the Web sites that Equifax and TRW maintain (you'll have to call Trans Union for more information); see figure 9.5.

To reach TRW on the Web, use the keyword

http://www.trw.com

Once you reach the TRW site, select Consumer Credit Information and then Consumer Credit. To find out more about Equifax, use the keyword

http://www.equifax.com

You'll find that Equifax provides less information (see fig. 9.6) than TRW, but if you're trying to correct a credit problem, you'll want to be thorough and contact both sites.

FIG. 9.5

TRW, a leading publisher of credit reports on consumers, maintains a site on the Web.

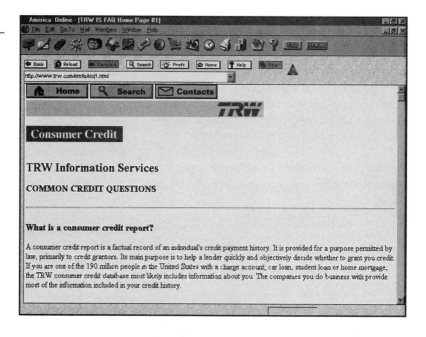

FIG. 9.6

The Equifax site can help you learn how to obtain a copy of the credit report Equifax publishes on you.

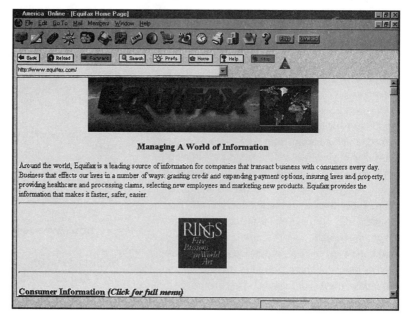

Equifax does not provide much information about its services, but it does show you the steps you need to take to obtain your own credit report.

Steering Clear of Scam Artists

Unfortunately, the Internet is full of scam artists who are trying to exploit people who are suffering from credit problems. Some of these scams offer little more than to sell you the credit report that Equifax, Trans Union, and TRW Equifax publish on you—the same reports that you can obtain for free or for a very low fee by yourself.

Other scams offer counseling. It's a classic case of preying on people who are in trouble. Investigations by the Federal Trade Commission have found that many of these "services" are completely bogus; after the services collect a fee, many vanish completely.

Learning to distinguish between such con artists and legitimate business is a necessity on the Internet. Scam artists have learned to take advantage of the free access everyone enjoys on the Internet. No one polices each of the services offered. When you're on America Online, you don't have to worry about these types of scams since AOL won't allow a fast-buck artist to prey on members. But once you're on the Internet, you have to rely on your own common sense to protect you.

Keep in mind that there's no special service that can correct credit problems without paying your debts. The road to a healthy credit rating begins by settling overdue accounts, and once your creditors have acknowledged that the debt is settled, you need to monitor your credit rating and make certain that it does not include errors.

Correcting Errors in a Credit Report

The process of correcting a credit report can seem like a bureaucratic nightmare, and most of us would rather have a root canal than tackle the job. But it's essential that you do whatever is necessary to repair your credit history as soon as you learn of any errors. If you wait, you'll find that needed records have a way of getting lost and that the wheels of justice can turn very slowly in correcting the problem: the quicker you spot an error, the easier it will be to set the record straight. And the more you know about the process, the easier it will be.

A few resources on the Internet are available with factual information that can help you protect your rights and do the job without spending money on outside help. Reading through this information can help you save the expense of hiring a lawyer to do it for you.

Credit Advice from the Consumer Law Page

The Consumer Law Page is a Web site (see fig. 9.7) run by the law firm of Alexander, Rapazzini & Graham in San Jose, California. You can reach it by using the keyword

http://seamless.com/alexanderlaw/txt/ intro.html

The site is completely free and does not compel you to use the services of the firm. Rather, the site is an informational clearinghouse; you'll find dozens of valuable articles that explain your rights as a consumer and the steps you need to take in claiming your rights. Most of the articles are published by government agencies.

To find the articles that will help you fix your credit problems, select the search tool on the page.

After you've opened the Consumer Law Page, scroll down through the page. Near the bottom of the page, you'll find the Search the Entire Site text box; enter the term you want to search. Type in **credit history**, click the Search the Entire Site button and select Search. A list of articles on the topic will appear. Click any of these articles, and you'll see a straightforward discussion of the topic. When you find a page that has useful information, be sure to print the page or save it.

You can also find articles on the Consumer Law Page by selecting the Brochures button. The page that opens is organized into subject areas. Scroll down to the area on Credit, and you'll find more than two dozen articles that will guide you through the steps you'll need to take in order to repair a credit problem.

FIG. 9.7

The Consumer Law Page provides articles that explain your rights as a consumer and a creditor.

Credit Information from the U.S. Federal Trade Commission

One of the advantages of the Consumer Law Page is that it's well-organized, and the most relevant information is easy to find. If you want to dig deeper, or just feel better going to the source, you will want to visit the Web site maintained by the government agency in charge of protecting the rights of consumers, the Federal Trade Commission (see fig. 9.8).

At its site, the FTC publishes official reports about daily business at the agency but if you dig deep enough, you'll find a wealth of information about consumer credit issues. Many of the articles on the Consumer Law Page were copied directly from this library.

The following steps will guide you to the information on resolving credit problems.

1. Use the AOL keyword

   http://www.ftc.gov/index.html

   The AOL Web browser will open and display the Web site of the Federal Trade Commission.

2. Scroll down and select the link Information Services and Other Sources.

3. A list of Pointers to Sites of Special Interest will open. Select U.S. Government Gophers. A Gopher Menu page will open.

4. Scroll down to find the choice Federal Trade Commission Consumerline. Select this option. A list of sub-directories will open.

5. Select ConsumerLine and another list of sub-directories will open.

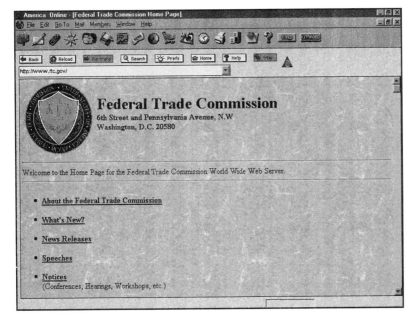

FIG. 9.8

The Federal Trade Commission is the federal agency charged with the task of protecting consumers.

6. Select Publications and another list of sub-directories will open.

7. Select Consumer Credit. A list of reports on consumer credit issues will open (see fig. 9.9).

In the list of reports that opens, look for "Fix Your Own Credit Problems" and "Solving Credit Problems." Here you'll find the same basic steps that any credit repair bureau would follow (that is, if they were actually going to do something to help you). You'll be able to follow these guidelines and correct problems in your credit history on your own.

If all this seems like too much work and you're thinking about hiring one of those services that promises to magically fix all of your credit problems, be sure to read "Credit Repair Scams." In this document, the Federal Trade Commission reports on their investigations into some of the credit repair agency rip-offs and provides tips on how to distinguish between a scam and a legitimate service.

Shopping for Insurance

Insurance is a necessity for everyone who cares about protecting the things they've worked so hard for. A mortgage lender usually requires that you maintain a homeowner's policy, and your state probably requires that you maintain auto liability insurance, but no one can force you to own other important types of insurance, like health and life insurance. If you've put off buying insurance for these important areas, your online account may be just what you need to help you protect yourself and your family. You can learn about the ins and outs of each of these types of policies—and you may save money on the premiums you'll pay.

FIG. 9.9

A list of articles published by the Federal Trade Commission help consumers repair their credit problems.

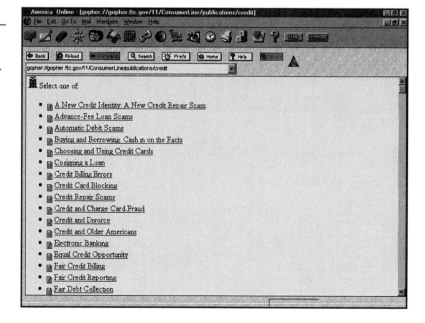

Learning About Your Choices for Insurance

One reason people put off buying the insurance they need is that they find it confusing or don't fully understand what's involved. Buying insurance may not be the most fun you'll ever have, but owning the right policies could make the difference between a comfortable lifestyle and poverty if you or your family ever suffers from unexpected problems.

While insurance agents will be happy to provide you with an education on your options, you're more likely to save money if you learn the basics from an impartial source who doesn't care which insurance company you choose, only that you do buy the insurance you need. If you have any questions about the types of policies you need—or the value of buying insurance at all—you can find most of the answers you need on AOL and the Internet.

Insurance Net: Answers and Links to Information

At the Insurance Net Web site, you may find the answers to all of your insurance questions, but if you don't, you'll certainly be sent in the right direction. This site provides reports that explain many of your options and a long list of links to other sites on the Internet (see fig. 9.10).

The links include Web sites run by commercial interests (such as insurance companies and brokers) and non-commercial organizations (such as federal agencies, like the Federal Emergency Management Agency, and trade organizations, like the Insurance Resources Center).

> "You're more likely to save money if you learn the basics from an impartial source."

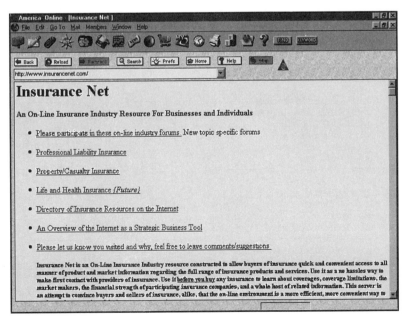

FIG. 9.10

The Insurance Net Web site is a clearinghouse for information available on the Internet about insurance policies.

Money-Saving Ideas from the Insurance Information Institute

The Insurance Information Institute educates the public on insurance issues, and at its Internet site, the Institute publishes a number of brochures that can help you choose the right policy. You can find the site by clicking on a series of links from the Insurance Net Web site, but if you want to go there directly, enter the keyword

gopher://ns1.infor.com:4200

Once connected to the site, select the link Insurance Information Institute—Consumer Brochures. You'll see a list of reports with valuable tips, like "Twelve Ways To Lower Your Homeowners Insurance Costs," and "How To File an Insurance Claim" as shown in figure 9.11.

Be sure to print or save a copy of any report that seems relevant—after all, the keyword isn't exactly easy to remember.

Choosing Among the Many Types of Life Insurance

Most of us know that insurance is a contract that we (or an employer) buy to ensure we'll receive financial benefits if a problem occurs. A homeowner's policy pays benefits if fire or a disaster damages your home, and a life insurance policy provides death benefits to the beneficiary of the policy if the insured dies. But what's the difference between whole life and term life? And how much do you need anyway?

FIG. 9.11

The site maintained by the Insurance Information Institute is full of money-saving advice.

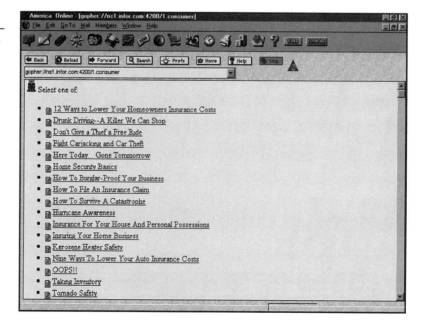

Life insurance is one of the most difficult types of insurance to buy because there are so many options. The following resources should help you tackle this important decision.

AAII's Help in Using Insurance as an Investment

While most insurance policies are a form of protection for a possession or a person, life insurance is often bought to provide protection and an investment. That's because whole life policies are designed to provide old-age benefits as well as death benefits; part of the money you pay in as a premium is invested. When you choose a whole life policy, you also choose the type of investment.

In the section of AOL run by the American Association of Individual Investors (AAII), you'll find a library of articles that explain the different types of policies and will help you understand the reasons why you would want to use them in your own investment strategy. The following steps will guide you to these valuable reports:

1. Connect to AOL and enter the keyword **aaii**. The opening screen for the American Association of Individual Investors opens.

2. Select scroll down the list of topics and select Insurance. A window opens with a list of reports, as shown in figure 9.12.

The reports you find here can be printed or saved to disk from the File menu.

Learning the Cost of a Term Policy

A large and growing number of pages on the Web offer to provide free quotes for term life insurance. Many of these sites are little more than advertisements for a single insurance brokerage company that is hoping to interest you in one of the policies the broker offers.

The information you'll find at these sites is about the same as you could get by making a phone call to different insurance brokers, but they may be more efficient since you can visit the sites any time of the

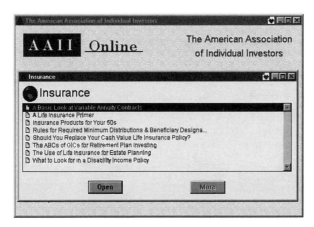

FIG. 9.12

Reports in the AAII section on AOL can help you choose insurance policies that fit into your investment strategy.

day or night to get a quote. To find a list of sites where you can get a quote, use the keyword

http://www.infoseek.com

The AOL browser will open to display the Web search tool, InfoSeek Guide. Enter **insurance quotes** in the Search text box. InfoSeek Guide will display a long list of Web sites where you can find quotes, as shown in figure 9.13.

"There's no charge for either service, and no agent will call you."

Only a few of these sites will offer you quotes from a broader range of insurance companies. These sites are not completely impartial since they receive a fee from all of the companies represented in their database. But they're worth including in any effort to shop for life insurance since they will give you quotes from over 100 different companies. See Table 9.2 for a list of these sites.

When you search from the QuickQuote site, you'll receive quotes from several companies immediately. The IQ and Quotesmith services do not give you the quote right away; instead, the quote is mailed to you. There's no charge for either service, and according to guarantees at the site, no agent will call you, so you have nothing to lose by trying all three.

A Spreadsheet for Comparing Life Insurance Quotes

Once you've received a few quotes, you may end up more confused than ever. You'll receive similar quotes when you compare equivalent types of

FIG. 9.13

Many Web sites offer free quotes on insurance; you can find a list by using the InfoSeek Guide Web search site.

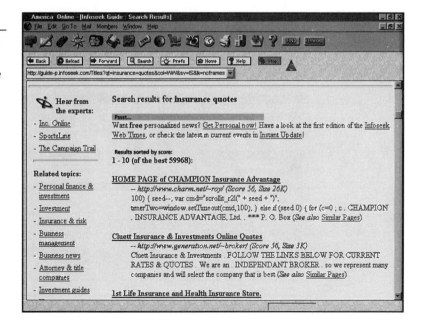

TABLE 9.2   Web Sites with Life Insurance Quotes

Service	Web Site
IQ, Insurance Quote Service	http://www.iquote.com
QuickQuote	http://www.quickquote.com
Quotesmith Corp.	http://www.quotesmith.com

insurance but many brokers will ask you to choose between term and whole life insurance. Whole life comes in many varieties including universal life, permanent life, and variable life, but the basic difference among insurance is quite straightforward.

Term life insurance is a simple policy: you pay a fixed amount (the premium) for the term of the policy, and your beneficiary will be entitled to a fixed benefit (the value of the policy). At the end of the term, you'll pay a higher premium (insurance premiums are based on tables that include age and other risk factors).

A whole life insurance policy will pay your beneficiaries a fixed benefit but the premiums do not change. Instead, you pay the same amount year after year, but you pay a higher premium in the early years than you would with a term policy. With a whole life policy, you will also be entitled to a cash payout at the end of the policy's life. In essence, some of the premium in a whole life policy goes toward an insurance policy, and some of it is invested for you.

Experienced investors prefer term policies because they know they can do a better job of investing the money than an insurance company and without the middleman. If you're not a committed investor, a whole life policy may be a better value since it will force you to invest.

One way to decide between the two is to enlist the help of a spreadsheet. Figure 9.14 shows a spreadsheet comparing sample term and whole life policies.

Normally, the difference between a term and a whole life policy seems mysterious. The whole life sounds great because you receive a small payment every year, and after a fixed number of years, you receive a large cash payment. But you also pay more every year than you would for a term policy.

The spreadsheet compares the real cost of each policy. The sample screen shows actual quotes for a $250,000 term and whole life policy for a 40

FIG. 9.14

A spreadsheet that you can download from AOL compares quotes for term and whole life insurance policies.

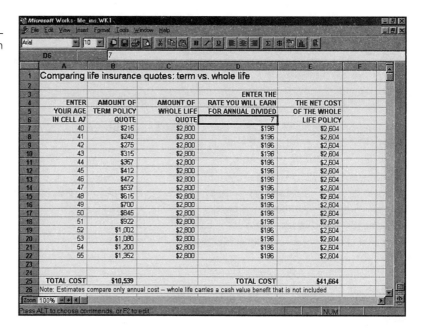

	A	B	C	D	E	F
	ENTER	AMOUNT OF	AMOUNT OF	ENTER THE RATE YOU WILL EARN	THE NET COST	
	YOUR AGE	TERM POLICY	WHOLE LIFE	FOR ANNUAL DIVIDED	OF THE WHOLE	
	IN CELL A7	QUOTE	QUOTE	7	LIFE POLICY	
7	40	$215	$2,800	$196	$2,604	
8	41	$240	$2,800	$196	$2,604	
9	42	$275	$2,800	$196	$2,604	
10	43	$315	$2,800	$196	$2,604	
11	44	$357	$2,800	$196	$2,604	
12	45	$412	$2,800	$196	$2,604	
13	46	$472	$2,800	$196	$2,604	
14	47	$537	$2,800	$196	$2,604	
15	48	$615	$2,800	$196	$2,604	
16	49	$700	$2,800	$196	$2,604	
17	50	$845	$2,800	$196	$2,604	
18	51	$922	$2,800	$196	$2,604	
19	52	$1,002	$2,800	$196	$2,604	
20	53	$1,080	$2,800	$196	$2,604	
21	54	$1,200	$2,800	$196	$2,604	
22	55	$1,352	$2,800	$196	$2,604	
25	TOTAL COST	$10,539		TOTAL COST	$41,664	

Note: Estimates compare only annual cost -- whole life carries a cash value benefit that is not included

year-old male. Column B totals the annual premiums for the term policy; the whole life policy is a little more involved since you need to subtract the payment you'd receive each year before you calculate the annual cost. You can download this spreadsheet from AOL and plug in the quotes you receive for yourself, using any type policy. You'll find the spreadsheet by using the keyword

http://www.mcp.com/que/desktop_os/ money

10

Facts That Will Make You a Better Consumer

Your number one job as a consumer is to protect your own interests. You'll find plenty of help online to help you buy safe products and save money along the way.

Making the most of your money requires more than shrewd shopping and aggressive bargaining. A little bit of research can go a long way toward stretching your hard-earned dollars in the marketplace—and protecting you when things go wrong. The fact is, the laws provide clear guidelines on how you must be treated as a consumer, but unless you're aware of those rights, you won't be able to claim them. In this chapter, you'll learn where to find clear information from official government agencies.

You'll also find out about detailed research the government performs on products, both to ensure their safety and to protect consumers from fraud and defective manufacturing. And, you'll find out how to take advantage of the lab-testing and product research performed by major magazines without spending a fortune on magazine subscriptions or moving into the library.

Finally, you'll learn about message boards where you can talk to other consumers who have already bought the products you're eyeing. With the tips you learn here, you'll be able to find a jury of your peers who can help you decide before you buy.

Over time you'll find that knowing your options before you enter a store will save you time, effort, and aggravation.

Product Research You Already Bought...with Your Taxes

Everyone knows that the U.S. government does a lot of research on the products and services that are sold throughout the country. Billions of dollars are spent to fund agencies whose main goal is protecting consumers, like the Food and Drug Administration and the Consumer Product Safety Commission. Most of the money is spent on enforcing the law, but the government also creates reports as a byproduct of that research to educate the public. Most Americans hear about these reports, but normally you hear only snippets from a specific finding used in a sound bite prepared for a TV news report.

As a consumer and a taxpayer, you have the right to read all of the reports that are being generated for your benefit. All you have to do is ask, but first you have to know what's available and how to get it. Until the advent of online access, you needed to

write or call the agency that created the report, but you probably wouldn't have known what you were looking for or where to start your search. Technology has changed all that. Today, you can connect to one of the sites run by government agencies on the Internet. You'll either find the phone numbers you can call to learn about consumer-oriented reports or you can print the reports right then and there.

Many federal agencies maintain attractive Web sites that are easy to navigate. But very few of these Web pages have the hard facts you'll want to have as a consumer. The best source for product information—especially information on product recalls and safety alerts—are Gopher servers, and many government Web sites lead you to a Gopher server that's filled with documents about the agency's services. For example, the Consumer Product Safety Commission operates a Web site (see fig. 10.1), but aside from showing you the official logo of the commission, it does little more than direct you to the Commission's Gopher server.

A Gopher server is not glamorous. You connect to it using the same America Online (AOL) browser you use to view Web pages, but when you're connected to a Gopher server, you see a directory of folders that looks like the File Manager on a Windows system. You'll see lists of folders that organize documents. Sometimes, you'll have to click three or more times to dig down through subfolder after subfolder before you find the document. But many of the documents you'll find are full of invaluable information that you can print or save to your hard disk.

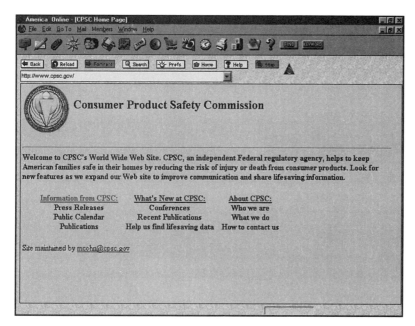

FIG. 10.1

Many government Web sites are little more than pretty faces; the real information is stored on Gopher servers.

The Consumer Product Safety Commission on the Web

The Consumer Product Safety Commission (CPSC) has a big job. It was created by Congress to "protect the public against unreasonable risks of injuries and deaths associated with consumer products." By its own count, more than 15,000 *types* of products are included in that mandate—since hundreds of specific models are sold in some categories, that means the Commission is responsible for hundreds of thousands of individual products. Some other government agencies monitor specific products; the Food and Drug Administration monitors the food, drug, and cosmetic industries; the Department of

Transportation oversees the safety of moving vehicles; and the Treasury Department monitors the sale of alcohol, tobacco, and firearms. All other products are within the scope of the Consumer Product Safety Commission.

The Commission runs a Web site that you can view by using the AOL keyword

http://www.cpsc.gov

Figure 10.1 shows the Commission's Web site. It's not a bad-looking page, but you won't find much here other than links to the agency's Gopher site, as shown in figure 10.2. So you should save yourself a step and start your research by using the keyword

gopher://cpsc.gov

FIG. 10.2

The Consumer Product Safety Commission runs a Gopher site that's filled with valuable product safety information.

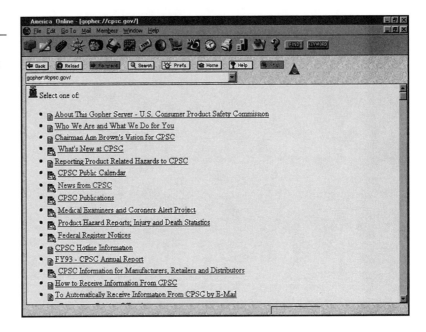

At its Gopher site, the Commission publishes reports about safety problems that it has found in certain types of products and advice on how to avoid injury. You'll also find news about product recalls and reports about changes that the agency has convinced manufacturers to make to products that are short of a recall. As a consumer, you'll want to know about any of these changes when they're made to a product you're planning to buy. Products recalls can go on for weeks. A dangerous product may continue to sit on store shelves and be sold to consumers as the official notice is passed from the manufacturer's headquarters to the headquarters of the stores carrying the merchandise and down to the store managers. You could easily buy a product that was recalled a month ago. While the laws require a manufacturer to alert customers about a recall, you won't be notified unless you return the product registration card that should be in the box. So even when the system is working—which means the registration card is in the box, you return it, and the company notifies you

within days of receiving your registration—you may be using a recalled product for several weeks.

Of course, very few products out of the thousands on the market are ever recalled. But when a product is recalled, it's usually because there's a fairly serious risk of injury. And on a number of occasions, companies that agreed to recall a product did not actually follow through; the products stayed on the market, and consumers who owned the faulty products were never notified.

Learning About Product Recalls

At the Commission's Gopher site, you can read through a list of the press releases that the Commission has issued. All of them are dated, and even though the Commission issued these to encourage the news media to publicize the recalls, many of these press releases were not widely reported.

▼ TIP

Reading through the press releases that are available at the Consumer Product Safety Commission's Internet site can help you learn about product recalls that were not widely reported by the press.

Most of the press releases announce an agreement that the Commission negotiated with a manufacturer about a product recall announcement. The press release will identify the product and explain how it may cause injury. Some press releases report that the

Commission has filed a lawsuit against a manufacturer that is unwilling to cooperate in rectifying a product safety problem; a few report the settlement of such lawsuits.

The following steps will guide you through the many folders where the press releases are stored:

1. Log onto AOL and use the keyword

   gopher://cpsc.gov/

   The AOL browser will open and display the opening page of the Consumer Product Safety Commission's Gopher site on the Internet (see fig. 10.2).

2. Select News from CPSC. A list of folders opens. Select CPSC Press Releases, 1990-1996.

3. A list of folders opens, showing the press releases organized by year. You can select any of the folders, but you'll be more efficient if you start with the most recent folders. Some day you may get around to reading the documents in all of the folders, but it will take a very long time. Once you select a folder, you'll see a long list of titles for each of the press releases (see fig. 10.3).

4. Select any of the titles and you'll see the full press release. If you own the product or know someone who does, you'll want to print the press release or save it to your hard disk. Select File and choose the option to Print or Save the page.

FIG. 10.3

You can learn about product recalls and other product safety problems in press releases issued by the Consumer Product Safety Commission.

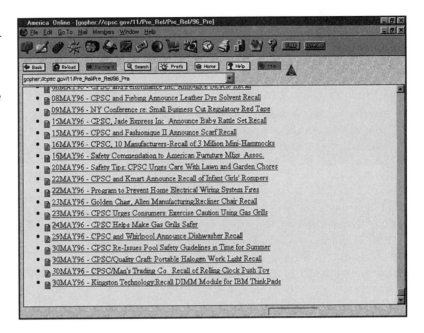

America Online - [gopher://cpsc.gov/11/Pre_Rel/Pre_Rel/96_Pre]

File Edit GoTo Mail Members Window Help

Back   Reload   Forward   Search   Prefs   Home   Help

gopher://cpsc.gov/11/Pre_Rel/Pre_Rel/96_Pre

- 08MAY96 - CPSC and Performance Inc. Announce Bicycle Recall
- 08MAY96 - CPSC and Fiebing Announce Leather Dye Solvent Recall
- 09MAY96 - NY Conference re: Small Business Cut Regulatory Red Tape
- 15MAY96 - CPSC, Jade Express Inc. Announce Baby Rattle Set Recall
- 15MAY96 - CPSC and Fashionique II Announce Scarf Recall
- 16MAY96 - CPSC, 10 Manufacturers-Recall of 3 Million Mini-Hammocks
- 16MAY96 - Safety Commendation to American Furniture Mfgs. Assoc.
- 20MAY96 - Safety Tips: CPSC Urges Care With Lawn and Garden Chores
- 22MAY96 - CPSC and Kmart Announce Recall of Infant Girls' Rompers
- 22MAY96 - Program to Prevent Home Electrical Wiring System Fires
- 23MAY96 - Golden Chair, Allen Manufacturing Recliner Chair Recall
- 23MAY96 - CPSC Urges Consumers: Exercise Caution Using Gas Grills
- 24MAY96 - CPSC Helps Make Gas Grills Safer
- 29MAY96 - CPSC and Whirlpool Announce Dishwasher Recall
- 30MAY96 - CPSC Re-Issues Pool Safety Guidelines in Time for Summer
- 30MAY96 - CPSC/Quality Craft Portable Halogen Work Light Recall
- 30MAY96 - CPSC/Man's Trading Co.: Recall of Rolling Clock Push Toy
- 30MAY96 - Kingston Technology:Recall DIMM Module for IBM ThinkPads

How To Get Product Recall Notices Sent to You

As you'll see when you visit the site, there are a fair number of product recalls—on average, about five or six a week. It can be difficult to absorb all of them during a single visit.

You may want to subscribe to the Consumer Product Safety Commission's mailing list. The Commission will add your e-mail address to the list of people who receive the press releases on the day they're issued. It costs nothing, other than the time you'll spend reading the message while you're connected to America Online.

▼ **T I P**

You can protect yourself from buying unsafe products by subscribing to the Consumer Product Safety Commission's mailing list. News of recalls will be sent to you automatically.

The process of subscribing to the list will be familiar to anyone who's already taken part in an Internet mailing list. The Commission's mailing list is managed by the "listserv" program. Even though you subscribe to the list through an ordinary e-mail message, chances are your message will never be seen by a human. The e-mail message is read by the listserv program which manages the job of adding names to the mailing list, sending out the mail, and removing the names of people who send in a sign-off message.

Here are the steps you'd take to put your name on the list:

1. Connect to AOL and select Mail, Compose Mail. The Compose Mail window opens.

2. In the To box, enter

   listproc@cpsc.gov

3. Press Tab twice to move to the Subject box. The AOL mail manager requires a subject, so you can enter anything here you like; the automated listserv program that receives your message will ignore the subject.

4. Press Tab to move your insertion point to the body of the message. Enter

   sub CPSCINFO-L *FirstName LastName*

   using your own name for FirstName and LastName. (You can use either your real name or a nickname; the entry on this line is used only to assign a return name in any messages you send to the list). Your screen should look like figure 10.4.

5. Check your spelling and then click the Send button.

Within a few hours you will receive an e-mail message that either confirms that you've been added to the list or reports a problem. If you don't receive a confirmation within a day, check your spelling carefully and try again. Once you've been added to the list, you'll start to receive mailings within a few days. If you find that you're not reading the messages, you can remove your name from the list by following the same steps but, in Step 4, rather than the line that begins with sub, use this line

signoff CPSCINFO-L *FirstName LastName*

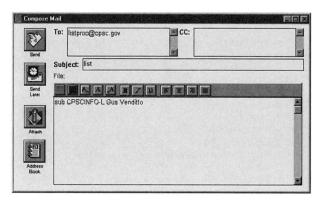

FIG. 10.4

Add your e-mail address to the Consumer Product Safety Commission mailing list and you'll be notified of every product recall.

Safety Advice from the Consumer Product Safety Commission

Not all of the Commission's findings result in product recalls. The Commission also publishes brief reports that identify hazards you may experience in products that are not defective. These reports include advice on selecting the best products and tips on using them after you've taken them home.

You'll find the reports on the Commission's Gopher site. Select the link CPSC Publications. A list of

product categories will open, ranging from Children's Furniture to Power Equipment, as shown in figure 10.5.

Some of the reports discuss problems that may develop with a particular product, but others cover broader topics, such as how to avoid problems that are endemic to used cribs, and hazards that often develop with aluminum cookware. The reports in this section are short, and you should be able to read through the material that is relevant to your lifestyle in one sitting.

FIG. 10.5

Reports from the Consumer Product Safety Commission include shopping tips and advice on using products safely.

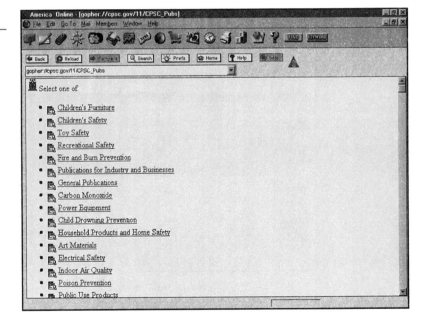

Sounding the Alarm for Dangerous Products

The information that the government provides comes from ordinary consumers who've reported a problem. If you know of an injury that you feel was caused by a poorly designed or defective product, you may want to report it to the Consumer Product Safety Commission. The e-mail address for reporting hazardous products is

amcdonal@cpsc.gov

At the Commission's Gopher site, you'll find detailed instructions on the information that you should submit under the heading Reporting Product Related Hazards to CPSC.

Car Recall Notices, the Government's Official List

You won't find any information about motor vehicles in the files of the Consumer Product Safety Commission. The safe manufacture of cars, trucks, and vans is monitored by the National Highway Traffic Safety Administration (NHTSA), a division of the U.S. Department of Transportation. Information that can help you choose and maintain a car is located at NHTSA's Internet site.

Occasionally, you'll hear news reports of a large recall that NHTSA ordered, but many other recalls take place quietly, and if they're reported in the news, only a small item is printed. The reports that make headlines are usually very broad recalls that affect hundreds of thousands of cars, often affecting a

year's worth of production in one model. But smaller recalls take place all the time, sometimes affecting the cars or trucks produced for a few months in a model year. Recalls also can affect child-safety seats and the parts used to repair cars. Normally, manufacturers are required to notify their customers, but unless you've completed a registration card after buying the product, the manufacturer would never be able to find you. Which leads to the question, Would your mechanic call you up and tell you that the brake hose assembly he just installed in your car was recalled?

You can find out for yourself which products have been recalled by reading through the NHTSA press releases. Fortunately, it shouldn't take more than a few minutes to catch up on a year's worth of reports:

1. Connect to AOL and use the keyword

   http://www.dot.gov/affairs/nhtsain.htm

   The Web browser will open and display the National Highway Traffic Safety Administration's Public Affairs electronic information page.

2. Select the link Published Auto Recalls. A page will open with links to the monthly list of recalls (see fig. 10.6).

3. Select a link and the press release will open. You won't need to read the entire report; scroll down through the page and look for the names of the cars and other products.

4. If you find a product that's relevant to you, select File, Print or File, Save.

5. To read through other reports, select the Back button on the browser toolbar. The list of links to monthly recalls will appear once again.

FIG. 10.6

You can find the government's list of car and truck recall notices at the Web site run by the NHTSA.

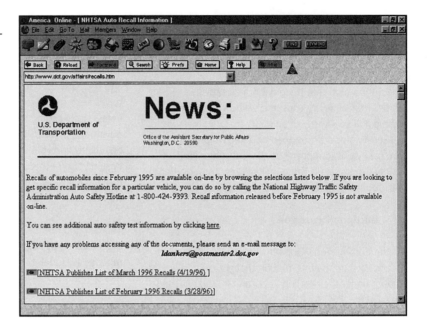

Although the list of recalls is issued monthly, they do not appear until after the month is over. Sometimes they appear months after the end of a month. For example, the September recall list may appear in late October or even late November.

The Consumer's Resource Handbook: Free for Downloading

The Consumer Product Safety Commission and the National Highway Traffic Safety Administration are the two federal agencies with the most extensive library of reports for consumers. But other government agencies also publish information that can help consumers. The job of coordinating this sea of information falls on the shoulders of the Consumer Information Center.

The Consumer Information Center is a government agency charged with informing the public about the thousands of publications that are available from the government. Many of these publications are available for a nominal fee of 25 cents or a dollar. However, at the Center's Web site, you can read and print many of the documents for no charge above the cost of your online connection (see fig. 10.7).

One of the Center's most popular documents—the Consumer Information Catalog—can be downloaded directly from the Web site. This handbook is a collection of tips from dozens of federal agencies on some of the bigger consumer issues, ranging from how to write a complaint letter to how to shop for a home mortgage. You'll find contact information for government agencies that can provide more information, including state consumer affairs offices. And you'll find guidelines on how to research products before you buy and a summary of your rights as a consumer after you've made a purchase.

FIG. 10.7

The Consumer Information Center helps consumers find publications available on products and consumer issues.

The following steps will guide you to the Consumer Information Catalog so you can read it online or download it as a text file that you can use on a word processor after you log off.

1. Log on to AOL and use the keyword

   http://www.pueblo.gsa.gov

   The Web browser will load and display the opening page for the Consumer Information Center, as shown in figure 10.7.

2. Select the link Browse the Consumer Information Catalog. A page will open with links that allow you to download a complete copy of the catalog or to view individual chapters (see fig. 10.8).

3. If you choose to download the catalog, you'll have a choice of downloading the document as a text file that can be opened with any word processor, or as a compressed ZIP file. The ZIP file is less than half the size of the uncompressed file, but you will need to expand the file with an un-zip program on your system before you can use it.

If you're not sure if you really want to download the complete catalog, you can view sections of the catalog while you're connected to the page. Scroll down the page and you'll see a graphic that displays a menu choice for each chapter (see fig. 10.9).

FIG. 10.8

You can download the
Consumer Information
Catalog directly from a
Web site.

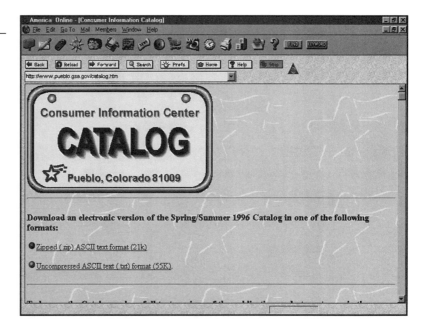

FIG. 10.9

You can read sections of
the Consumer Information
Catalog directly from a
Web site.

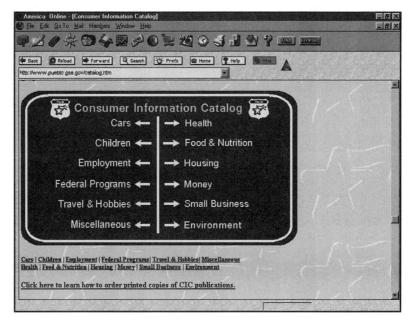

Consumer News Highlights

The entire catalog may be one of those documents that sounds great but you're not sure whether you'll really use it. To help you decide whether you want to spend time downloading the file, you can read bulletins that the Consumer Information Center makes available at its Web site; these short articles describe the documents in the catalog.

You can find the list of bulletins either by selecting the link Consumer News from the main Web page, or by using this keyword

http://www.pueblo.gsa.gov/consnews.htm

When you reach the page shown in figure 10.10, you'll find that the bulletins are organized by categories.

Here's a summary of the categories and some recent bulletins:

◆ Cars ("Underhood Tips To Help You Keep Your Cool")

◆ Children ("Toys & Play")

◆ Employment ("Telecommute America")

◆ Federal Programs ("Buying Federal Property")

◆ Food & Nutrition ("A Consumer's Guide To Fats")

◆ Health ("Nonprescription Pain Relievers")

◆ Housing ("12 Ways To Lower Your Homeowners Insurance Cost")

◆ Money ("66 Ways to Save Money")

◆ Miscellaneous ("Online Scams")

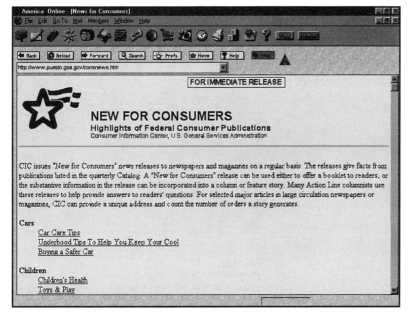

FIG. 10.10

The Consumer Information Center publishes bulletins that describe many of the brochures you can order.

Each bulletin will give you a flavor of the type of information you'll find in a longer brochure published by a government agency. Here you'll find information on how to order the original.

Product Tests and Ratings from Consumer Reports

Consumer Reports is best known for its print magazine with detailed comparison reports on products. The magazine's reports are one of the only independent sources of product testing information for many types of products; virtually every type of product is scrutinized and rated in the magazine's test labs. Blue jeans, toothpaste, cameras, tools—if you buy it, they've probably done a report. To help ensure that there's no hint of bias in any of the reports, the magazine does not accept advertising of any kind.

On America Online you'll find excerpts from many of the magazine's articles, including the popular ratings. The *Consumer Reports* section of the America Online service is organized into categories.

◆ Automobiles, including road tests, new car profiles, and new car ratings.

◆ Electronics, with recommendations on radio, television, video, and stereo.

◆ Food and Health, including recommendations about nutrition, treatments, and food products.

◆ Home and Workshop covers a wide range of products and services including appliances, clothing, and toys.

◆ Money with advice on personal finance issues.

It's easy to browse through the entire library. To see an overview of the collection, use the keyword **consumer reports**. Figure 10.11 shows the opening menu.

To see the most recent reports, click the picture of the magazine's cover in the upper right corner of the window. A list of reports will open; click any one of these reports to read the text (see fig. 10.12).

You won't find every article in the magazine, but you can do something online that you can't do with the printed magazine. You can print a copy for your own personal use on your printer, or save it to your hard disk.

▼ **T I P**

Even if you subscribe to *Consumer Reports*, you'll want to use the online version. You can find the articles you want faster by using the Search command, and you can print a copy of any article to take with you to the store.

FIG. 10.11

Consumer Reports organizes its collection of articles by product category.

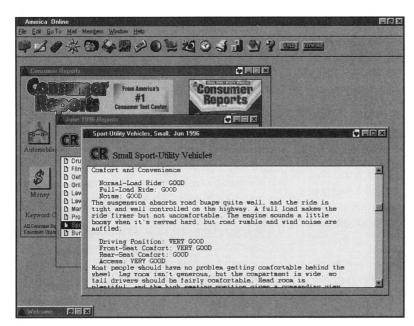

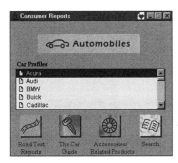

FIG. 10.13

Reports in the Automobiles category are organized by manufacturer and according to articles that appear in the print version of *Consumer Reports.*

Browsing by Category

When you first explore the *Consumer Reports* area, you'll want to click each of the category buttons in order to get a perspective on how the section is organized. Each button has a slightly different menu that is tailored to the unique characteristics of the reports in that section.

Many of the categories are organized on very general lines. When you select the Food and Health button, for example, you see a menu that allows you to choose from a list of all articles within the category or to choose individual buttons that will divide the articles into just those concerned with Food and those concerned with Health products.

The organization of the Automobiles section is a little more complicated. Click the Automobiles button and you'll see a list of car manufacturers, and four new buttons (see fig. 10.13).

Select the name of a car manufacturer and you'll see a report with a brief summary of each model currently in the manufacturer's line. Each button offers you a different type of report.

 Road Test Reports are articles that appeared in the magazine in recent years. Each one has a different perspective, such as "family sedans" or "mid-sized coupes."

 The Car Guide is a list of the articles that appeared in *Consumer Reports'* last special issue devoted to the new car model year. Here you'll find a profile for almost every model on the market.

 Accessories/Related Products are reports on things car owners would need, such as car wax, jumper cables, and tires.

 Search opens the general *Consumer Reports* search command; you can perform a search on any of the categories, not just cars.

No matter which category you choose, once you have selected an individual report, you can read it online, print it, or save it to your system, using the commands on the File menu.

Finding Reports on a Specific Product

One of the advantages that *Consumer Reports* on America Online has over the printed magazine is that you can search through all of the articles for any term. Even if you have been a longtime subscriber to the magazine and have 10 years' worth of magazines neatly organized on your bookshelf, you'll find it's easier to use the library on America Online. By the time you look through the table of contents in the printed magazines to find a particular article, you could have logged on to America Online and performed a search that would display the report you want. You may still want to keep those old back issues; they have pictures and some ancillary material, like diagrams, that you won't find online. But you'll find the Search feature is much faster than looking through your old issues.

You won't have to look far to find the Search command; it's on the main menu and on every one of the category menus. When you click any of these Search buttons, the same window will open. You can search for any type of product no matter which category you were in when you selected the button. Type in the term you're looking for and click List Articles; you'll see all of the individual reports. Figure 10.14 shows a search for the word "refrigerator."

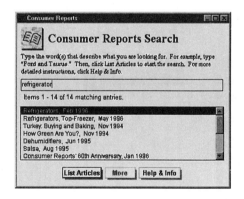

FIG. 10.14

Something you can't do with the printed magazine: the Search command will find every article that mentions a word or phrase.

When you're looking for something specific, it pays to refine your search term. In figure 10.14, the search on "refrigerator" found 14 reports. That may be the appropriate amount of information if you're starting from scratch in your fact-gathering expedition. But if you've already narrowed your shopping down, you can save time and effort by using a search term that is more specific.

For example, if you've already been to the stores and are considering two or three brands, you might want to use the manufacturer's name along with the product category. Figure 10.15 shows one way to conduct a search for refrigerators that is restricted to articles that mention two popular brands. By using the search term, "GE and Frigidaire and refrigerator," you can limit your findings to the more manageable number of three reports, rather than the original number—14 reports.

You'll find it's worth experimenting a little with the search terms when you're researching a very crowded product category, like cars. Playing with the search term will take only seconds, but reading

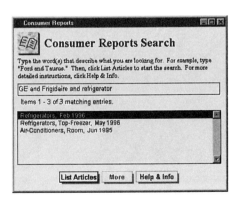

FIG. 10.15

Refining a search in the *Consumer Reports* library of articles can save you time and connect charges.

through pages and pages of reports that are not relevant will not only cost you extra connect time—it may tire you out before you find the information you really need.

Taking Only What You Need

If you're doing a broad search on product information, you may find you'll get more from the report if you save it to your system and then do some editing with a word processor to make it more usable. For example, you may want to delete the products you don't want to buy from your report before you print out a copy. You can then take your edited copy to the store with you.

You may even want to take it a step further and build a little worksheet that can help you keep track of the information you find while shopping. Here's how you could save the information from the *Consumer Reports* database and then use it to build a spreadsheet:

1. Connect to AOL and use the keyword **consumer reports**. The main *Consumer Reports* menu opens.

2. Select Search. The Search window opens.

3. Enter as much information as you can about the product you're seeking. Press Enter.

4. A list of articles appears in the bottom of the Search window.

5. Select one article; it appears in a new window.

6. When you find material you want to save, such as a comparison table, highlight it with your mouse (to do this, move your mouse pointer to the first word in the section, hold down the left mouse button, move the pointer until the entire area is highlighted, and release the button).

7. Select Edit, Copy from the main menu (see fig. 10.16).

8. Open the word processor or spreadsheet you'll use to store the information. Depending on which program you're using, you may need to open a new file. To switch between applications in Windows, press Alt+Tab; to switch between applications on a Mac, click the Finder button.

9. With a new, blank file open, select Edit, Paste. The text you copied from the *Consumer Reports* article appears.

You can now use your word processor or spreadsheet to edit the article, removing any text you won't need and adding your own notes. If you copy *Consumer Reports* tables into a word processor, you'll find that they will appear in the correct column format only if you use a fixed-pitch font, like Courier. (A fixed-pitch font assigns an equal value to every

character and space, while proportional fonts, like Times Roman, give a different amount of space to each character and space, distorting the appearance of a table.) You can fix a distorted table after it's in your word processor by highlighting the text and choosing a proportional font.

Figure 10.17 shows how the data in figure 10.16 looks after it was imported into a Microsoft Works word processing document and formatted with Courier New, a fixed-pitch font.

If you use a spreadsheet like Microsoft Excel or Lotus 1-2-3, you may want to import *Consumer Reports* tables into a spreadsheet, rather than a word processor. The spreadsheet will guide you through the process of converting the report's spaces to spreadsheet columns; it will take a few minutes, but the time will be worth it if you're planning a major shopping expedition. You'll want to refer to the table often.

FIG. 10.16

When you're ready to use the information in a *Consumer Reports* article to help you comparison shop, you'll want to print just a small part of an article.

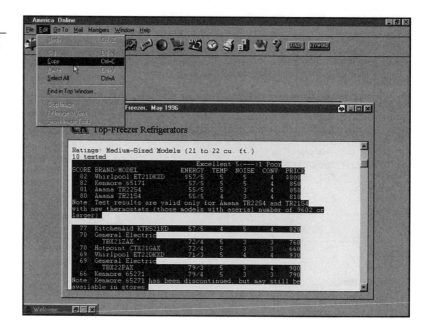

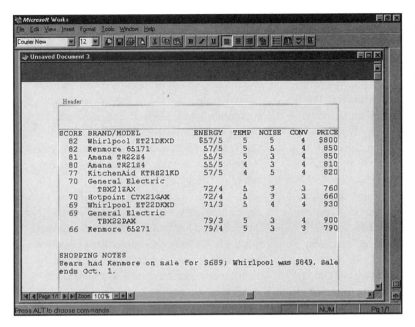

FIG. 10.17

Once you've copied the text into a word processor, you can keep notes.

Microsoft Works, on the other hand, cannot easily convert the *Consumer Reports* tables; you'd need to spend time performing cumbersome find-and-replace operations in a word processor in order to convert the spaces between columns into tabs before you can display it in a word processor.

◆ **CAUTION**

Remember that *Consumer Reports* material is protected by copyright. You can copy it to your own system and use it, but you will be in violation of the copyright if you distribute it to a group or charge others to use it.

Asking Your Online Neighbors for Opinions

No matter how clever and elaborate commercials become, the most powerful form of advertising is still "word-of-mouth." Every marketer knows that you care a lot more about what your friends and acquaintances think than what ads say. Who wouldn't rather hear from someone who's spent their own money on a product than from a paid endorsement?

One of the best things about your AOL account is that your circle of friends and neighbors is greatly expanded every time you log on. You can eavesdrop on fascinating conversations about the products you're planning to buy, before you take the plunge.

"Eavesdrop on fascinating conversations about the products you're planning to buy, before you take the plunge."

If you want to open up your search to the larger population of the Internet, visit the newsgroup (keyword: **misc.consumers**). The consumer discussion on any given day will be dissecting just about every product you can think of, from deodorants to credit cards. It's a good place to go when you want to cast a wide net, but you'll probably find your time is more productive if you concentrate on areas where people with a special interest in the product gather.

Click the Life, Styles & Interests button which appears on the AOL Channels menu, and you'll uncover a greater variety of merchandise than you would on a trip to the mall.

On the Life, Styles & Interests channel, just about every conceivable product from books and boats to wheels and weddings has its own forum. Most of the people who visit these forums are just ordinary consumers who've taken a special interest in one of these products—perhaps because they're thinking about a purchase or because they're dissatisfied with a product and are looking for suggestions on how to resolve the problem. But mixed in with the ordinary folk are genuine experts who either work in the field or spend considerable time following developments as a hobby.

An online forum is the perfect place to meet such experts. You don't have to fear being cornered at a party for hours as your expert expounds at great length on all the latest developments in the field—and throws in his or her own theories on why the world is in such bad shape. Instead, you can ask questions from the safety of your own desk, and when the detailed answers show up on the message board, just scroll through the response until you find the tidbit of information that you'll need to know before you go shopping.

You can see a list of all the sections from the list of Highlights and Features that appears on the main Life, Styles & Interests menu. For most purchases, you'll have no trouble spotting the right message board. Looking for a camera? Select Photography. Thinking about buying a boat? Go to the Boating selections.

Some of the forums have nothing to do with merchandise. There are forums for special interests, too, such as veterans groups and science fiction fans. If you're looking for a car or any kind of electronic equipment, you could become exhausted just looking for help in making your decision. The following sections will help you conserve energy as you gather information.

Talking About Cars with Other Drivers

To find a central resource for all of the car-related information on AOL, use the keyword **wheels**. A menu will open with a list of topics (see fig. 10.18).

FIG. 10.18

Wheels is the hub for car resources on AOL.

Many of the resources listed on the Wheels menu are Web sites and features designed for car enthusiasts. The best place for shoppers to talk to other consumers are the two sites on AOL run by the popular car magazines—*Car & Driver* and *Road & Track*—and an AOL forum devoted to car talk called the Auto Message Center.

In the areas run by the magazines, you can search through the articles that appeared in the print editions, including current articles and back issues. Since both magazines specialize in evaluating high-performance vehicles, you may not find them to be the best source of information on station wagons and economy cars for the family. But if you enjoy the magazines, you'll want to read any reviews that appear on a car you're thinking of buying (see fig. 10.19).

Both magazines also run message boards. Occasionally, you'll find writers and editors from the magazines here but generally most of the messages come from readers. You'll find many of the readers are very knowledgeable and care deeply about cars, so it's a good place to ask advice.

You'll also want to post questions or solicit opinions at the Automotive Message Center; you can reach it from the Wheels menu. This enormous message board maintains separate discussions on dozens of different car models and specialties, such as French cars and Italian cars; there's even a folder for a car many people forgot: Studebakers!

FIG. 10.19

At *Car & Driver*'s AOL section you can read articles from the magazine and talk to other readers.

Stereos, TVs, and Gadgets

Before you buy your next electronic toy—whether it be a laser disc player, an over-priced stereo amplifier or even a plain old television set—you may want to solicit the opinions of the regulars at the Consumer Electronics section. Changes in technology are adding new features to even the simplest stereo devices, so you may want to find out what others are saying before you go shopping. Select Consumer Electronics from the Clubs & Interests menu or use the keyword **consumer electronics** (see fig. 10.20).

You may have to spend a few minutes looking through the menus to find the right place to ask your question. Nearly 100 folders are maintained and within some of the folders; there are over a dozen categories. For example, you'll find just nine folders

on the Video Games Message Board, but dozens of categories lurk just below; select Nintendo and you'll find 38 separate categories.

Finding the right area can help you avoid a bad purchase. Ask about a new piece of equipment and you'll be able to solicit opinions on how good it is, what you can expect to pay, and whether it's likely to become obsolete any time soon.

▼ TIP

When you first look through a folder, you can avoid seeing old messages with the Find Since button. First, highlight the folder you want to browse, then click the Find Since button and type in **7** to see only messages posted in the last week.

FIG. 10.20

The Consumer Electronics forums cover hundreds of individual discussions.

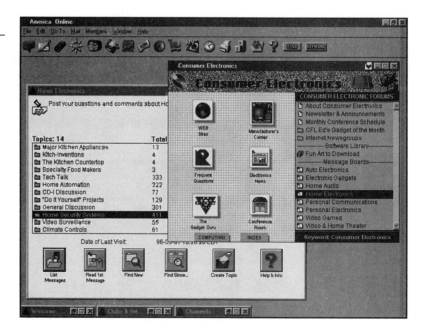

11

Looking for Bargains

Shopping by computer is all about choice. When you know how to use the tools, you can compare products and prices in a way never before possible.

You see the ads everywhere. When you jump from site to site on the Web, small colorful boxes hint that a great deal is just a click away. Unfortunately, many times all you find is information from a single manufacturer for products at prices that are higher than you'd pay at the local mall.

Spend a few minutes looking at the products for sale and you might conclude that shopping online is a rip-off. But you'd be mistaken. A few tools are available that can help you compare products and prices with an ease that has never before been possible. In this chapter, you'll find out how to go beyond the flashy graphics and hunt for true bargains.

What's for Sale Online

The range of merchandise for sale online is growing from week to week. New companies are being formed to sell at online sites, and established companies are developing their own retail operations. So if you didn't find something last week, don't assume it's not available today.

For the most part, products being offered online are not being purchased online. Instead, Web sites are being used to provide detailed information about the merchandise including toll-free numbers you can call to place an order. The fact is, most people would agree that an 800-phone call is an easier way to order a product than completing a form where you have to type out all the details about your order and your credit card.

So what's the point? The value of shopping on the Web is to find businesses you would never have heard of without the Web's amazing reach. Buying a pair of socks or a head of lettuce will never be common online. But shopping for items you can't find locally will be very popular. In the time it takes to find your car keys, you could locate a shop on the other side of the country that has just the item you need. And once you know how to use the available tools, you'll be able to compare prices at stores that are miles apart, in just a few minutes.

Putting Credit Card Worries to Rest

One reason that few companies offer merchandise for sale at their online sites is the possibility of a credit card number being intercepted. When you're connected to the public Internet, the information that moves over the public network passes through dozens of other computers. A well-educated thief could set up shop for the purpose of intercepting credit card transactions and then place phony orders. As a consumer, you have little reasons to worry about this possibility. You're protected by federal laws that limit your liability on credit card charges; if you didn't sign a receipt, the vendors are liable, not you. And even though the chance of someone perpetrating this type of fraud is remote, the possibility of a significant loss has chilled the atmosphere. In fact, few companies are willing to risk the possible losses. (For more information, see the section "Cash Across the Net" in Chapter 9.)

In coming months, experts expect this problem will be solved by security schemes that encrypt transactions so credit card authorization codes cannot be stolen. For the security technique to work, you'll need to be running a Web browser program that is capable of encoding the information at both ends. You won't have to do anything, as long as you're running the most recent version of the AOL browser software or a browser that provides security. The software at the remote site will be able to detect the security in your browser and will communicate directly with it.

That doesn't mean scam artists will go out of business. When shopping online, use the same common sense you would use when buying merchandise from a store. A purchase is always an act of trust; if you don't believe the company you're dealing with is acting in good faith, don't buy. And always review your monthly credit card bills closely to make sure the statement reflects only purchases you authorized.

Searching the Web for Products

The tools that make online shopping so easy are the Web search sites. These are Web sites that have one goal: to help you find other Web sites that have information on a specific topic.

As with any set of tools, some are better at particular jobs than others. In the tests I ran for *Internet World* magazine, I found InfoSeek Guide, shown in figure 11.1, to be the best tool for the type of broad-based search you'd want to perform in shopping.

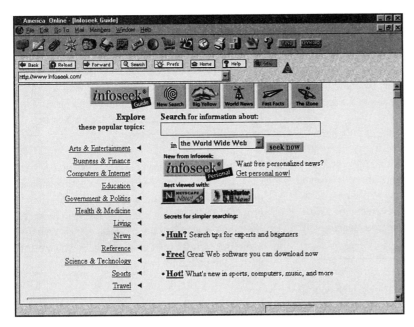

FIG. 11.1

Tests have shown InfoSeek
Guide to be one of the
best tools for finding
products for sale on the
Internet.

InfoSeek Guide excels at understanding a search
request with several words, has one of the largest
databases of Web pages, and does one of the best
jobs at staying current. You may find you prefer one
of the other search engines. Later in the chapter,
you'll see how Excite is great for finding classified
ads. And WebCrawler, which is run by a division of

America Online, is easier to use since it opens when
you select the Search button on the browser.

Table 11.1 shows the other search tools that you may
want to try. There are a few others that I did not
include; in my view, this table reflects the sites that
did the best in my review.

Table 11.1	Web Search Sites	
Name	**Keyword**	**Best feature**
Alta Vista	**http://www.altavista.digital.com**	Most comprehensive
Excite	**http://www.exite.com**	Classified ads in newsgroups
InfoSeek Guide	**http://www.infoseek.com**	Understands detailed search requests, and is very comprehensive
WebCrawler	**http://www.webcrawler.com**	Finding names of companies

The software design intelligence that goes into a good search engine is quite remarkable, and explaining it adequately would require an entire book. But the most important thing you need to know is that a search engine creates an enormous database that stores details on as many Web pages as the search software can handle.

▼ **T I P**

When looking for information with a Web search tool, be as specific as possible. With millions of pages on the Web, you'll be overwhelmed with information unless you refine your search with as many details as possible.

When you conduct a search, the Web search engine looks through that database to find the term you entered; the search will show you the listing it has for every site in its database which has some mention of this term. The better Web search engines will display the matches according to a relevance-ranking system. Sites that seem to have a large amount of information on the topic should be at the top of the list; sites that have only a small reference to the search term within a large page will be at the end of the list. Most people who use the Web search engines find what they're looking for within the first ten or twenty sites, even though most searches report fifty matches or more.

Conducting a Product Search

You have to be a bit of a detective when searching for bargains online. Many people who run Web sites online are shouting for attention, so it's easy to get distracted when you're looking for something in particular.

Your goal when setting out to shop online is to cast a wide net at first and then to quickly filter out the sites you'll find that are not relevant. Just about any search term you can use in looking for product information will find dozens of sites that are on a completely different topic. So be prepared to perform a few searches. It won't take long. Each search is performed in a few seconds.

When you start your search, you should already have some ideas about the brands you're considering and the type of materials. But if you are too specific at first, you may eliminate many vendors who haven't specifically mentioned the products in their Web pages but carry a broad product line. So you'll want to start with a broad term and then narrow the search.

Let's say you were looking for furniture. A number of furniture catalogs and manufacturers have Web sites that offer an overview of the company's product line; some show pictures of their pieces and others provide only a small amount of information but claim to offer competitive prices. After you've visited a local showroom, you will probably know the specific models you want. When you go online, you may find that you can buy the same merchandise and save hundreds of dollars if you order from a dealer in another state.

Here's how you'd execute the search:

1. Log on to AOL and use the keyword

   http://www.infoseek.com

   The main InfoSeek Guide screen opens, as shown in figure 11.1.

2. In the search box, type the search term (for example, **furniture**) and press Enter. Pay attention to spelling and capital letters. (If you

include a proper name in your search term, be sure to use capital letters.) Within a few seconds, a new screen will display a list of Web sites where the term is mentioned (see fig. 11.2).

3. Don't be too quick to select the first site you see. (If you were searching for the word "furniture," more than 100 sites will turn up.) The first site in the list is likely to have relevant information, but something further down the list may be an even better choice. When you've chosen the site you want to see, double-click the highlighted title. The AOL Web browser will display the site.

4. After you read through this page, you can return to the list of sites found by InfoSeek by clicking the browser's Back button. Once this page returns, you can visit any found site by double-clicking the highlighted title. You can

continue to go back and forth between the four sites and the list of sites by using the browser's Back button.

5. The first page displays only ten matches; once you've read through this page, you'll find a highlighted link at the bottom of the page for the Next 10 Results (see fig. 11.3). Select this link to see more pages that are about your search topic.

Any time you find a page that seems to have valuable information, be sure to create a bookmark so you'll be able to find the page again. If you're doing some serious shopping, you will want to create a new folder in your Favorite Places list devoted just to the places you find on this shopping expedition. (If you need help recording a Favorite Place folder, refer to the section "Favorite Places: An Expanding Folder" in Chapter 1.)

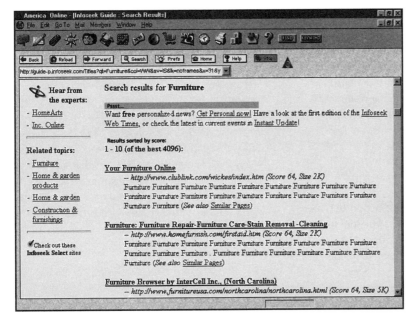

FIG. 11.2

A search for the term "furniture" finds dozens of Web sites in InfoSeek Guide.

FIG. 11.3

When you reach the end of a search results page, you'll find a link to the Next 10 Results.

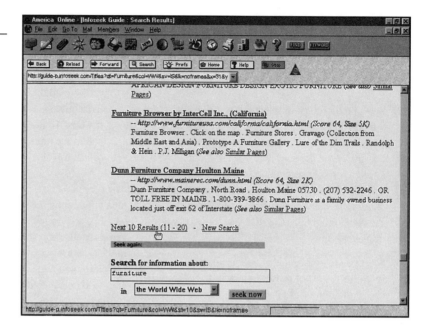

Honing In on Details

Your first broad search on the category will help you to understand the range of services available. For example, many small shops that custom-build furniture are using the Web to hawk their wares, but you'll also find a few catalogs that carry nationally known brands, including the models you may have chosen from a visit to local stores.

▼ **TIP**

InfoSeek Guide makes a distinction between capital and lowercase letters, so be sure to capitalize proper names. Most other Web search engines do not distinguish between upper-and lowercase letters.

You may get lucky and find the absolute best catalog with the best prices on your first search, but in most cases you'll need to refine the search. If you are interested in a specific brand, try using the manufacturer's name in your search, for example, "Ethan Allen furniture" or "Pennsylvania House furniture."

When using a name, it's important to include more details than just the name. If you search for Ethan Allan, you'll find historical Web sites that mention the man. If you search for Pennsylvania House, you'll find any site that mentions the state of Pennsylvania and a "house" including people in Pittsburgh who are selling their home.

Ask To See Similar Merchandise

Another technique for focusing on a specific type of Web site is to use the Similar Pages option. Every listing in a list of search results from InfoSeek Guide will include this as a link. When you select Similar Pages, InfoSeek Guide reads the words in its database for this page and creates a new search query for pages that have words in common with this page. Figure 11.4 shows the results of selecting Similar Pages for a furniture gallery.

Not only will the Similar Pages option find a few pages that may have been ignored the first time, it will save you from scrolling through a long list. You may want to use it repeatedly in your search. Every time you find a Web site that seems "just perfect," select Similar Pages from this site's listing rather than

stopping your search. You may find something that's "even more perfect."

May We Suggest...?

As you conduct a search, InfoSeek Guide does more than just report individual sites. It also suggests new search categories that may interest you. These appear to the left of the page as text links. For example, in a search on "furniture," InfoSeek Guide displays "Home & garden products" and "Shopping for office supplies." When you select these links, you'll see a list of sites on these topics. It could be a distraction if you know exactly what you're looking for, but if you're open to suggestions, it may uncover some unique possibilities that wouldn't have occurred to you otherwise.

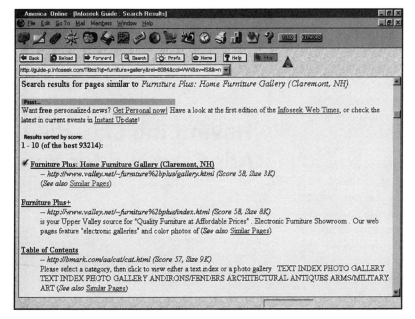

FIG. 11.4

You can focus on a product category by choosing the Similar Pages option in InfoSeek.

You'll also find that during your search, ads for products similar to the one you're researching will appear at the top and bottom of the InfoSeek Guide display. The software is designed to display advertisements according to the types of products you want. One reason why you may want to click on these links to see the main page is that the company posting the ad is obviously actively seeking customers through the Internet; the company will have more information than you're likely to find elsewhere. Some Web sites you find may be relatively inactive, posted months ago and ignored since then. Following the links to ads is one way of finding information about a company that really wants to sell products over the Internet.

Going Direct to the Manufacturer

Often when you're shopping in retail stores, the people selling the product know very little about the products. Manufacturers can't have their own representatives everywhere, and stores can't afford to train their staff in every detail of the products in the store. When you're shopping online, you can bypass the middleman and go right to the source, finding information from manufacturers of products that you'd never be able to find otherwise.

For example, in the search for "furniture" shown in figures 11.2 through 11.4, most of the sites found were re-sellers. But if you had decided you wanted to buy furniture from Ethan Allen, before you invest thousands of dollars, why not take a few seconds to see what the folks at headquarters have to say? Of course, you *could* pick up the phone and call the company, but what would you say? When you contact the company's Web site, you can browse

through information that you won't find in a catalog. Figure 11.5 shows the first Web site found by using the search term "Ethan Allen furniture."

You may not be able to buy from the manufacturer—many companies refuse to sell to the public in order to gain the loyalty of the stores that carry their merchandise. But you may be able to learn about models that the stores in your area don't carry. You could find information that may help you save money. Perhaps the list price of the product was recently lowered or a new line of merchandise is coming (and when a new line comes out the old line is usually discounted).

One benefit of visiting the site of a manufacturer is to learn about other stores in your area. The Ethan Allen site has a store locator that's easy to use (see fig. 11.6). Click on your state and the screens that appear will help you find other stores in your area. Not every Web site provides such a handy tool, but more companies are adding this technique every day.

Once you know the phone numbers and addresses of other stores in your area, you'll be able to comparison shop with little effort.

Having the Classified Ads Searched for You

When you're looking for a used car, used furniture, or any of the other types of merchandise sold through the classified ads of newspapers, your AOL connection will let you search through the equivalent of a hundred papers in just a few seconds.

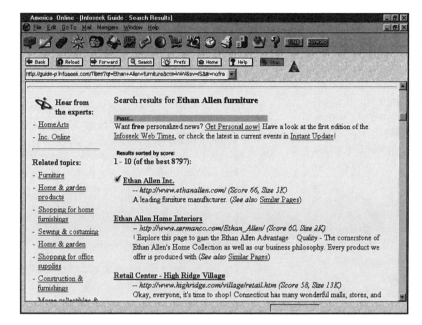

FIG. 11.5

One of the best reasons to shop online is to get information directly from manufacturers.

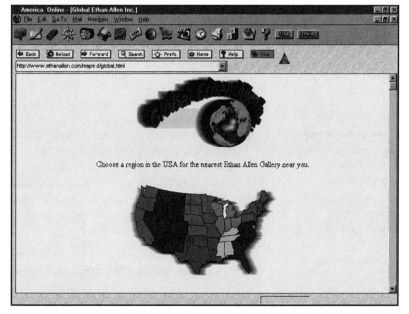

FIG. 11.6

At some manufacturer's Web site, you can locate all of the stores in your area that carry the company's products.

The Web search engine Excite creates a database of all the messages posted in newsgroups where classified ads appear. The system works very well since the database is kept fresh; only messages posted in the last two weeks are kept in the database. You may not want to buy a car from someone on the other side of the country, but for some types of merchandise, it may not matter. People sell skis, magazine collections, furniture, and anything else that might be listed in a newspaper classified ad. And you may find the seller is just around the corner.

The same rules apply to buying through the classifieds as apply when buying through newspaper classified ads. You're buying directly from another person, so no consumer protection agency will be able to help you if the sale goes sour. And when buying merchandise from someone in a different city, you also have to negotiate the shipping expense and the issue of who's responsible if the merchandise is damaged in transit.

Searching the Classifieds with Excite

Newsgroups on the Web are similar to message boards on America Online (AOL) except that anyone with an Internet account can post a message on a newsgroup, which means it's open to more than 20 million people around the world. You can read through the newsgroups on your own (keyword: **newsgroups**) but if you want to search the classifieds, the Excite search will be much faster.

The following steps will guide you through a search of the classifieds with Excite:

1. Connect to AOL and enter the keyword

   http://www.excite.com

   The AOL Web browser will open and display the Excite title page.

2. Enter a general description of the type of product you're searching for. Don't get too specific. If you're looking for a Ford Taurus, don't enter the year or details like A/C and radio. Just enter "ford taurus" (it doesn't matter if you use capital or lowercase letters in Excite); see figure 11.7.

3. Click the Classified button. A black dot will appear next to the word Classified.

4. Click the Search button that appears next to the search term. The search will begin.

5. A list of titles from classified ads will appear (see fig. 11.8). Each title should tell you something about the merchandise being offered, but since the titles are written by the person who posted the ad, it may not be very descriptive. You'll also see the date it was posted, the e-mail address of the person who posted the ad, and the newsgroup where it was posted.

6. If you want to limit your search to nearby locations, pay attention to the newsgroup that appears in each listing. Some newsgroups were created specifically to help people post "for sale" ads within the region. The newsgroup name will include the name of a city or the state abbreviation, followed by forsale. For example, ads posted from tx.forsale are from people in Texas; nj.forsale is for New Jersey.

7. When you find an ad you want to read, click the title. The ad will appear in the browser window.

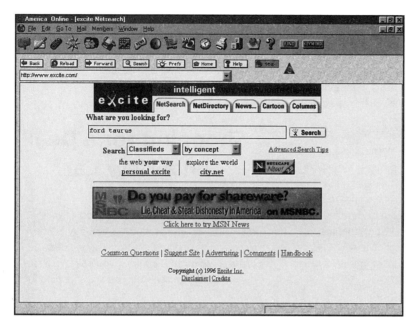

FIG. 11.7

You can search through classified ads on the Internet with Excite.

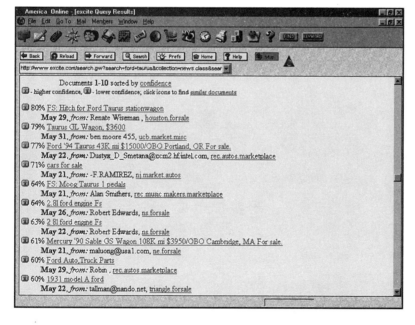

FIG. 11.8

A search on classified ads will be limited to ads that were posted within the last two weeks.

8. If you want to respond to the message, click the highlighted e-mail name at the top of the message. The AOL Compose Mail window will open with the name of the seller already entered in the To field (see fig. 11.9). Write a message, click Send, and the message will be mailed.

After reading through the messages, you may become interested in seeing other postings in a particular newsgroup. To see everything currently available in the newsgroup—including old messages that Excite ignores—click the newsgroup name. You can select the name either from the list of classified ads that appear directly after the search or from the heading of the individual message. The AOL newsgroup reader will open, displaying a list of other messages posted.

Once you've discovered the classified newsgroups, you may want to clear out your garage and sell some of your old valuables. Table 11.2 shows a list of the newsgroups you'll want to explore.

Shopping for a Deal on a New Car

After the purchase of a home, for most of us, the next most expensive product we ever buy is a car. Saving a few hundred dollars on just one new car purchase can dwarf the money you'll save in a lifetime of clipping grocery coupons and shopping for sales.

Table 11.2   Newsgroups That Run Classified Ads

Newsgroup	Type of Merchandise
alt.forsale	Anything
misc.forsale.computers	Computers and peripheral equipment
misc.forsale.non-computers	Anything
rec.antiques.marketplace	Antique furniture, rugs, pottery, and so on
rec.arts.books.marketplace	Old books and magazines
rec.audio.marketplace	Amplifiers, stereos, turntables, and so on
rec.autos.marketplace	Cars
rec.photo.marketplace	Cameras
rec.skiing.marketplace	Skis, ski boots, poles
regional.forsale nj.forsale, tx.forsale	Regional newsgroups (for example, and so on)

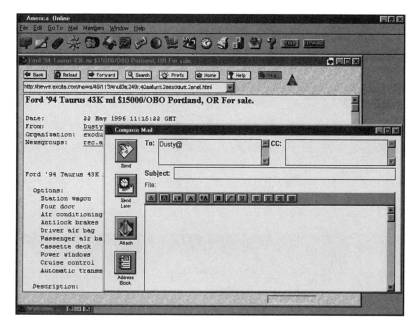

FIG. 11.9

After you read a classified ad, if you want to respond, you can compose a message by clicking the name of the person who posted the message.

Unfortunately, the best way to save money on a new car demands a certain negotiating skill that most of us don't have. Not only do you need to research car prices and dealer discounts, you have to be willing to go toe-to-toe with the dealer in bare knuckles negotiating. Most of us are no match for the dealer, and we're happy when the dealer offers to shave a few hundred dollars off the list price so we can bring the negotiating session to an end.

AutoVantage is an online service that does the shopping for you. You ask for prices on a new car, and AutoVantage obtains actual offers from several dealers that will be hundreds of dollars lower than the sticker price. While you may be able to negotiate a better deal, most people will not. A test conducted by ABC-TV found the price obtained with AutoVantage was lower than the price customers who negotiated with dealers were able to obtain.

You can learn more about the service by using the keyword **autovantage** (see fig. 11.10).

To use the system, you'll need to register. The annual fee is about $48, but trial registration offers are usually available. In addition to the central car shopping service, an AutoVantage membership also includes discounts on car service and parts.

When you're ready to buy a car, you complete an AutoVantage form where you specify the model and any options you want. AutoVantage submits the request to several dealers in your area who will respond with a firm price. You can't negotiate this price, although you can talk directly to the dealer about changes to the option package. AutoVantage doesn't have fancy graphic displays. Figure 11.11 shows the character-based display: an old-fashioned mainframe terminal entry screen.

FIG. 11.10

AutoVantage can help you find the best price on a car purchase or obtain discounts on service.

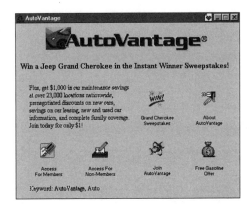

FIG. 11.11

AutoVantage doesn't offer the fancy graphics you normally see on America Online, but it may get you a better price on a new car.

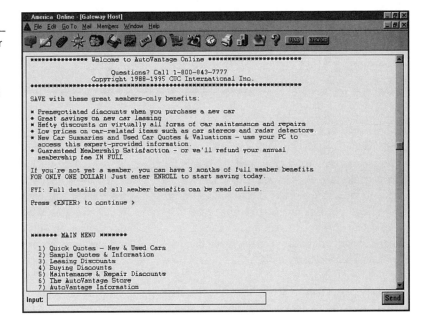

Once you register, you can talk directly to AutoVantage representatives using an 800 phone number or by sending a message from America Online. To learn more about AutoVantage online, select the About AutoVantage button on the opening screen.

Creating Your Own "Big Buy" Spreadsheet

As you shop for big ticket items—both online and in stores—you'll be taking lots of mental notes.

Whether you're buying a car, furniture, or anything that will take a big dent out of your savings, you'll feel better and make a better decision if you use your computer to help you keep track of all the numbers you'll encounter.

A spreadsheet can help you add up the different prices you'll find and total the impact of all those options you'll need to consider. While one often forgets about small charges like shipping and sales tax, they can add up. And, when you shop online, you may be able to save the sales tax you would have to pay if you bought from a local store, but you may have to pay additional shipping costs that wouldn't be required in a local purchase.

The spreadsheet Big_Buy can be downloaded from The AOL Money Guide page on the Web. Use the keyword

http://www.mcp.com/que/desktop_os/ money/

and look for the link to spreadsheets. The spreadsheet is designed to help you track purchases simply by typing in the prices you're quoted (see fig. 11.12).

The spreadsheet in figure 11.12 uses sample numbers, but the spreadsheet you download will not have actual data; instead, you'll find zero values for each line. To use the spreadsheet after you've downloaded it, follow these steps:

1. Open your spreadsheet program and select File, Open. Select Big_Buy from the folder where you stored the file.

2. When the file opens, change the labels in column A to identify the product and options you're considering.

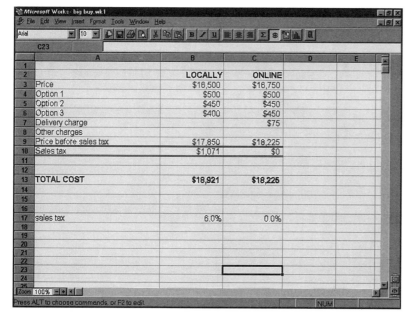

FIG. 11.12

You can download this spreadsheet to help you track big purchases.

	A	B	C
2		LOCALLY	ONLINE
3	Price	$16,500	$16,750
4	Option 1	$500	$500
5	Option 2	$450	$450
6	Option 3	$400	$450
7	Delivery charge		$75
8	Other charges		
9	Price before sales tax	$17,850	$18,225
10	Sales tax	$1,071	$0
13	TOTAL COST	$18,921	$18,225
17	sales tax	6.0%	0.0%

3. Scroll down to find the cell for sales tax and enter the percentages charged in your area and the sales tax that an out-of-state vendor may charge you. When entering sales tax, remember it's a percentage. For a tax of six percent, enter .06.

4. Enter the prices you've been quoted. The totals for "Price before sales tax", "Sales tax," and "TOTAL COST" will be automatically calculated.

5. After you have adjusted the file using your own data, select File, Save As and enter a new file name to identify the product you're tracking, such as "taurus" or "livingrm."

Keep the original file to use in tracking other purchases.

Strolling Through Online Malls

Your online connection can help you be a tough comparison shopper for big purchases, but it also brings a new twist to an old pleasure: online malls where you can browse at your leisure.

Strolling through an online mall may not provide as much exercise as a visit to the mall, but you don't have to fight for a parking space, wait on long lines at the register, or wrestle your packages to the car. No, you just sit in the quiet of your den and browse through pictures the same way you'd leaf through the pages of a catalog (see figure 11.13).

FIG. 11.13

When you shop JC-Penney's online catalog, you can select from categories of merchandise.

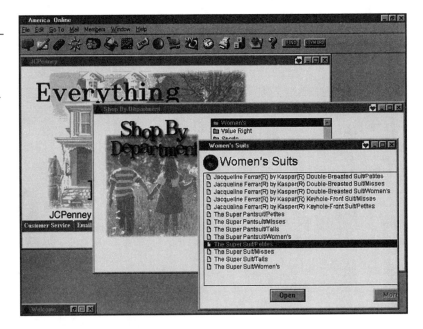

The benefit of shopping online is that you can quickly find items by selecting folders grouped by category. When you're ready to order, you don't have to make a call, you just complete an order form online. Merchandise will be shipped directly to your home.

The easiest way to shop online is by using the Marketplace on America Online. Because your credit card information is already stored in America Online's files, any purchases you make go through quickly. You can also shop at malls on the Internet but you'll need to open an account, using your credit card information. As discussed earlier in the section, "What's for Sale Online," credit card purchases on the Internet are still relatively limited because of the lack of security controls. However, when shopping through America Online, you won't have to worry about the possibility of having your credit card number stolen.

The Marketplace at America Online

The Marketplace is organized like a mall that was designed for your convenience, rather than the merchant's. You reach the mall either by selecting the Marketplace button on the AOL Channels menu or by using the keyword **marketplace** (see fig. 11.14).

Browsing through the categories can be just as pleasant as a trip to the mall and a lot less work. Select any category and you'll see a list of merchants. For example, select Entertainment & Music and you'll see a list that includes FAO Schwarz, MTV, Tower Records, and Warner Bros. Studio Store (the list of merchants is changing all the time).

FIG. 11.14

The Marketplace features special offers (on the left) and a directory of all the shops, organized by category (on the right).

▼ T I P

When you're having trouble finding a holiday gift, browse through the vendors at AOL's Marketplace. Many have special offers on their main menu in the weeks before major holidays.

You can also choose to see all merchants from the Marketplace menu by clicking the List Alphabetically button. When you choose any merchant from the list, you'll see unique menus created by the store's designers, and part of the appeal of online shopping is to sample the graphics on each screen. Chocolate lovers will want to see what Godiva Chocalatiers is showing, and gadget fans will enjoy browsing through The Sharper Image online.

Every merchant has an opening page where a special is featured; often, the specials are seasonal, which can be a big help in shopping for gifts. Mother's Day, Father's Day, Valentine's Day, and Graduation are all cause for sales at the Marketplace.

To browse through the catalogs of each merchant, select categories that interest you. Usually, you'll have to select a broad category, and then a narrower category before you see the list of products. Select Women's Dresses in the Eddie Bauer catalog and you'll see over a dozen types of dresses within each category. Once you select a category, you'll see a list of specific styles and sizes. Select one of these and you'll see a full description, including the price, and in most cases, you'll also see a color photograph, as in figure 11.15.

Every menu for a specific product includes a Click Here To Order button. If you decide to purchase the item, you'll be asked a series of questions; for clothing, you'll be asked to specify the size and color. Many items come with a choice of gift wrapping. If it's gift wrapped, you'll be asked to enter a message that will appear on the card. Once you complete the order, you'll have a chance to review the details. Select Cancel at any time if you're not satisfied.

AOL will retain a copy of the orders you've placed, which it calls a Shopping Cart. At any time after you've ordered products, you can check your shopping cart to see the items you're buying and the total amount you've spent.

Shopping the Malls on the Internet

The Internet has a few shopping malls but none can equal the experience of AOL's Marketplace. Perhaps in a few years, you'll find shopping malls on the Internet with the wide range of products you can find now on AOL, but today, most malls carry merchandise from only a limited number of merchants.

The Internet Shopping Network is the largest and best-organized mall, but the merchandise is almost exclusively from computer and software companies (see fig. 11.16). You'll find a few specialty items, such as flower deliveries, but only a few.

You can reach the site by entering the keyword

http://shop.internet.net

In order to simplify the process of buying products at the mall, you need to register, which will store your credit card information and address on the mall's computers. The Internet Shopping Network uses the encryption available in AOL's browser when you transfer your credit card information. You'll only need to submit the information once; when you register, you'll receive a user name and password that will allow you to order products without completing another form.

FIG. 11.15

You'll see a picture for most merchandise on sale in the Marketplace.

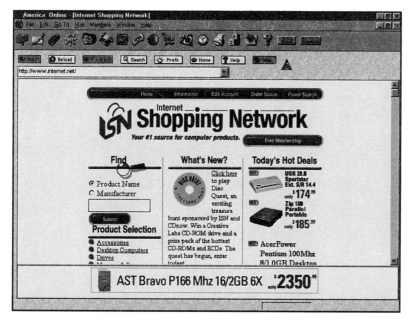

FIG. 11.16

The Internet Shopping Network is the largest mall on the Internet.

▼ **T I P**

New malls are in development. To check for recent openings, use InfoSeek Guide with the
search term, "shopping mall."

While Internet Shopping Network is the largest mall,
it's not the only place to buy computer products on
the Internet. CompUSA, the large computer retailer,
runs its own Web site (keyword: **http://
www.compusa.com**) and many software publishers
and computer manufacturers operate their own sites.
Internet Shopping Network offers the advantage of
one-stop shopping, but you may want to compare
the prices with those offered elsewhere. Use the tips
suggested earlier in this chapter in the section,
"Conducting a Product Search" to see what else is
being offered.

12

Buying and Financing a House

Whether you're just thinking about buying a home, or seriously trying to sell your current home, you'll find that the tools available both online and on your hard disk can save you time and aggravation.

The Information Superhighway has changed few areas of commerce as much as real estate. Just a few years ago, the only way to sell a house was through the newspaper classifieds or a realtor. Today, many realtors are taking their listings to the World Wide Web and to America Online's Real Estate Center. Full-color photographs and detailed property fact sheets are posted online. Once you know how to search, you'll be able to see many of the houses now on sale without ever leaving your computer.

Not everything has changed about the home buying process. You'll still want to hire a professional inspector before you close the deal. You still need to shop for a mortgage. And, chances are, you'll still agonize over whether you can afford the house of your dreams.

This chapter will show you the tools you can use to help in every step of the process. You'll learn how to search for a house online. You'll find out where you can get information to guide you through the hiring of home inspectors and a mortgage banker. And you'll learn how to crunch the numbers on your home purchase in a spreadsheet that you can download for free.

Free Advice for Home Buyers

Free advice is easy to come by. Just about everyone you meet is ready to give you an opinion on where you should buy a house and what type you should get. But you may want to supplement some of this with hard information from an authoritative source. Since the government is responsible for establishing many of the systems you'll be contending with as a home buyer and a mortgage owner, you may want to start your search with publications from government agencies.

Chapter 10, "Facts That Will Make You a Better Consumer," goes into great detail on the Consumer Information Center Web site, a government agency which distributes publications that can help consumers. One of the many topics covered by the center is Buying & Financing Housing. You'll find about a dozen booklets available directly at the site that you can save to disk or print. Use the keyword

**http://www.gsa.gov/staff/pa/cic/
housing.htm**

When the AOL browser displays this page, you'll see brief descriptions of booklets. Each one explains an issue faced by home buyers, like adjustable rate mortgages, homeowner's insurance, and professional home inspection services. The Consumer Information Center sells these brochures to people who order by phone, but from AOL, you can see the brochure simply by clicking its title, as shown in figure 12.1.

Once you've selected a brochure you want to keep, select File and then choose either Print or Save.

Learning About Mortgages

First-time home buyers usually enjoy visiting homes for sale and have fun learning about the real estate market in their area.

FIG. 12.1

The Consumer Information Center's Web site offers free literature to help consumers shop for real estate and mortgages.

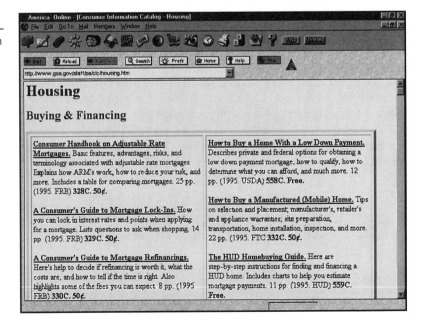

On the other hand, few people really want to invest as much effort into the process of buying a mortgage. But the fact is, unless you're independently wealthy and will be paying cash for your dream house, you're going to learn about mortgages whether you like it or not. People who fail to approach the process of applying for a mortgage seriously could find themselves without the mortgage they need in order to close a deal. You don't want to learn from your mistake after you've lost the house you wanted to buy because your mortgage application was denied.

Learning about mortgages before you select a house will also help you buy the best house you can afford. The cold reality is that your income and credit history will qualify you for a certain mortgage size. Maybe you are willing to live on a diet of bread and water for the next 30 years to buy a $300,000 home, but you'll never convince a bank of that. The mortgage application process requires detailed financial information from you and your spouse. The bank or mortgage company will decide how much money it will lend you based on this information.

The Paperwork You'll Need To Complete

Fortunately, you can learn much of what you'll need to know at The Mortgage Mart, a Web site that you'll find on AOL by using the keyword

http://www.mortgage-mart.com

The site, shown in figure 12.2, not only explains the terminology and procedures, but also has sample forms you can review.

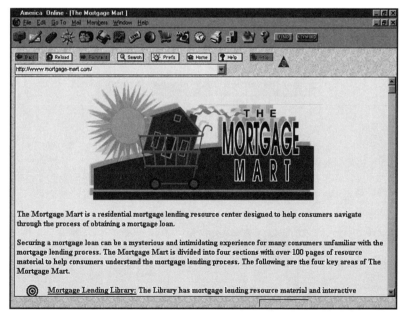

FIG. 12.2

The Mortgage Mart provides detailed information on the process of shopping for and obtaining a mortgage.

You'll be able to read explanations of the mortgage lending process, including very specific details on the types of forms that are being used by loan officers today. You'll find out which documents you'll need to supply, such as a recent pay stub and copies of bank account statements. You can read a description of the title-search process that you'll need to authorize before you can buy property. And you can search through an enormous glossary that explains many of the new terms you'll encounter as you buy a house (see fig. 12.3). Select the Lending Library option on the main Mortgage Mart page, and then select Definitions to see the Glossary.

The information available at The Mortgage Mart site is designed to help you buy a mortgage, but because the process of obtaining a mortgage is so central to the process of buying a house, you'll learn just about everything you need to know about buying a house here.

How Much Mortgage Can You Afford?

Sadly, many people start their home buying efforts without a clear idea of what they can afford. Only after they've fallen in love with a house and settled on a price do they learn that they can't obtain the mortgage they need. Or, they may learn that they need to provide paperwork, like old tax returns, that isn't readily available. By the time they're able to complete the application process, the deal may have soured.

At The Mortgage Mart site, you can prepare yourself for the process of applying for a mortgage so you won't be hit by unpleasant surprises at the last minute. You can see samples of the forms that are currently being used by many lenders, so you'll know what kind of information you'll need to have. And

FIG. 12.3

You'll find explanations for hundreds of terms that are used in real estate purchases at The Mortgage Mart.

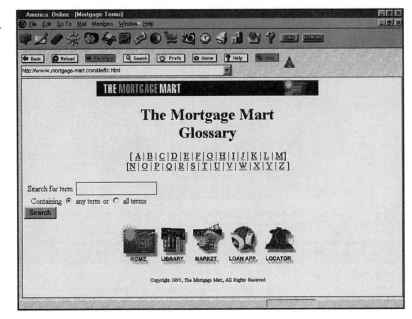

you can complete a Loan Pre-Qualifier application that will let you enter your own personal information and learn the maximum mortgage that you will be able to get, as shown in figure 12.4.

The calculation performed here may be off by a few dollars, but it's likely to be a very close indication of the size of mortgage you'll be able to get. Most lenders follow similar formulas in deciding on the amount of credit they're willing to extend. No matter how much charm you exert on the loan officer, the size of the mortgage you'll be able to get is based on a formula that looks at your current total income, any outstanding obligations (student loans, car payments, alimony, and so on) and the cost of the property (including property taxes). Some lenders are not willing to take on as much risk as others, so you might not be able to get the same size mortgage from every lender.

To use the calculator, follow these steps:

1. Connect to AOL and use the keyword

   http://www.mortgage-mart.com

   The main Mortgage Mart Web page opens.

2. Select the link Mortgage Lending Library. A list of resources opens.

3. Select Pre-Qualifier. The screen shown in figure 12.4 opens.

4. Complete the form with information on yourself and your spouse. For monthly income enter your total income (before taxes); for monthly obligations, include a total of all fixed payments (loan installments, child support, alimony, tuition).

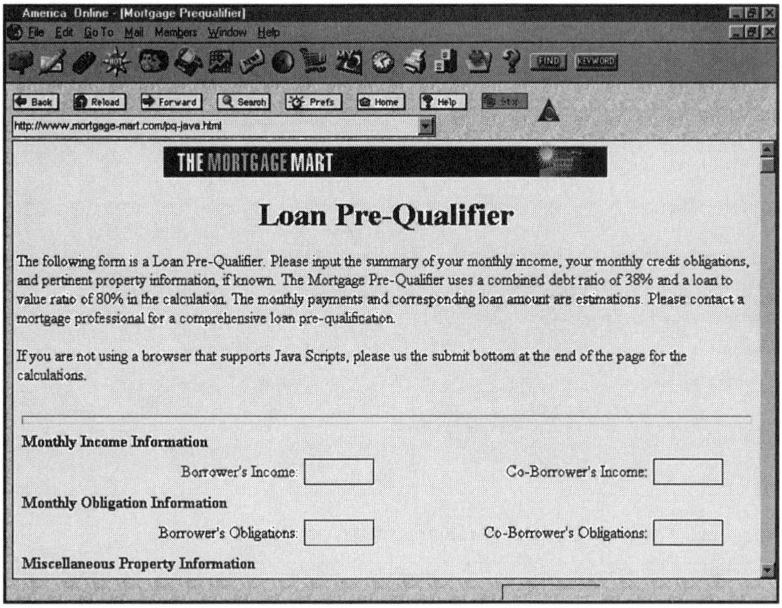

FIG. 12.4

The Loan Pre-Qualifier will calculate the size of the mortgage you'll be able to get, based on your income.

5. When you've completed every box, scroll to the bottom of the page and click the Submit Form button. If you make a single error, you can type over the information in the box where you made the error. But if you want to start over and complete the form from the beginning, click the Rest button. Once you're satisfied that the answers are accurate, click the Submit Form button. A report will appear, showing the maximum mortgage you'll be able to receive, as shown in figure 12.5.

Mortgage Mart offers no guarantee that you'll be able to obtain this much in a mortgage. The number will be accurate only if you've entered accurate information about yourself. And you could be turned down for a loan because the lender believes the house is worth far less than you want to pay or the lender may decide you're not a good credit risk based on information that appears in your credit history.

If you have a problem with a credit report, refer to Chapter 9; the sections "Learning Your Own Credit History" and "Correcting Errors in a Credit Report" will help you fix problems that may have been reported to the lender.

▼ TIP

If you believe your past credit problems may prevent you from obtaining a mortgage, you may want to follow the advice in Chapter 9 before you begin the process of buying a house and applying for a mortgage.

FIG. 12.5

After you complete the Pre-Qualifier application, Mortgage Mart estimates the largest mortgage you're likely to obtain.

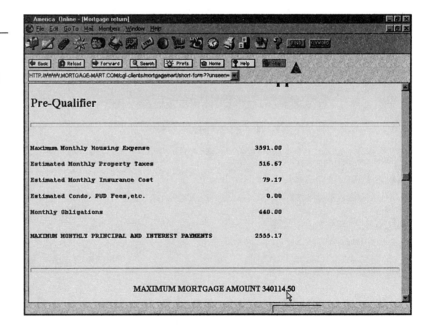

Shopping for the Best Mortgage Rates

Once you've learned about mortgages and the size of the mortgage you can obtain, you can start to shop for the best rate available to you. A little comparison shopping can save you a small fortune in interest payments. Over the course of the loan, you may save tens of thousands of dollars in interest—and it could be enough to significantly affect your lifestyle every month.

For example, on a $150,000 mortgage, you'll need to make a monthly payment of about $1,100 if your mortgage carries an interest rate of 8.0 percent, assuming a 30-year term (and not including taxes and insurance). But you'll pay $100 less every month if you can find a mortgage at 7.0 percent. Over the 30 year life of the mortgage, that's a savings of $36,000.

You may want to use the savings in mortgage rates to buy a bigger house. Using the example above, the couple who were prepared to pay an interest rate of 8 percent on a $150,000 mortgage would be able to have the same monthly payment ($1,100) but buy a house that cost $15,000 more, if a 7 percent mortgage could be found.

Most people shop for a mortgage by reading newspaper ads or hiring a mortgage realtor who charge for the service of finding a mortgage lender. There is a better way. Sites on the World Wide Web can show you comparisons of the rates now being offered around the nation. Limit your shopping to the banks and mortgage companies with the best rates and you may save hundreds of dollars a month on your interest payment over the amount you'd pay without the comparisons. The reason is that many of the banks offering the lowest interest rates don't advertise the rates; they're often smaller banks with lower profiles.

A number of companies publicize themselves as being a good source for mortgage information on the Internet, but most show you only the rates offered by a small number of lenders who pay a fee to be included in these informational sites. Use one of the sites and you can still miss the best rates being offered.

For a good introduction to mortgage prices, visit the Mortgage Center on America Online. Enter the keyword **mortgage** and select Mortgage Rates. On the main menu, you'll find a list of articles about current mortgage rates and some tips on how to shop for the best rates (see fig. 12.6).

When you're ready to apply for a mortgage, you'll want to find the lenders with the best rates. At AOL's Mortgage Information Center, you'll find lists of rates that have been offered in recent weeks. These lists are compiled by HSH Associates, a company that's in the business of selling information to consumers about mortgage rates. It surveys almost every bank and mortgage lender every week and compiles comparative lists of the best rates. It does not take fees from the lenders; instead, it charges borrowers a small fee to see the current surveys.

The excerpts from recent HSH Associates reports offer a general idea of current mortgage rates, but you'll want the most recent survey when you're prepared to apply for the loan. To obtain a copy, you'll have to visit HSH's Web site and purchase a report. You can select the Web site from the Mortgage Center main menu or by using the keyword

http://www.hsh.com

FIG. 12.6

The Mortgage Information Center has tips on shopping for the best mortgage rates, and a list of lenders with the rates they're offering.

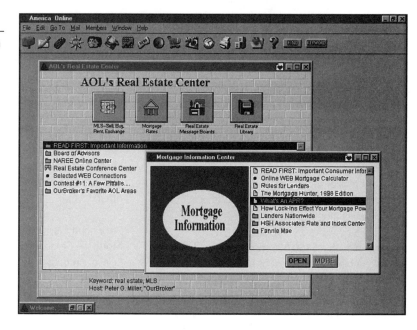

To see the company's recent calculation for average mortgage rates, select the highlighted link on the first page that reads "daily national average mortgage rates." You'll see a page similar to figure 12.7.

If you visit this site at the beginning of your home buying search, you may want to assume that you'll be paying about a quarter of a percentage point below the average. That's because you'll be able to see the lowest rates in your area by ordering HSH's current report. So unless interest rates increase sharply while you're shopping for a house, you're almost certain to find rates below the national average in the report on current mortgage rates.

When you're ready to actually apply for a mortgage, you'll want to buy a report from the company. It shows a detailed list of the best mortgage rates in your area; the report shows application fees, information on how to lock in the rate, and phone

numbers for each lender. Unless you've been very lucky in your shopping, you're likely to find a number of lenders with rates that are at least a percentage point below the rates that you've seen publicized. Information on ordering the report is available at the HSH site; the cost is about $10. Updates are published weekly.

To go directly to a page with the phone number for ordering the HSH weekly report, use the keyword

http://www.hsh.com/mtgrates.html

You'll be able to receive the report as an e-mail message. The report will arrive as a text attachment that you can print or edit with any word processor. You may want to keep notes as you use it, since you'll be calling the banks and mortgage companies mentioned and adding the names of loan officers and more details about the loans offered.

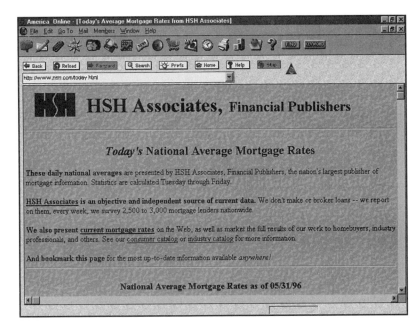

FIG. 12.7

HSH surveys over 2,500 mortgage lenders in preparing its database of current mortgage rates.

PC users can also order a database from HSH that has much of the same information in the e-mail report but you can search the data. You'll need to download PCMU, a program HSH offers at this Web page (it's available only for DOS). The program must be decompressed using an un-zip program after you download it; once you've got it running, you can open the database and search for lenders and types of mortgages available in your area.

Mortgage Software You Can Download

Many shareware programs have been written to help home owners and home buyers calculate the price of

a mortgage or answer common questions like whether to choose an adjustable rate or a fixed-rate mortgage. You'll find extensive choices for the PC and Mac by using this keyword:

http://ibc.wustl.edu/mort/mort_links.html

Figure 12.8 shows you some of the files you'll find at the site.

Some of the files are worksheets that you can load with your own spreadsheet, and others are share ware programs that are provided on an evaluation-only basis. If you use the program, you should pay the small registration fee.

FIG. 12.8

This list of mortgage-related programs includes calculators and worksheets you can run in your spreadsheet program.

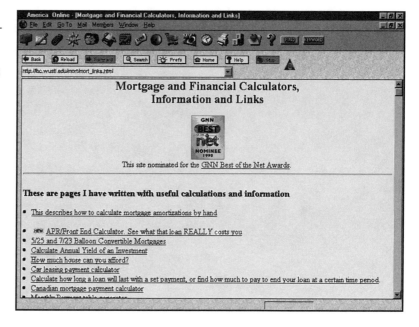

Running the Numbers in a Homebuy Spreadsheet

Shopping for a home can be a bewildering process. You're flooded with numbers—asking prices, property taxes, mortgage rates—at a time when you're trying to evaluate neighborhoods, kitchen decor, and color schemes. It's enough to make you want to check into a hotel and stay there!

Buying a home can be the best investment you make, but the only way you'll know if it will work for you is if you take charge of the numbers. Fortunately, it's not at all difficult to keep track of the situation if you use a simple spreadsheet. You can download the basic worksheet I wrote (with plenty of help from my

attorney and brother, Michael Venditto). It's available from America Online, using the keyword

http://www.mcp.com/que/desktop_os/ money/

You can download HOMEBUY.WK1 for Lotus 1-2-3, HOMEBUY.WKS for Microsoft Works, or HOMEBUY.XLS for Microsoft Excel.

The spreadsheet is organized to help you compare three different homes. Plug in the numbers for each situation and the spreadsheet will show you the two numbers that matter most to a home buyer.

◆ Your monthly payment

◆ The cash you'll need to close the deal

Figure 12.9 shows the spreadsheet, with numbers already entered for several different scenarios.

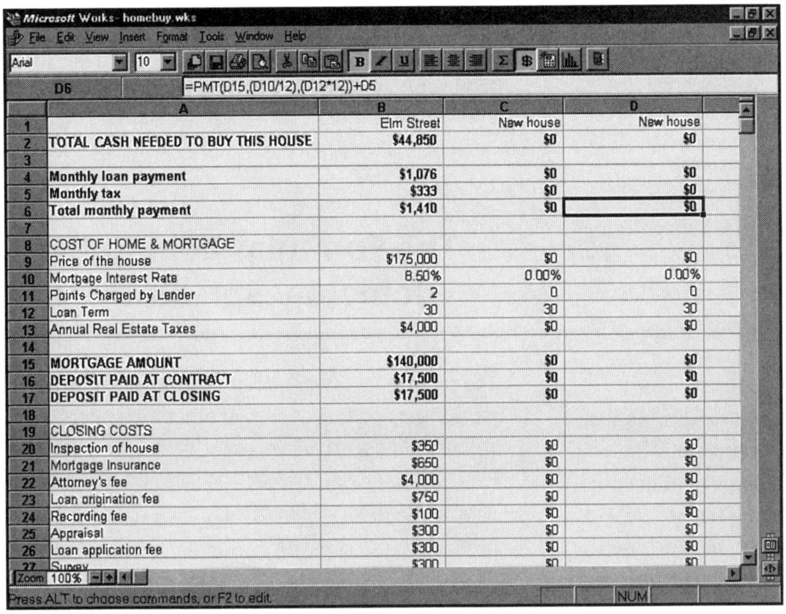
Microsoft Works - homebuy.wks

D6 =PMT(D15,(D10/12),(D12*12))+D5

	A	B	C	D
1		Elm Street	New house	New house
2	**TOTAL CASH NEEDED TO BUY THIS HOUSE**	**$44,850**	**$0**	**$0**
3				
4	**Monthly loan payment**	**$1,076**	**$0**	**$0**
5	**Monthly tax**	**$333**	**$0**	**$0**
6	**Total monthly payment**	**$1,410**	**$0**	**$0**
7				
8	COST OF HOME & MORTGAGE			
9	Price of the house	$175,000	$0	$0
10	Mortgage Interest Rate	8.50%	0.00%	0.00%
11	Points Charged by Lender	2	0	0
12	Loan Term	30	30	30
13	Annual Real Estate Taxes	$4,000	$0	$0
14				
15	**MORTGAGE AMOUNT**	**$140,000**	**$0**	**$0**
16	**DEPOSIT PAID AT CONTRACT**	**$17,500**	**$0**	**$0**
17	**DEPOSIT PAID AT CLOSING**	**$17,500**	**$0**	**$0**
18				
19	CLOSING COSTS			
20	Inspection of house	$350	$0	$0
21	Mortgage Insurance	$650	$0	$0
22	Attorney's fee	$4,000	$0	$0
23	Loan origination fee	$750	$0	$0
24	Recording fee	$100	$0	$0
25	Appraisal	$300	$0	$0
26	Loan application fee	$300	$0	$0
27	Survey	$300	$0	$0

Press ALT to choose commands, or F2 to edit.

FIG. 12.9

Homebuy is a spreadsheet you can download and use to track a home purchase.

In the spreadsheet, the numbers displayed in bold are calculated by formulas already entered. The numbers in a normal font will be entered as you learn specific prices and terms of the mortgage. While the calculation of the price of the home and the mortgage rate contributes heavily to the cost of a house, they're not the only costs.

Closing the deal on a home purchase will incur a long list of expenses. Many of these costs can be controlled by comparison shopping (the inspection, for example) but others are completely out of your control (the state's loan origination fee). You'll have to pay some fees because of the rules in your state and others because of requirements of your mortgage lender; the spreadsheet accounts for just about all of them. In the sample shown here (and the file available for downloading), I've included just about every possible closing cost you could encounter, so you may find the total runs a little high. Your attorney will be able to give you a more accurate summary for your own area (including the fee he or she will charge).

The Homebuy spreadsheet is set up to total all of these expenses and then include them in the formula in cell B2 which calculates "TOTAL CASH NEEDED TO BUY THIS HOUSE."

Using the Homebuy Spreadsheet

Using the spreadsheet is very simple. After you download and open it with your spreadsheet, replace the numbers for the following information.

- Price of the house
- Mortgage interest rate

- ◆ Points charged by lender (if any)

- ◆ Loan term (in years)

- ◆ Annual real estate taxes

- ◆ Closing costs

Don't replace the figures in the cells that are formatted in bold. These cells contain formulas that use the information you enter; the formulas will calculate "TOTAL CASH NEEDED TO BUY THIS HOUSE" and the monthly payments.

The spreadsheet assumes that you'll be buying the house in the most common arrangement. After you reach an agreement, you pay a 10 percent deposit upon signing a contract, and at the time of closing you will pay another 10 percent of the purchase price; your mortgage lender will supply the remaining 80 percent. If you plan to pay a higher amount for either deposit, you can enter the amount, and the spreadsheet will still accurately calculate the amount of cash you need and your monthly payments.

"The spreadsheet helps you understand the cost early in the process— before you fall in love with a house that is out of your price range."

The most difficult figures to obtain in creating your estimate are the closing costs. The sample spreadsheet can help you gain an idea of what you may pay. I used typical costs for New York state, but you'll find different prices where you live. You won't be able to estimate these expenses down to the penny. Your realtor can give you the closest approximation. The spreadsheet's greatest value is to help you

understand these costs early in the process—before you fall in love with a house that is out of your price range. You'll get a general idea of what to expect, and you'll be able to take these costs into your calculation.

The Formulas Behind the Homebuy Spreadsheet

The spreadsheet won't cover every situation. If you're rebuying a condo, you'll have other expenses. And if you're selling a home, you may want to factor in the resale value of your home. Adjusting the spreadsheet to your needs will be fairly easy once you understand how it was constructed.

Figure 12.10 shows the same spreadsheet but it displays the formulas in each cell so you can understand how to customize the spreadsheet.

The most valuable formula in the calculation uses the PMT or payment function. Aside from this financial function, the rest of the spreadsheet does little more than a calculator would. It multiples the purchase price by .1 to calculate a 10 percent deposit. It totals up all the closing costs and adds them to the contract deposits to calculate the "TOTAL CASH NEEDED TO BUY THIS HOUSE." Of course, a spreadsheet is far more valuable than a calculator could be since the spreadsheet lets you change numbers without entering the totals each time.

The payment function has been available in just about every spreadsheet written; it's used to calculate the payment on a loan (or investment) that has fixed installments. The structure of a payment function is

PMT(*principal,rate,term*)

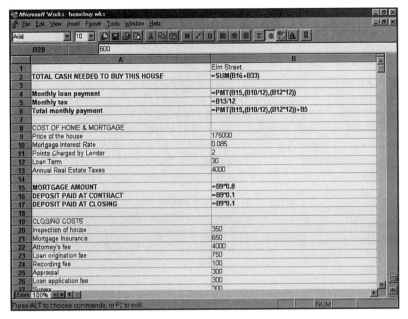

	A	B
	Microsoft Works - homebuy.wks	
	File Edit View Insert Format Tools Window Help	
	Arial ▾ 10 ▾	
	B28	600
1		Elm Street
2	TOTAL CASH NEEDED TO BUY THIS HOUSE	=SUM(B16+B33)
3		
4	Monthly loan payment	=PMT(B15,(B10/12),(B12*12))
5	Monthly tax	=B13/12
6	Total monthly payment	=PMT(B15,(B10/12),(B12*12))+B5
7		
8	COST OF HOME & MORTGAGE	
9	Price of the house	175000
10	Mortgage Interest Rate	0.085
11	Points Charged by Lender	2
12	Loan Term	30
13	Annual Real Estate Taxes	4000
14		
15	MORTGAGE AMOUNT	=B9*0.8
16	DEPOSIT PAID AT CONTRACT	=B9*0.1
17	DEPOSIT PAID AT CLOSING	=B9*0.1
18		
19	CLOSING COSTS	
20	Inspection of house	350
21	Mortgage Insurance	650
22	Attorney's fee	4000
23	Loan origination fee	750
24	Recording fee	100
25	Appraisal	300
26	Loan application fee	300
27	Survey	300

Zoom 100%
Press ALT to choose commends, or F2 to edit. NUM

FIG. 12.10

The Homebuy spreadsheet shown in formula view; note that the values in the CLOSING COSTS section are entered only to provide an example of typical expenses.

In this spreadsheet's payment calculation, the *principal* is the amount of the mortgage, the *rate* is the interest rate, and the *term* is the number of years. In cell B4, the spreadsheet calculates the monthly loan payment using the value B15 for principal, which is the price of the house minus the two deposit payments (or 80 percent of the full price). The spreadsheet will still work if you enter a specific contract amount rather than allowing the spreadsheet to calculate the contract.

The rate used in the PMT formula must be the rate applied to each payment. Because you want to determine the monthly payment and are starting with an annual interest rate, the spreadsheet formula must divide the rate by 12.

The term used in a PMT formula must be the total number of payments, not the number of years, so the formula in our spreadsheet multiplies the number of years by 12.

Finding the Perfect House, Without Venturing Outdoors

Now that you're armed with the tools you need to know how much of a house you can afford, you can start shopping with confidence. But your AOL connection can streamline something as time-honored as the house-hunting expedition.

Hundreds of realtors now operate Web pages to hawk their wares. Many of these sites are little more than on-screen calling cards. But many realtors have extensive online listings that let you search by neighborhood, price range—even by the number of bathrooms. With a little online surfing, you can cut down

> **"Spend a few minutes sizing up the local offerings online, and you'll enter the realtor's office a knowledgeable buyer."**

on the number of weekends you'll spend in the backseat of a realtor's sedan, trudging from house to house.

Any experienced home buyer will tell you that realtors will only show you the most desirable properties if they're convinced you know the local market. After all, someone has to buy the white elephant that's been sitting on the market for the last two years. Until the realtor has had a chance to size you up, you're likely to see the leftovers. Spend a few minutes sizing up the local offerings online and you'll enter the realtor's office a knowledgeable buyer who's already seen quite a few houses on the market.

Finding the Houses for Sale in Your Area

While there are quite a few real estate realtors online, finding the realtors in your area—or the area where you plan to move—will require a little detective work. You can find realtors using the same technique you'd use in comparison shopping. In Chapter 9, the section "Searching the Web for Products" has a detailed explanation of how to find things on the Web. The following steps are a quick summary of that discussion:

1. Connect to AOL and use the keyword

   http://www.infoseek.com

   The opening screen for the Web search engine InfoSeek Guide will open.

2. In the empty Search for Information About box, type in **real estate** and the city or state you're interested in, for example, **real estate and dallas**, as in figure 12.11. You may want to add the state name, but it's not necessary.

3. Click the Search Now button; within a few seconds, InfoSeek Guide will display a list of Web sites that contain information on real estate in your area. To view any of these pages, click the highlighted title (see fig. 12.12).

Once you've found a list of realtors, you can start your tour of the area. You can jump back and forth between the sites listed in InfoSeek Guide and the individual pages. To help you stay organized in your search, you may want to create a Favorite Place for this page, because once you start visiting the sites you may become distracted and lose track of the list of realtors.

Ired: Internet Real Estate Directory

Finding realtors using InfoSeek Guide is a little cumbersome, since the listings are not very well-organized. Occasionally, you'll find one of the listings has nothing to do with real estate in your area—after all, the only thing you've really done is find Web pages with the words "real," "estate," and your area in them. If a lawyer was writing about "estate taxes," there's a good chance this page would show up.

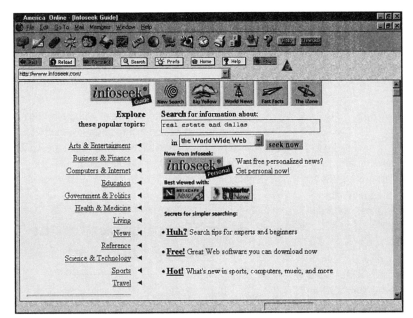

FIG. 12.11

Use InfoSeek Guide to locate realtors in your area.

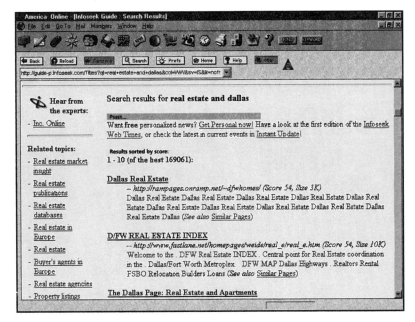

FIG. 12.12

You'll find many real estate realtors have sites for every large metropolitan area in the United States and Canada.

One alternative is Ired, the Internet Real Estate Directory; see figure 12.13.

This Web site was created to help buyers find the realtors who are on the Internet. You can display the site by using the keyword

http://www.ired.com

Not only does the Ired directory save time by listing only realtors, you'll find that the listings are easier to browse since they all appear on the same page rather than stretched over several pages, as in the InfoSeek Guide.

To find a realtor in a specific area, display the Ired home page and select USA Links. You'll see an alphabetical listing of the states; select the state and you'll see a list of cities and towns. Once you've selected the area you want, you'll see a list of links to many of the realtors who have Web sites in that area. Figure

12.14 shows the listing of sites you'd find by searching for Westchester, NY.

Select any of the listings on this page to display the Web site of a realtor in the area. Some realtors will display photos of homes at their site, but others may only advertise the realtors' services without listing available property. Keep in mind that few realtors are completely committed to their Web sites, so you will still need to call a realtor to learn about all of the listings in the area.

HomeScout Looks for the House You Want

HomeScout sounds like the miracle that the tired home buyer has been waiting for. You type in details

FIG. 12.13

Ired, the Internet Real Estate Directory, provides a guide to realtors on the Web.

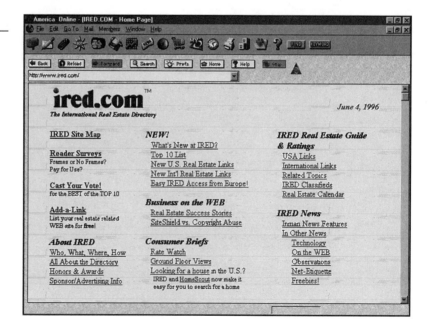

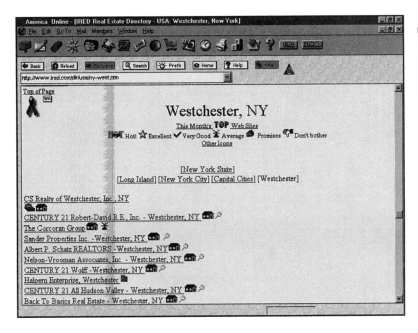

FIG. 12.14

Ired's listing of realtors in a specific area is easy to browse; each listed realtor operates its own Web site.

about the house you want to buy, and HomeScout finds the listing—in about two seconds and at no charge.

You'll find this Web wonder by using the keyword

http://www.homescout.com

On the main page, you'll find a form where you enter criteria about the house you're seeking (see fig. 12.15).

▼ TIP

Shopping for real estate online can give you a quick overview of the type of real estate available and the prices. It will also lead you to realtors in the area.

The HomeScout Web site is similar to InfoSeek Guide and other Web search engines, except that HomeScout creates a database that's limited to real estate listings. You can search the database by completing the form with details on

◆ City

◆ State or province

◆ Maximum price

◆ Minimum price

◆ Minimum bedrooms

◆ Minimum bathrooms

Once you've entered something in each field, select the Search button and HomeScout searches its database. In a few seconds, you'll see a list of links to houses in the database that matches your criteria. Each link will open a page that displays information about a home (see fig. 12.16).

FIG. 12.15

On the opening page for HomeScout, you'll find a form where you enter your criteria for the right house.

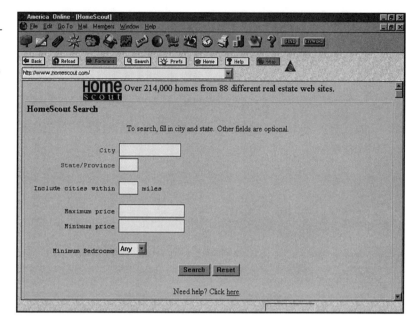

FIG. 12.16

A typical home listing on the Web; this one was found with HomeScout.

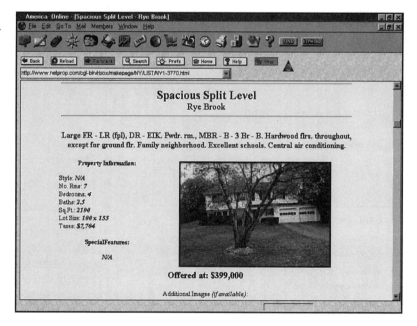

Some of the pages you'll find have photos. Most pages are operated by realtors, and to see the house, you'll need to call the realtor and set up an appointment.

Since you'll probably end up using a realtor, you may want to use HomeScout just to get a general idea of what's available. When you're ready to actually leave your computer and start touring real houses, you may want to go back to Ired and start calling the realtors you find in the area.

When your search becomes serious, you may want to repeat your search of InfoSeek Guide. It may uncover "for sale by owner" offers that will not show up in Ired or HomeScout.

Multiple Listings at AOL's Real Estate Center

You won't see a picture of houses for sale at AOL's Real Estate Center, but you will be able to quickly locate available houses and learn a good deal of information about the property. Both realtors and homeowners can create a "for sale" entry in the Real Estate Center's database, so you may find quite a few houses listed here by owners that you won't find through the Web sites dominated by realtors. And because each listing includes an extensive database report, you can learn a great deal of information about each house listed. You can also learn about houses and apartments for rent.

▼ **T I P**

When you're ready to sell your house, the Real Estate Center will let you advertise the property for free. You can avoid unwanted calls by posting only your e-mail address.

Here's how you would search for a house in a particular city.

1. Connect to AOL and enter the keyword **mls**. The main menu of the Real Estate Center appears.

2. Select the option MLS, Sell, Buy, Rent, Exchange.

3. Select the Enter Database button. A search dialog box opens.

4. Enter the name of the city or other details about the type of property you want to find. Press Enter. A list of properties appears in the bottom half of the window.

5. To see more listings, select the More button.

6. Select any property from the list. A window will display details on the property that were supplied by a realtor or the homeowner, as shown in figure 12.17.

FIG 12.17

At AOL's Real Estate Center, you can find properties put up for sale by a realtor or a home-owner.

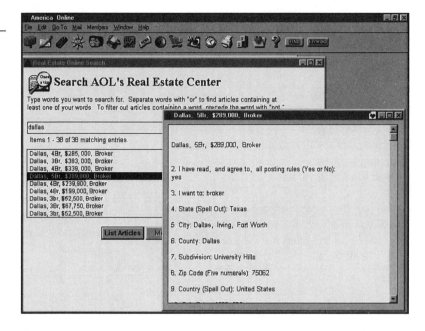

If you want to contact the seller, you'll find an e-mail address near the bottom of the listing; a few listings also include a phone number. All of the listings are based on a database form, and if the seller has not entered all of the information on the form, it may seem cryptic. If you're having problems understanding the language, download a copy of the database form from the main menu.

13

Planning Ahead To Meet College Costs

Whether you're helping a high schooler or preschooler, planning ahead can make college a better experience for everyone in the family.

Paying for a college education is the most serious financial strain most families ever experience. Only the wealthy are able to shoulder the expense without dipping into savings, and only the truly gifted can hope to win a full scholarship. Unless you start a college savings fund years ahead of time, you'll find the cost of the average college can quickly deplete the family's savings.

Parents who have plenty of time before their children are ready for school can take advantage of the miracle of compounded interest. If you're not already aware of how much difference this can make, the spreadsheets described in this chapter will show you very clearly how you can make savings grow and help you decide if you're saving enough now.

Parents who don't have much time to build a portfolio will also benefit from exploring college costs online now. You'll be able to compare the real cost of college (including living expenses and fees) to find a college you can afford. And a number of Web sites will help you find scholarships and financial aid packages that can defray some of the cost.

What Will It Cost?

Preparing for college expenses is especially difficult because educational costs keep rising. In recent years, college tuition and other expenses have

> "You can get a general idea of what colleges cost by reviewing the College Handbook on America Online."

risen faster than the inflation rate, increasing the burden on parents. While the college cost inflation rate has slowed down in recent years, it's still running higher than the inflation rate—6 percent for college costs compared to 4 percent for the overall economy. That means planning for college requires the extra step of accounting for inflation.

Learning About Costs

While every college has unique needs and sets its own expenses every year, you can get a general idea of what colleges cost by reviewing the College Handbook on America Online (AOL).

The Handbook's menus let you search for colleges by name and find a summary of the current curriculum and costs.

1. Connect to AOL and enter the keyword

    college board

    The opening menu for the College Board will appear, as shown in figure 13.1.

FIG. 13.1

The College Board has a collection of articles that can help you understand the options available for financial aid and how to apply.

2. The College Board's main menu lists a number of good articles that can help families plan for college expenses. But to find the database with current costs for specific schools, select the College Handbook button. A list of options will open.

3. Select Search the Handbook. A dialog box opens.

4. Enter the name of a college and select the List Articles button.

5. Select a school from the list and double-click the name. A window opens with information about that school. Scroll down the document and you'll find sections with information on Annual Expenses and Financial Aid, as shown in figure 13.2.

You can print this document or save it to a file from the File menu.

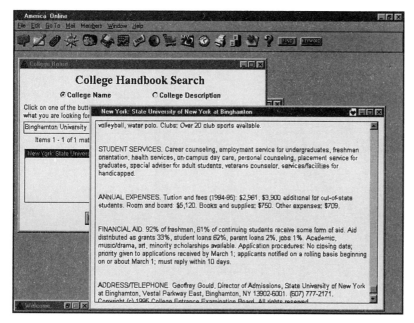

FIG. 13.2

The College Handbook includes descriptions of most colleges and universities, including a summary of costs.

You can also search the database of colleges to find schools that offer specific courses of study in the region you choose. For example, in Step 3, if you select the College Description option and use the term "art history and boston," then only schools that include both "art history" and "boston" in the school description will appear.

Projecting Tomorrow's College Costs in a Spreadsheet

Knowing how much college costs today is only half the battle. Once you've found the cost for school today in the College Handbook database, you need to determine what it will cost when your young students are ready—and after inflation has pushed the price higher. Even parents of preschoolers will benefit from an attempt to project the expenses they'll be faced with when their children are ready. Fortunately, a spreadsheet makes this a fairly simple job.

Figure 13.3 shows a spreadsheet that takes today's college tuition and projects the cost using the current inflation rate. You can use the figures you find at the College Handbook and your children's ages to see how much you'll need to save.

> "Knowing how much college costs today is only half the battle."

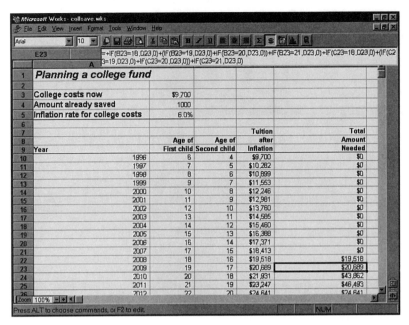

FIG. 13.3

The top half of the Collsave spreadsheet projects tuition using current figures and the inflation rate now affecting college costs.

This spreadsheet, Collsave, can be downloaded from AOL using the keyword

http://www.mcp.com/que/desktop_os/ money

At this Web site, you'll find a version for Lotus 1-2-3, Microsoft Works, or Microsoft Excel that can be downloaded. This spreadsheet will help you build a college fund that can meet the needs of one or more students, even if they're still in diapers. The examples shown here are taken from the part of the spreadsheet designed for families with two children; the Collsave spreadsheet you can download has distinct sections for families with one, two, or three children.

Using the spreadsheet is simple. Once you download the file and open it in your own spreadsheet program, enter values for "College costs now,"

"Inflation rate for college costs," and the current ages of each child. With this information entered, the spreadsheet will calculate the expenses for a college education for each year forward. To find out how much you'll need to have, scroll down until you find the tuition in the year each child is 18.

The spreadsheet uses variables for several key figures: college cost, children's ages, and the inflation rate. It assumes that the children will start college at the age of 18. The spreadsheet will estimate exactly how much you need to put aside every year in order to meet the bills during college years. You'll be able to adjust the file periodically, using a different figure for tuition, inflation rate, or the children's ages. And because it shows you the projected cost each year in the future, you'll be able to check the spreadsheet in years to come and see if your plan needs adjustment.

Figure 13.3 shows typical costs in 1996 for a public college, but you'll be able to use costs for any college. The spreadsheet formulas will calculate the affect of inflation. Currently, college costs are rising at about 6 percent a year (higher than the general inflation rate) but because there's no way of telling what the inflation rate will be in the future, the spreadsheet treats inflation as a variable.

You don't need to understand the formulas behind the spreadsheet, but knowing how it was created will be useful if you want to customize the file or create a different application. You could use the same principle to create a spreadsheet for planning any big purchase that requires years of savings.

How the Collsave Spreadsheet Works

The formulas in figure 13.3 use only multiplication and addition. The screen shows the spreadsheet in Microsoft Works, but it works the same way in Lotus 1-2-3 or Microsoft Excel.

In column D, college costs are calculated each year. To make it easier to keep track of the amounts in building this spreadsheet, I created a Range Name for tuition and the inflation rate (the range names are Tuition and Inflat, respectively). The second cell in the Tuition column, D10, calculates the affect of inflation on the tuition; to do this, you need to multiply tuition by the inflation rate (to calculate the

expected increase) and then add the current tuition to that number. The formula is

=(Tuition*Inflat)+Tuition

The cells for the following years calculate the affect of inflation, too, but the amount to be used in this calculation has changed. You don't want to use the current tuition; you want to use the tuition projected for the previous year. So the formula in cell D11 multiplies inflation by the tuition in cell D10, using the formula

=+D10(D10*$Inflat)

From this point on, the formula doesn't vary. The cells in rows below multiply inflation by the tuition in the cell above. In building the spreadsheet, the formula in cell D11 can be copied into the cells below. When the copy operation is performed, the spreadsheet will automatically adjust the value for the tuition to the cell below. To make sure the spreadsheet uses the value in the one cell where the inflation rate is stored, the formula includes the dollar sign ($), establishing Inflat as an absolute reference (rather than a relative reference).

The ages are also calculated so the spreadsheet will be flexible enough to be used for different children and updated in the years to come (feel free to share the spreadsheet with friends and relatives). This formula is very simple, because it adds one year in each row. The formula used in cell B10 is

=+B9+1

The cell reference in this formula is relative—it does not have a dollar sign—so when it is copied to the cells below, the spreadsheet adjusts the formula to the new location. For example, when cell B10 is copied to cell B11, the formula changes to

=+B10+1

Building a spreadsheet this way is fast and makes it possible to try out new values with little work. But these calculations are just the foundation. Now that you have a way to project college costs for when today's students will be ready, you can begin to use that information for real planning.

Finding the Real Cost for the Entire Family

To find the amounts you're likely to be paying in the future, you can read down the spreadsheet and find the value in the Tuition column for the years when your child is of college age. But if you have more than one student, you'll be paying double that amount in the years when both are in college.

You can have the spreadsheet perform this calculation with a simple multiplication (times 2) formula. But you want the amounts doubled only in the years when both students are of college age. It's possible to have the spreadsheet perform the calculation only in the years when the amounts are doubled if you use an IF formula. You also need to make an assumption of college age; this spreadsheet assumes college bills will be faced for four years, when the student is between 18 and 21.

An IF formula looks at the value in a cell, and if it meets the criteria entered in the formula, the spreadsheet will perform one operation (known as the "true" value). If the criteria is not met, the spreadsheet will perform an alternate operation (the "false" value). You can use the IF formula to look at

the values in the cells where the ages were calculated; if the value is 18, 19, 20, or 21, then the tuition for that year should be added to the current cell. If the age is anything other than one of those values (the "false" value), a zero will be added.

Advanced spreadsheets, like the newest versions of Microsoft Excel and Lotus 1-2-3, allow nesting within an IF formula, so it would be possible to write a single formula that would test for numbers less than 18 and greater than 21. But in order to make the spreadsheet work in Microsoft Works, you need to enter the formula repeatedly, looking for the age in each year. For example, the formula in cell E27 begins with the entry

=IF(B27=18,D27,0)+(IF(B27=19,D27,0)

It then continues with repetitions of the IF formula to test through ages 20 and 21, and then repeats again for the second child. You can see the entire formula for cell E26 in the formula entry box in figure 13.4.

If it sounds overly complicated, don't be concerned. You won't need to touch the formula unless you plan to customize the spreadsheet. All you need to do is enter a current tuition, inflation rate, and child's (or children's) current age(s), and the spreadsheet does all the work. You can scroll down to see the total college expense that you'll be facing for the years when your children are between 18 and 21. Learning how to use the IF formula will be helpful when you decide to build a spreadsheet that helps you make a decision about a future event. The IF formula can evaluate calculated numbers and perform new calculations based on the answers.

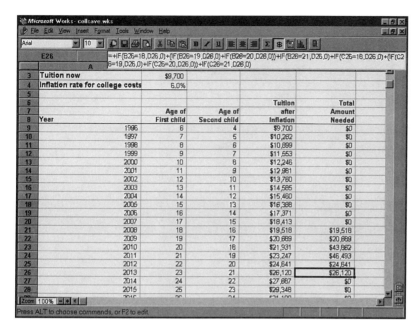

FIG. 13.4

Using an IF formula, the spreadsheet will add the tuition only in the years when the age equals 18, 19, 20, or 21.

Managing Your College Fund

Once you've entered the age(s), inflation rate, and tuition in the top part of the spreadsheet, you will want to scroll down to the bottom half, where you can learn how much you need to be saving every year in order to pay the college bills. This spreadsheet was designed to take the projections of college costs and use them to create a realistic savings plan.

You're able to do this by using a standard spreadsheet function called FV for Future Value. It can calculate the amount that a regular savings plan will generate over the years. To use the FV formula, you need to know three things:

◆ Amount saved each year

◆ Interest rate

◆ The time period for the saving plan

You don't have much control over the time you have left (other than asking your children to defer college for a few years). But you do have some control over the interest rate, and this spreadsheet should illustrate the importance of wise investing.

Figure 13.5 shows the bottom of the spreadsheet in Microsoft Works. The versions of the spreadsheet for Microsoft Excel and Lotus 1-2-3 also include an entry for the amount of current savings, in addition to yearly contributions, taking advantage of the more advanced FV formula in those programs.

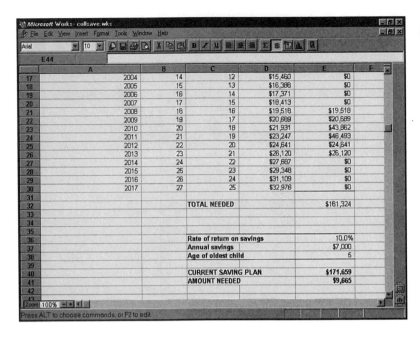

	A	B	C	D	E	F
17	2004	14	12	$15,460	$0	
18	2005	15	13	$16,388	$0	
19	2006	16	14	$17,371	$0	
20	2007	17	15	$18,413	$0	
21	2008	18	16	$19,518	$19,518	
22	2009	19	17	$20,689	$20,689	
23	2010	20	18	$21,931	$43,862	
24	2011	21	19	$23,247	$46,493	
25	2012	22	20	$24,641	$24,641	
26	2013	23	21	$26,120	$26,120	
27	2014	24	22	$27,687	$0	
28	2015	25	23	$29,348	$0	
29	2016	26	24	$31,109	$0	
30	2017	27	25	$32,976	$0	
31						
32			TOTAL NEEDED		$181,324	
33						
34						
35						
36			Rate of return on savings		10.0%	
37			Annual savings		$7,000	
38			Age of oldest child		5	
39						
40			CURRENT SAVING PLAN		$171,659	
41			AMOUNT NEEDED		$9,665	
42						

FIG. 13.5

Enter the amount you contribute to a college savings plan annually, and the spreadsheet will let you know if your plan is on track.

The spreadsheet uses the amount you projected for college costs and the allows the user to enter the interest rate expected, the amount currently being set aside, and the current age of the oldest child.

The spreadsheet uses these values in the FV formula (which is in cell E40, next to Current Savings). The age of the oldest child is subtracted from 18 to determine the number of years that the savings plan will be in effect. The numbers are on the conservative side; they assume that you'll want to save up the entire amount before the kids have a single college bill. Because the fund will continue to earn interest even after small amounts of money are deducted, there's a good chance you'll have a surplus (which will probably be used for other necessities, like trips home).

Figure 13.6 shows the spreadsheet in a formula view. Most users will never want to touch the formulas, but you may want to customize the spreadsheet. For example, if your children will not attend school from the age of 18 to 21, you'll want to change the calculation to the year when they will be incurring college costs.

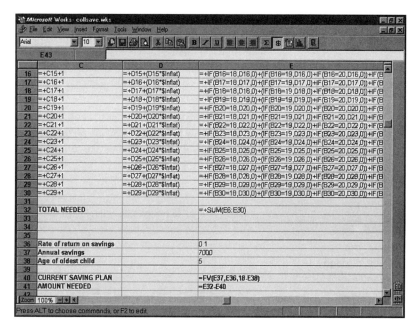

FIG. 13.6

A look at the formulas used in the projections for the college saving plan.

If you're not sure of the investment rate you're likely to achieve with your investment philosophy, here's a general idea of which figures to use: 6 percent if you buy CDs; 8 percent if you buy bonds; and 10 percent if you invest in the stock market. Because it's impossible to accurately predict the rate of return from any investment other than low-interest paying bank accounts, it's important to remember that this spreadsheet is only a general guide.

One benefit of using the spreadsheet is to help you understand the importance of having an aggressive investment plan when saving for a long-term goal. Don't risk your money in volatile investments (like aggressive stock funds or speculative stocks) if you have only three or four years to save. And while you need to be careful in choosing the investment vehicle for a college education, no matter how long you have to save, if the children are still young, you'll

have enough time to withstand the ups and downs of a few stock market cycles and may want to choose growth-oriented and dividend-paying stocks for your college fund. Just be sure to move the money into less volatile investments, like CDs or money market funds, within three or fours years of when you'll need to pay the bills.

Most people will want to concentrate on the figure that they have greatest control over: annual savings. Your goal is to try different amounts in this cell until you find the figure that will produce a very low number in the cell Amount Needed. If the number in this cell appears in parentheses, you're in luck; the number is negative, meaning you have more than you need. If the result in Amount Needed is high, don't despair; the following sections show you where to look for help.

Finding Financial Aid

Financial aid information can be hard to come by. School counselors can help to some extent, but no counselor will be able to keep track of the thousands of programs available across the country. Many programs are available only to students who attend a particular college. Others are available only to children and guardians of professional organizations. The standard way of finding financial aid is to pick a school and then ask about financial aid packages.

▼ **TIP**

The College Board can guide you through the process of finding financial aid and completing the application process. Enter the keyword **college** and select the menu option Paying for College.

Using your AOL account, you can start to look for financial aid before you select a college. The following sections guide you to the right places.

CollegeNet: Linking to Resources

A good place to start your search is at CollegeNet. This Web site is a kind of clearinghouse for information about colleges. You'll be able to find the Web sites that hundreds of colleges run, and you'll find links to information about financial aid.

To find CollegeNet, use the AOL keyword

http://www.college-net.com

From the opening menu, you can search for colleges by name or by region. If you select a region, you see a list of nearly every school in the area; the names of colleges that have Web sites will be highlighted. Select the link to display the college's Web site.

To find information on scholarships, loans, and grants, select the Financial Aid option on the main menu. A page full of links to other sites on the Web opens (see fig. 13.7).

Some of these sites will be of only limited value; many of the links did not work when I tried them. But new sites are added regularly, so you may want to visit here periodically to see what's new.

Determining Your Eligibility for Financial Aid

Sallie Mae is a financial institution that helps fund a large share of the loans available to students. Its Web site is an excellent source of information on the different types of aid available and the procedures you'll need to follow to obtain them. When you're seriously looking for financial aid, be sure to visit the "How To Pay for College" page on the Sallie Mae Web site (see fig. 13.8). You can find it by using the keyword

http://www.salliemae.com/consumer/ howtopay

By reading through this page and following each of the links that explain the terms, you'll end up with plenty of information on the options available and the formulas that college administrators use to award financial aid. You'll be able to see some of the forms that financial aid applicants are currently asking students and their parents to complete.

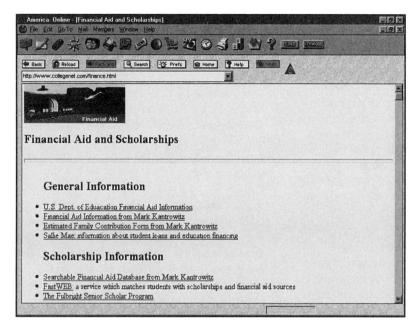

FIG. 13.7

CollegeNet is a Web site that can help you find college aid resources on the Web.

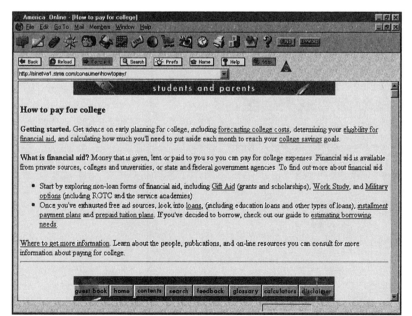

FIG. 13.8

On Sallie Mae's Web site, you'll find "How To Pay for College," a guide to the various types of financial aid available.

Perhaps the most valuable resource is a calculator that will allow you to perform the same calculation that many financial aid administrators will use to determine your eligibility. This calculation is known as the Expected Family Contribution (or EFC) and it is always performed before awarding financial aid to a student. It uses the family's income and assets to determine how much the college expects the family should contribute to the expenses. To find the calculator, display the How To Pay for College page, select the highlighted text "eligibility for financial aid," and then select "estimating your EFC." The calculator is shown in figure 13.9.

To complete the form, you'll need know the student's assets and income, and the parent's assets and income. After you enter this information and select Calculate, you'll see your EFC, the amount colleges will expect you to pay.

Where To Find Scholarships and Grants

Once you have a general understanding of your options and the likelihood of receiving a financial aid package, you can began a search for the packages that are currently available. FastWeb is a Web site that helps students find the aid packages that may be open to them.

You can complete a questionnaire that will create a profile for the student in an attempt to find scholarships or grants that are available. Because many of these awards are limited to members of a particular group, they're often not widely known. Some awards are reserved for members of a union, while others are designed to help students pursue a specific field of study.

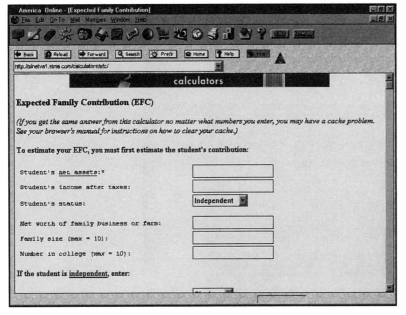

FIG. 13.9

Sallie Mae's Eligibility for Financial Aid Calculator allows you to see how your family's situation will be reviewed by college administrators.

Completing the questionnaire will take just a few minutes, and the service is free, so any family that's looking for financial aid will want to use it.

1. Log on to AOL and enter the keyword

   http://www.studentservices.com/fastweb/

   The FastWEB home page opens (see fig. 13.10). Select the option Begin the FastWEB Scholarship Search.

2. The first step guides you through the process of creating a FastWEB mailbox. Enter your name and a user ID that you select just for your FastWEB mail. (FastWEB will send information on available awards to this mailbox, not to your private e-mail account.)

3. Your mailbox information will be displayed; select the On to Step 2 button.

4. Enter your address and phone number; select the On to Step 3 button.

5. You need to enter demographic information, including the student's birth date, race, and ethnic origin. Select the On to Step 4 button.

6. You need to enter information about the student's scholastic information, including the student's grade level, and current grade point average. A key entry on this screen asks for the student's career objective and hobbies; because some scholarships are offered by professional and trade groups, be sure to enter all objectives that may apply. After you've completed all entries, select the On to Step 5 button.

FIG. 13.10

The FastWEB site can help families find grants, scholarships, and financial aid packages.

7. The information entered on this screen may be the most important in helping your student find available scholarships (see fig. 13.11). This screen is designed to match the student with specific scholarships offered by unions, non-profit organizations, corporations, and trade groups. The questions concentrate on the parent's activities. Be sure to read the list of options closely and select as many organizations as apply; hold down the Ctrl when you're selecting multiple choices. When you've read through all the choices, select the On to Step 6 button.

8. On this screen, enter up to three colleges the student would consider attending (including the school where he or she may already be enrolled). Select the All Done button.

9. If any of your answers are ambiguous, you'll be asked to clarify. Once the information is clear, FastWEB begins processing. A response will take anywhere from 15 minutes to an hour. You'll need to return to the FastWEB mailbox to see the report.

10. To return to the FastWEB mailbox, enter the keyword

http://www.studentservices.com/fastweb

and select the option FastWEB Mail Box. You'll need to enter your name and user ID.

If you took the time to carefully complete the form, you have a good chance of finding a list of scholarships in your mailbox. The report you'll receive shows details about each scholarship program, including a description of the types of students who are eligible and instructions on how to apply. You'll even find a suggested form letter that you can edit with your word processor.

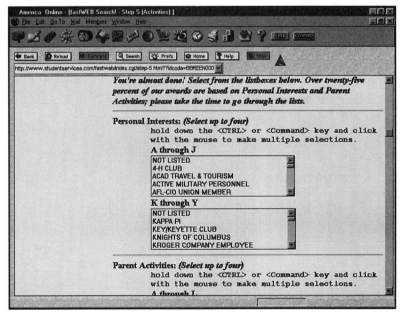

FIG. 13.11

The FastWEB questionnaire asks questions about the student's and parents' affiliations to find scholarships that may be available to your family.

▼ T I P

Many financial aid packages are offered by trade groups and clubs, so be sure to enter every possibility when you complete the FastWEB questionnaire.

You'll receive the greatest number of responses within a day, but you should check back again because the FastWEB service receives new information about scholarships, and so a new report may arrive after some time has passed.

14

Planning for Retirement

Whether your retirement seems like a distant dream or an approaching train, it pays to be prepared. Time is on your side—but only if you start saving for retirement early enough.

Just a few short years ago, anyone who had a million dollars was considered wealthy. But for most Americans, having a million dollars at retirement age will be only enough to ensure a modest lifestyle. Thanks to a steady rate of inflation, Americans who are under the age of 50 will need to build a retirement that's well over a million dollars if they hope to enjoy a comfortable retirement.

For most Americans, the difference between today's comfortable retirement income and tomorrow's problem is the disappearing pension. Only a relatively small number of today's workers will be entitled to a pension that provides a fixed income. Unless you're one of the fortunate few, you'll want to spend some time planning your investments so you can amass the sizable retirement fund you'll need to have when you stop working.

In this chapter, you'll learn about some online resources that can help you understand some of the available options. And you'll learn how to run your own spreadsheets that can help you accurately project the amount you'll need to save and keep track of your progress in years to come.

The skills you'll learn in this chapter will go a long way toward helping you achieve financial security in the decades ahead.

Learning About Social Security Benefits

Most Americans realize that Social Security retirement benefits won't be enough to provide a comfortable retirement. A growing number of people doubt they'll receive any Social Security benefits at all, believing that the fund will run dry long before they're old enough to claim benefits. The future of Social Security is in the hands of Congress—and voters—and no matter what you believe will happen, the best attitude is to treat Social Security as just one variable in your plan.

Even if you are confident you'll collect retirement benefits, knowing how much to expect is a challenge. When a worker covered by Social Security claims retirement benefits, the Social Security Administration uses a complicated formula that indexes the worker's annual earnings to account for inflation and then finds the average monthly income for the 35 years when income was highest. It applies a formula to this amount to determine the monthly benefit. Of course, the formula is subject to change, based on the whims of Congress and the affect of annual cost-of-living increases.

To find out exactly how the Social Security system works, you can visit their site on the Web. Enter the keyword

http://www.ssa.gov

The AOL Web browser opens and displays the Social Security Administration's home page, shown in figure 14.1.

Scroll down and you'll find a number of links to information on the site. Select FAQs (Frequently Asked Questions) to find answers to some of the

FIG. 14.1

There's no way of knowing whether the fund will be around when you retire, but you can visit the Social Security Administration's Web site today to learn about the benefits plan.

most commonly asked questions on benefits, payroll taxes, and a wide range of topics. The information covered here will be most relevant to people who are about to claim benefits.

How Much Can You Expect from Social Security?

If you're trying to learn how to project the amount of your retirement, you have a couple of choices. You can ask the Social Security Administration to prepare a summary of your current earnings and an estimate of the retirement benefits you'll receive, or you can read an explanation of how retirement benefits are being calculated today.

To see the Social Security summary, you need to request a Personal Earnings and Benefits Statement (PEBS). You can request one directly while you're connected to the Web site, but the statement will be mailed to you (not by e-mail, by postal mail).

For a more immediate answer, you can read the publication "How Your Retirement Benefit is Figured," which provides a detailed explanation of the formula used to determine retirement benefits. It won't have any information about your account, but it gives the exact formula that will be used to calculate benefits. The publication is presented only in either Adobe Acrobat PDF or PostScript PS formats, so you may need to download additional software to read the files. PDF files can be read with the Adobe Acrobat reader, a software program that displays formatted documents on-screen with the fonts and page layout intact; the reader is available for free; PS or PostScript files can be read with applications that have PostScript drivers installed.

▼ **T I P**

You'll find answers to many common questions about Social Security at the Web site. Documents cover everything from how cost-of-living increases are determined to how you apply for a Social Security number.

Adobe distributes its Acrobat Reader for free, and since you can use it to view other documents in the future, you may get a lot of use out of the file. The following steps guide you through the process of obtaining this document and then how to download the Acrobat software you'll need.

1. Log on to AOL and enter the keyword

   http://www.ssa.gov/programs/ programs_intro.html

2. The AOL browser loads, displaying a list of Social Security publications available online (see fig. 14.2).

3. Select the link LIST OF PUBLICATIONS. A page opens with a list of publications about retirement benefits.

4. In the paragraph, How Your Retirement Benefit Is Figured, select the highlighted link pdf. The AOL browser displays a dialog box asking whether you want to configure a viewer to display this file; select No.

5. A File Save dialog box opens. Either accept the file name and download folder or select a new one. Select the OK button, and the file will be downloaded.

6. To view this file, you'll need the Acrobat Reader. You can download it from Adobe's Web site. In the Web browser's location box, type

FIG. 14.2

An explanation of how the Social Security Administration calculates retirement benefits is available on the Web.

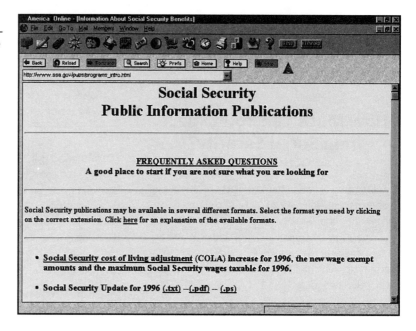

http:/www/adobe.com

and press Enter.

The main page for Adobe's Web site opens.

7. Select the link Products. You'll see a choice of Adobe products.

8. Select the link Adobe Acrobat. You'll see a page with information about the product. Select the link Download Adobe Acrobat.

9. You'll see a choice of software platforms, including Mac and Windows. Select your platform to see a page with instructions on how to install the file and an option to begin the download.

After the file is downloaded to your system, you'll need to install it by running the Setup program. The program gives you the option of configuring the AOL Web browser to recognize Adobe Acrobat files in the future. You can choose this option, but it's not necessary to view the Social Security retirement benefits file.

To view the file, run the Acrobat Reader and open the file you downloaded from the Social Security Web site, shown in figure 14.3.

Downloading the Acrobat Reader may seem like a like of trouble to go through just to read one pamphlet, but after you display the document, you'll understand why the Social Security Administration uses the Acrobat format. You can magnify sections of the document to get a better view or zoom out to get a better perspective.

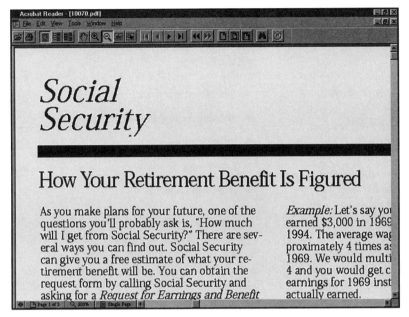

FIG. 14.3

The Social Security explanation of retirement benefits after it was downloaded and displayed in the Adobe Acrobat Reader.

Creating a Realistic Retirement Plan

Whether you download the Social Security booklet or not, you won't know the precise amount of your benefit until you retire. That shouldn't stop you from trying to project your retirement income today. All plans for retirement require some level of projection. No one can reliably predict what inflation will do to the value of the dollar or how growth in the economy will affect investments tomorrow.

The best retirement plan will be flexible enough to allow for frequent adjustment, depending on opportunities you encounter, changes in your lifestyle, and fluctuations in the inflation rate.

Keeping those needs in mind, I created a couple of spreadsheet files that can be adapted to just about

any personal situation. The following sections explain how to download them from AOL and use them. After that discussion, you'll learn about a shareware program you can download for a different perspective.

How Much Income Will You Need for Retirement?

To build a realistic plan, the first fact you must face is inflation. It's not enough to invest and hope that you'll have enough to last through retirement. You'll need to devote some thought to how much you'll need before you can even hope to know if you're saving enough.

The starting point in building a plan is to decide on the amount you'll want to spend annually using today's living standards as a guide. Obviously, you'd like to have as much as possible, but you need to be realistic—you'll be funding this account.

Before you settle on the amount, keep in mind that your expenses are likely to be lower after you retire. If you own a home, the mortgage may be paid off, you won't be saving for your children's education, and you'll have no work-related expenses.

Once you settle on an amount based on today's standard of living, you'll be prepared to work with Ret_Need, a spreadsheet you can download from The AOL Money Guide site online (see fig. 14.4).

While the screens used show the spreadsheet in Microsoft Works, you can download a version for Lotus 1-2-3, Microsoft Works, or Microsoft Excel. You can download the file by using the keyword

http://www.mcp.com/que/desktop_os/ money/

The spreadsheet is designed to show you how much you'll be spending each year at retirement age. The calculations in this spreadsheet let you enter your own values for

◆ Retirement income

◆ Social Security & pension

◆ Inflation rate

◆ Current age

◆ Retirement age

The spreadsheet calculates the affect of inflation on the income you want to have, but because you can probably count on some outside income—for most people, that's Social Security—the spreadsheet deducts this amount from the projected income (after it's been adjusted for inflation, too). Pessimists who don't believe Social Security will be around when they retire can enter zero for this value. The rest of us

FIG. 14.4

The first step in preparing a retirement plan is to project how much you'll need to have.

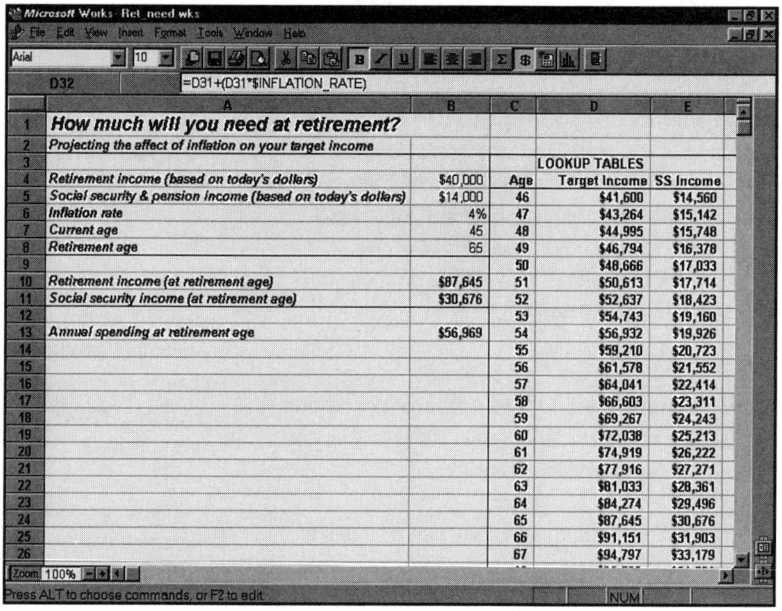

will want to include the benefit we expect to receive from Social Security as part of our retirement income.

If you're fortunate enough to be able to count on a defined-benefit pension plan which that grow over the years with cost-of-living increases, in addition to Social Security income, combine both amounts and enter the total for the cell Social Security & pension income (in today's dollars). Don't enter profit-sharing fund amounts or defined-contribution retirement plan amounts; those will be used in the retirement planning spreadsheet.

The amount the spreadsheet calculates as annual spending at retirement is the amount you'll need to withdraw every year from your retirement fund. You'll need to figure out how much you'll really need to retire. Only after you know this amount can you realistically build a saving plan that can meet your retirement needs.

The Design of the Ret_Need Spreadsheet

You won't need to change any of the formulas in the Ret_Need, but if you want to customize the spreadsheet, you'll want to know about the design. Figure 14.5 shows the spreadsheet in formula view.

The spreadsheet reads the values entered for retirement income and Social Security income, and then calculates how much they'll grow each year using the inflation rate entered. Because the spreadsheet needs to be flexible enough to work with a variety of ages, rather than calculate the income amounts for just one year, it builds a table. This table, in columns C, D and E, increases age by one and increases income by the inflation rate in every row.

To determine the amounts for Social Security and income at retirement age, the formulas in B10 and

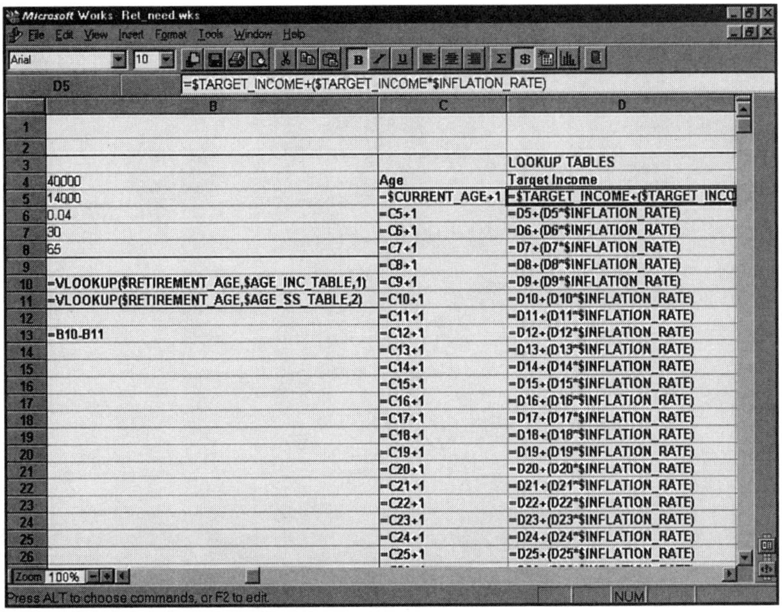

FIG. 14.5

The Ret_Need spreadsheet relies on lookup tables to determine the income and Social Security benefits to use at retirement age.

B11 use a VLOOKUP function to find the figures at retirement age. The cell that displays the answer to the question "How much will you need at retirement age?" (cell B13) subtracts Social Security income from the retirement income.

How Much Do You Need To Save?

Now that you have some idea of how much you'll be spending every year when you retire, you can build a realistic plan. The spreadsheet Ret_Save lets you use the Annual Spending amount from Ret_Need as the foundation of your plan.

This spreadsheet allows you to project the returns you'll earn on your current savings, IRA accounts, and any company profit-sharing accounts in your name. You can track different interest rates for each account, and you can experiment with different retirement ages (see fig. 14.6).

The screens in this book show the spreadsheet in Microsoft Works, but you can download a version for Lotus 1-2-3, Microsoft Works, or Microsoft Excel. You'll find the spreadsheet by using the keyword

http://www.mcp.com/que/desktop_os/money

To use the file, open it with your spreadsheet and enter values in the box at the top of the spreadsheet. You'll enter the following

- Annual spending at retirement age (the amount you determined with the Ret_Need spreadsheet)
- Amounts in each retirement account (IRA, profit sharing, and other savings)
- Return on investment or interest rate for each account

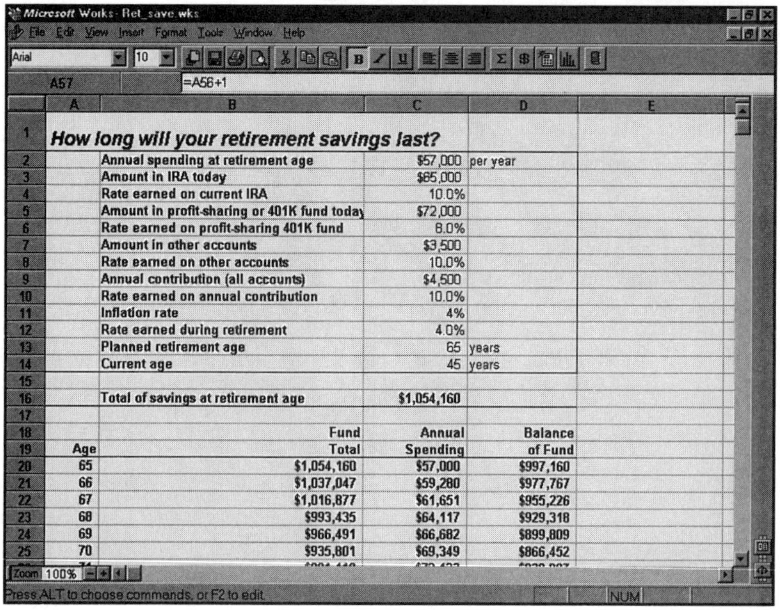

	A	B	C	D
1	*How long will your retirement savings last?*			
2		Annual spending at retirement age	$57,000	per year
3		Amount in IRA today	$65,000	
4		Rate earned on current IRA	10.0%	
5		Amount in profit-sharing or 401K fund today	$72,000	
6		Rate earned on profit-sharing 401K fund	8.0%	
7		Amount in other accounts	$3,500	
8		Rate earned on other accounts	10.0%	
9		Annual contribution (all accounts)	$4,500	
10		Rate earned on annual contribution	10.0%	
11		Inflation rate	4%	
12		Rate earned during retirement	4.0%	
13		Planned retirement age	65	years
14		Current age	45	years
15				
16		Total of savings at retirement age	$1,054,160	
17				
18		Fund	Annual	Balance
19	Age	Total	Spending	of Fund
20	65	$1,054,160	$57,000	$997,160
21	66	$1,037,047	$59,280	$977,767
22	67	$1,016,877	$61,651	$955,226
23	68	$993,435	$64,117	$929,318
24	69	$966,491	$66,682	$899,809
25	70	$935,801	$69,349	$866,452

FIG. 14.6

The Ret_Save spreadsheet shows you whether your current retirement savings will be able to fund your retirement.

- Annual contribution you plan to make in the future
- Return on investment for these future calculations
- Inflation rate
- Return you can expect on retirement savings (this rate will be low to reflect a conservative investment strategy)
- Planned retirement age
- Current age

The value you enter for return on investment will have a dramatic affect on the fund. If you're not sure of the return on your investments, as a general rule, enter 10 percent if you invest in growth-oriented stocks, 8 percent for government bonds, and 6 percent for CDs. Remember to enter percents as a decimal; enter **.1** for 10 percent or **.06** for 6 percent.

The spreadsheet keeps track of two distinct funds—the total you're saving and the annual withdrawals you're likely to make after you reach retirement age. When you change any one of the values at the top of the display, the spreadsheet calculates the affect on both funds.

To see how long your savings will last after retirement, scroll down. When the figure is displayed in parentheses, the fund is exhausted (parentheses are used to show negative numbers). Figure 14.7 shows a retirement plan that needs work. The fund will be exhausted at age 83.

Clearly, this is not a spreadsheet you'll use just once. You'll want to try out new values for each of the variables. If the inflation rates change, you can change the value in cell C11 to see the affect on your retirement plan. And when you receive a new statement on your IRA or profit-sharing accounts, you can update the file.

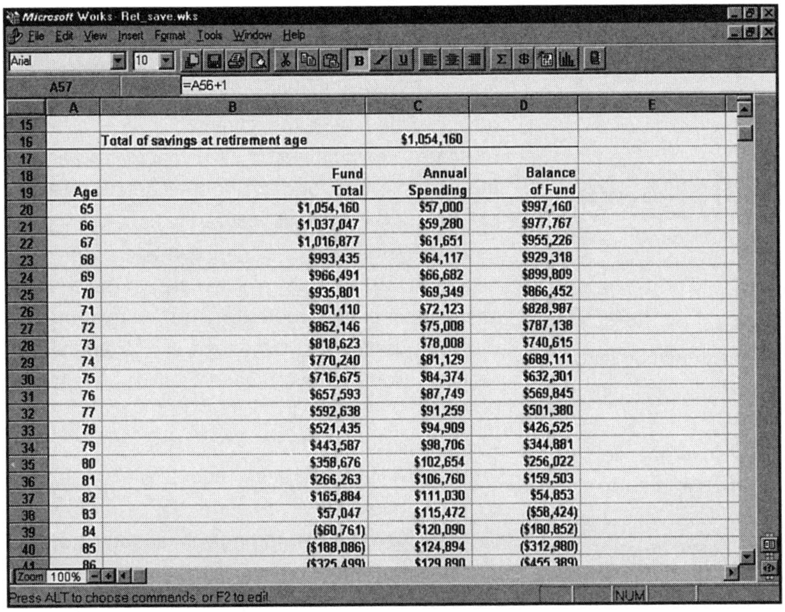

	A	B	C	D	E
15					
16		Total of savings at retirement age	$1,054,160		
17					
18		Fund	Annual	Balance	
19	Age	Total	Spending	of Fund	
20	65	$1,054,160	$57,000	$997,160	
21	66	$1,037,047	$59,280	$977,767	
22	67	$1,016,877	$61,651	$955,226	
23	68	$993,435	$64,117	$929,318	
24	69	$966,491	$66,682	$899,809	
25	70	$935,801	$69,349	$866,452	
26	71	$901,110	$72,123	$828,987	
27	72	$862,146	$75,008	$787,138	
28	73	$818,623	$78,008	$740,615	
29	74	$770,240	$81,129	$689,111	
30	75	$716,675	$84,374	$632,301	
31	76	$657,593	$87,749	$569,845	
32	77	$592,638	$91,259	$501,380	
33	78	$521,435	$94,909	$426,525	
34	79	$443,587	$98,706	$344,881	
35	80	$358,676	$102,654	$256,022	
36	81	$266,263	$106,760	$159,503	
37	82	$165,884	$111,030	$54,853	
38	83	$57,047	$115,472	($58,424)	
39	84	($60,761)	$120,090	($180,852)	
40	85	($188,086)	$124,894	($312,980)	
41	86	($325,499)	$129,890	($455,389)	

FIG. 14.7

A retirement plan in trouble. Based on projected savings and spending, this fund will run out at age 83.

One of the spreadsheet's main benefits should be to encourage you to pay attention to your investments and the returns you're earning. Most financial advisers warn that people with low-risk, low-interest retirement savings are in danger of failing to achieve the returns they'll need. Money market funds and CDs with 6 percent returns will not be enough. Returns of 10 percent—which has been the average rate of return from investing in the stock market over the last 50 years—will be needed.

Keep in mind that the spreadsheet's projections are based on broad assumptions. You cannot accurately predict the return rate of any investment, and even if inflation stays relatively constant, there will be minor fluctuations throughout the course of each year that the spreadsheet will not track. The spreadsheet assumes all of your retirement savings are in tax-deferred accounts. And during the retirement years, the timing of withdrawals can have a big impact on the rate at which your savings earn interest. In order to be conservative, the spreadsheet assumes the amount spent each year is withdrawn at the beginning of the year. Because you could earn interest on some of the money during each year, you'll be able to stretch it out a little longer.

The Design of the Ret_Save Spreadsheet

After you've downloaded the Ret_Save spreadsheet, you may want to personalize it. That should be fairly easy once you understand the underlying structure.

The Ret_Save spreadsheet is contained in one file, but it has three distinct parts. The rows at the top (shown in fig. 14.6) are for entering data. The values entered in each cell are used down below in a formula.

The second part is a table that appears at the bottom of the spreadsheet (rows 67 to 139) as shown in figure 14.8. This table projects the growth of saving in the years between the current year and retirement age. The information in this table doesn't need to be seen often, so it was placed down below, but the calculations are needed for the third part. The cells in this table track the growth of each account (IRA, profit-sharing, and so on) with a payment (PMT) using the interest rate entered for the account. For each year's growth in savings, the table also increments the age by one every row. The table is structured this way so that the spreadsheet can find the total for all savings at whichever age is entered for retirement, using a VLOOKUP formula.

The third part of the file is a balance sheet for the retirement years (rows 20 to 62). This section begins with the total amount in the fund at retirement age and decreases the fund each year. The amount withdrawn each year starts with the value entered for annual spending (cell C2), but we need to account for continuing inflation during retirement years; the subsequent rows increase the amount displayed under Annual Spending by the inflation rate that was entered earlier. But while inflation is eating away at our spending power, the retirement savings also will continue to earn interest. A PMT formula calculates the growth in this fund, taking the figure in Balance of Fund for the previous year as the principal and using the value entered as Rate earned during retirement (cell 12). Because most people will put their retirement money in more conservative investments than they used before retirement, the spreadsheet needs to allow for this additional interest rate.

One cell joins these three sections: the cell labeled Total of savings at retirement age (C16). This cell combines two different amounts, the total of savings from the funds you're starting with and the growth of your annual contribution. The formula used in this cell adds two different formulas; one uses the

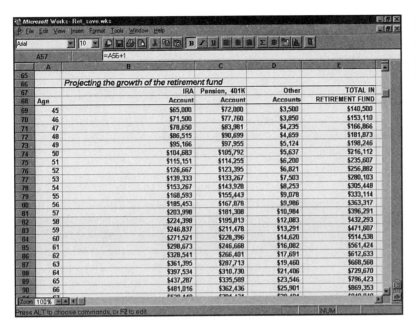

FIG. 14.8

The Ret_Save spreadsheet projects the total saved between the current age and retirement age. A PMT function is used to calculate the growth every year.

VLOOKUP function to find the total savings in the funds at the retirement age, and the other uses an FV (future value) function to project the growth of the annual contribution at the return rate entered for annual contribution.

To help keep track of all the variables, range names were assigned to many of the cells that were used in formulas.

Retirement Planning Shareware You Can Download

Retirement planning is such an important topic, you will want to see as many perspectives as possible. A number of commercial programs, like Quicken and

Managing Your Money, have calculators that can help you evaluate your plan. And a few shareware programs also are offered. Shareware programs can be downloaded at no cost above the connect charges you'll pay. But the program's license requires that you pay a relatively small registration fee to the publisher if you continue to use the software.

The FPLAN-KWIK Financial Retirement Planner

This simple program asks you to complete a short interview and then displays a report on your projected retirement income. The approach is similar to the one used in the Ret_Save spreadsheet, but FPLAN-KWIK has a few differences.

It bases its projections on monthly income, and it works more like a typical software application so the values you enter and the calculations are displayed on different screens. But FPLAN-KWIK does not show you the actual numbers after retirement years; instead it simply advises you whether your savings will be sufficient. Anyone who's serious about preparing for retirement will want both programs.

You begin the program by selecting the Data Interview button. You'll be guided through a series of questions that ask for your current age, the age when you hope to retire and so on. When you've answered all questions, you see a worksheet with all of your responses displayed in a form, as shown in figure 14.9.

On this screen, you can adjust figures, but don't spend too much time choosing the right numbers to enter. The goal of the program is to help you explore the possibilities. As soon as you've entered your best guesses for each field, select the Analysis Reports button. You'll see a screen that describes your situation in several paragraphs of text. It's a speech that you might hear from a professional financial planner at the beginning of an interview. The language can be obtuse but the information is valuable (hint: when

the report states, "Income retirement will be adequate by" a certain number of dollars, that means you'll have more than you need).

For a look at the numbers in table form—a form that's likely to make more sense—select the Summary Report button. This screen, shown in figure 14.10, displays the projections in each category and adds them up.

This report includes a conclusion that suggests changes to your savings plan that will reduce an expected shortfall. You'll want to move back and forth between the Summary Report and Data Worksheet to refine your plan (select the X button in the upper right corner to close a report or worksheet). Pay attention to the inflation rate. The program allows you to choose a general inflation rate and different rates for sources of fixed income (that gives you the chance to guess how much of an annual increase Congress will set aside for Social Security benefits in the future). Also, be sure to use a marginal tax rate of 0 if your retirement savings are in IRA's or other tax-deferred income accounts.

FIG. 14.9

In FPLAN-KWIK, you can track several sources of retirement income.

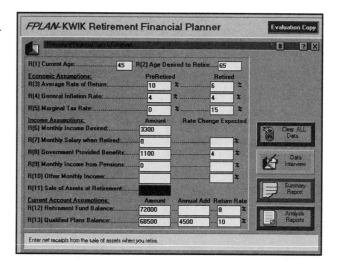

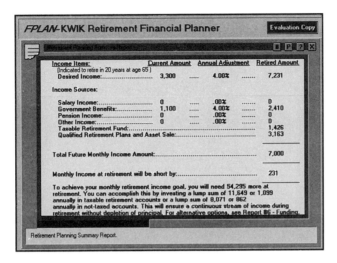

FIG. 14.10

The Summary Report screen displays projections about your retirement investments and an estimate on whether it will be enough to meet your goal.

Downloading the FPLAN-KWIK Retirement Planner

If you're ready to try the program, here's a set of directions that will help you download the file and set it up quickly.

1. Connect to AOL and enter the keyword **aaii.** The main menu for the American Association of Individual Investors Online opens.

2. Click the Software Library button. A menu of library sections opens.

3. Select Financial Planning from the list. A list of programs you can download appears.

4. Double-click the listing FPLAN-KWIK Retirement Planner. A window opens describing the program (see fig. 14.11).

5. Select the Download Now button. The Download Manager window opens.

6. You can either change the name of the file or the folder where AOL will store it. Normally,

AOL stores files in the \download folder which is inside the main AOL folder. Unless you have your own scheme for organizing downloaded software, you should accept AOL's selections and click OK.

7. The downloaded file is compressed in ZIP format. When you sign off from AOL, the file will be decompressed and stored in the FPLAN folder, within the AOL \download folder.

■ **NOTE**

If the file is not decompressed, you turned off the "automatically decompress at sign-off" setting. You'll need to decompress the file with an un-zip program. If you don't have one, change the setting by selecting the Members menu, then Preferences, and Download. Once you've selected the option to decompress files, repeat the download process.

8. After the program has been downloaded and you've signed off from AOL, you need to install the program. Use the Windows Run command,

FIG. 14.11

You can download FPLAN-KWIK from the software library run by the American Association of Individual Investors.

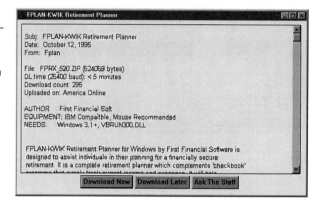

and select Browse; find the AOL download folder. You should see a new folder named FPRX_520 (the number may be different). In this folder you'll find a Setup program. Double-click it to begin the installation.

The installation routine gives you the option of storing the program in its own folder or creating a folder that you name. After the installation is complete, you'll find a new program group and icon for the KWIK Retirement Planner has been created. Double-click the icon to run the software.

Remember that this program is offered as shareware. You're free to evaluate the software but if you continue to use it you should register it and pay the $20 fee. Registration information is contained within the program.

Finding Advice for Estate Planning

Estate planning is a completely separate process from retirement planning. You use estate planning to ensure that your assets will go to people you love

after you die, rather than being lost to taxes and people who would otherwise have a claim to the property. Spreadsheets won't help you in creating this kind of strategy; you need to learn about the law in your area.

Learning the Basics of Estate Planning

While only a good lawyer can craft an estate plan that's likely to survive legal challenges, you can save money if you learn about the topic before you sit down in your attorney's office. Once you're there, your education is billed at hourly rates.

On AOL, you'll find some basic primers at the area run by Nolo Press. A library of articles covers everything from the purpose of a will to the mechanics of a charitable trust (see fig. 14.12).

To find the articles, use the keyword **nolo press**. When the Nolo Press main menu opens, select Reference Library. A menu will display different categories. Select Estate Planning to see the list of articles. You can print or save any article once it's displayed on-screen.

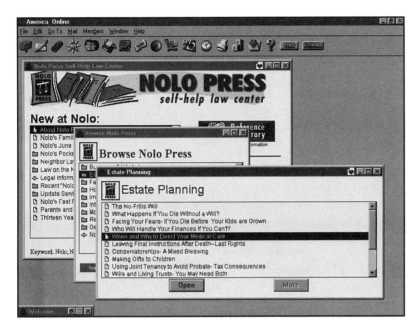

FIG. 14.12

A library of articles in the Nolo Press section covers the basics of estate planning.

Finding a Professional Estate Planner

If you decide your estate is large and complex enough that you need to create an estate plan, the first person to consult is your own lawyer. But if you decide you need more help, you can turn to the Web.

A growing number of estate planners now maintain Web pages. Many of these pages are little more than advertisements for professional services, but others contain detailed information on current issues that affect planners, including recent changes in tax policy and developments in case law.

▼ **TIP**

When planning your retirement, you may want to ask people who've already made the transition. You can ask questions at the message boards run by the American Association of Retired Persons on AOL. Keyword **aarp**.

A California attorney runs a page with links to pages run by many of the lawyers who specialize in estate planning, and to some other informational resources that can help you learn about the topic (see fig. 14.13).

You'll find this page by using the keyword

http://www.ca-probate.com/links.htm

FIG. 14.13

If you're shopping for an estate planner, this Web site is a good place to start.

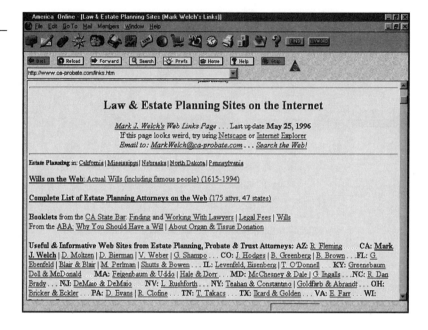

Keep in mind that local laws will be a factor in creating an estate plan, so you'll need an attorney who's licensed to practice law in your state.

C H A P T E R

15

Looking for New Opportunities

> The world changes fast, and you have to move with it if you want to keep that competitive edge.

Whether your goal is to amass a fortune or enjoy a comfortable lifestyle, making the most of your money requires vigilance. You need to always be on the lookout for new opportunities and new ways to invest your savings.

An online connection helps you find the information you need fast, but where do you look for it? This chapter is a start in the right direction. It will help you put out feelers for the trends that will affect your future financial picture without requiring that you devote all of your free time to the process.

The Next Big Thing: IPOs

We've all heard the stories about someone who got rich because he or she "got in early" and bought stock in a big company when it was still a small company. Aside from signing a multi-million dollar contract with a professional sports team or winning the lottery, there are few ways to strike it rich as quickly as an IPO.

IPOs are Initial Public Offerings, and they're like a coming-out party for a new company. These companies have been in business for a while but the shares were held by a small group of investors. When the initial public offering is made, new shares are issued and placed on sale at a public exchange (American Stock Exchange, NASDAQ, or the New York Stock Exchange).

> "Finding the 'next big thing' is the specialty of America Online's IPO section."

Aggressive investors—especially those who trade frequently—look for IPOs that are likely to open in a blaze of glory. When there's strong public interest in an IPO, the price of a share will rise dramatically in the first few days before it settles down to a consistent trading range. One of the most successful IPOs, Netscape Communications, tripled in price before it settled down. Cashing in on just one IPO can make up for a lot of mistakes elsewhere.

Because many hot IPOs trail off in the following weeks, leaving losses in their wake, most long-term investors shy away from the category, preferring to wait until the price on these new stocks settles down.

The interest in many IPOs is so strong that unless you have an active account with a stockbroker, you may not be able to buy an IPO at the price that's considered most desirable—the offering price. But within a few hours, you should be able to buy shares from the AOL's online stockbrokers, probably at a premium over the opening price.

The interest in IPOs is so strong that America Online introduced a new section within the Personal Finance channel devoted solely to discussion of IPOs.

Reports on IPOs in the Works and on the Street

Finding the "next big thing" is the specialty of America Online's IPO section. Investors who are aggressive in pursuing opportunities will find this section can help focus their research on IPOs with a variety of good source materials. Unless you work on Wall Street, you probably don't have access to the types of special reports that are featured here.

The IPO section is like a mini-mall for the resources on America Online that have information on IPOs. Open the IPO section by entering the keyword **ipo**, and you'll see a menu of resources that will help you track all of the new public stock offerings (see fig. 15.1).

FIG. 15.1

The IPO section brings together a wide range of resources on companies that are in the process of going public.

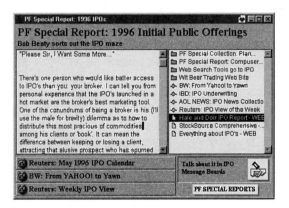

Some of the resources can help you learn about the general idea of IPOs, others report news on companies about to make their first offering, and others track the success of recent IPOs.

Articles that appear in the business publications with a presence on America Online, such as *Business Week* and *Investor's Business Daily*, are featured when they're on an IPO-related topic. Web sites that interest IPO hunters are featured as links on the main menu. But the most valuable feature is a calendar listing the month's newest IPOs. The calendar appears in AOL's Business News section among a long list of articles, but it's easy to find in the IPO section.

The calendar is an excellent resource for individual investors who want to track this hot field of investing. To see the list of stocks, first display the IPO main menu and then look for the menu listing for the current month's IPO calendar. Click the Go button next to the listing. For example, look for "Reuters September, 1996, IPO Calendar" (see fig. 15.2).

The calendar provides something that's hard for the small investor to obtain: the hard numbers on new offerings. While there's plenty of gossip and rumors surrounding IPOs, unless you have your own broker, you would have to do a lot of legwork to get the information in this calendar. You'll find the list of stocks that have filed with the SEC (Securities and Exchange Commission) to begin trading. You'll also find the date they are scheduled to start trading, the company that is bringing the stock to market (the underwriter), the number of shares that will be offered, and the price of the initial offering (per share).

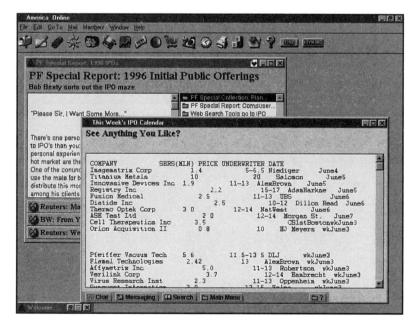

FIG. 15.2

Separating the facts from the gossip: the monthly IPO calendar.

Working with the IPO Calendar

Once this calendar is displayed, you can print it or save it to your hard disk using the File menu. If you're serious about buying stocks that are listed in a calendar, you could use the saved file as a starting point to make notes. For example, you might record notes on the progress of your research (the phone number of the underwriter and a note when you called the underwriter, asking for a copy of the offering).

Because the file is in text format with columns, you'll find it's easiest to use in a word processor if you use a fixed-pitch font. Since most word processors use a proportional font as the default font, the columns may be impossible to read when you first open the file. To make the columns line up properly, highlight all the text and then select a fixed-pitch font such as Courier.

Figure 15.3 shows how the file will appear after it is saved to a hard disk, opened with Microsoft Works word processor, and formatted in Courier.

The text document can be imported into a spreadsheet file fairly easily if you use Microsoft Excel or Lotus 1-2-3. When the file is opened, the spreadsheet will perform a conversion (parsing) of the spaces in the text columns into spreadsheet columns. Performing this conversion with Microsoft Works requires the tedious process of replacing the spaces between columns with tabs before it can be read by the spreadsheet. If you want to perform the conversion, refer to the section in Chapter 3, "Formatting Downloaded Statements with Microsoft Works;" unfortunately, the IPO calendar will prove more difficult to convert than the Disclosure financial statements used in that example because the spacing between columns in the IPO calendar is not consistent.

FIG. 15.3

The columns in the IPO format are easier to read if you format the text in a fixed-pitch font.

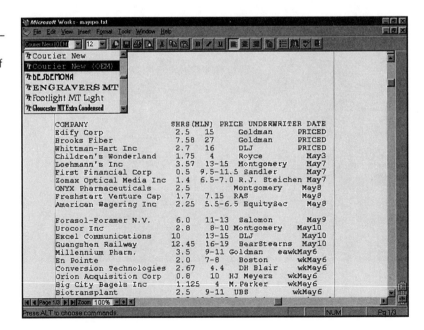

Talking About IPOs: Who's On, Who's Out, and Why

If you're thinking about investing in a newly issued stock, the message boards that can be reached from the main IPO menu are a good place to take a pulse of the market. The message boards are not solely devoted to the topic of IPOs; these boards are also accessed from the Company Research area and so a number of the folders cover other investment topics. The boards are moderated by Bob Beaty, a columnist in America Online's Company Research section, so many of the message folders discuss topics from his recent columns.

Here's how you can find the messages on upcoming and recent IPOs:

1. Connect to AOL and enter the keyword **IPO**. The main IPO section menu appears.

2. Click the Message Board icon in the lower right corner. The main menu for the message boards opens.

3. Select Browse Folders. A window displays the list of topics.

4. Select the IPOs: Past, Present & Future folder. A list of messages on IPOs appears, as shown in figure 15.4.

5. In the first screen, you'll see the oldest messages. To see newer messages, click the More Messages button several times; repeat until the More Messages button disappears, indicating that all of the messages on the board are now available.

6. Scroll down through the list of messages; any time you see a subject that interests you, double-click the subject to see the message.

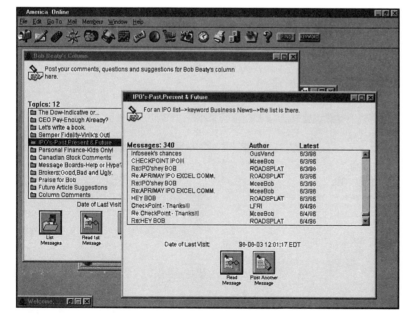

FIG. 15.4

Talking about new opportunity: in the IPO message board investors compare observations about newly issued stocks.

Reading what others are saying about a stock can be a good way to help you make up your mind. If you continue to be interested, you'll want to do more research. Chapter 3, "Researching Stocks with Hard Facts," discusses the basic techniques of stock research.

Talking About IPOs at The Motley Fool

You'll also find more discussion of IPOs in the Motley Fool message boards. Finding the IPO talk may take a bit of detective work, but it's worth the trouble. You'll need to dig for the messages on new stocks—partly because thousands of messages are posted every day in the hundreds of message boards, and partly because some of the Motley Fool's message boards have been so busy that they've been retired and replaced with new folders. The following steps will take you directly to the IPO message boards:

1. Enter the keyword **motley fool**. The main Motley Fool menu opens.

2. Click the Message Boards button. The main window for Motley Fool's Message Boards opens.

3. In the list of boards, select the Let's Talk Investment Approaches folder. The message board control window opens.

4. Select the Browse Folders button. A window opens, displaying a list of several dozen topics.

5. Read through the list of topics until you find the Init Public Offerings folder. The folder will be numbered; if the previous folder was retired in recent weeks, you may see two folders. Select the one with the highest number to see the more recent messages. If the previous folder was retired longer than a few weeks ago, only one Init Public Offerings folder will be available. Select the folder and you'll see a list of recent messages, as shown in figure 15.5.

FIG. 15.5

Finding the Motley Fool's message board where IPOs are discussed requires a bit of detective work.

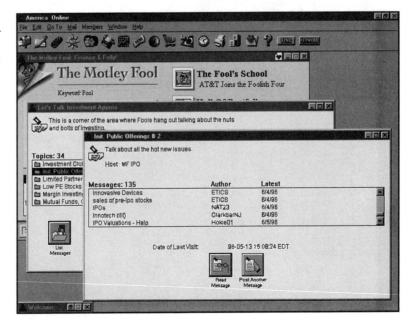

6. In the first screen, you'll see the oldest messages. To see newer messages, click the More Messages button several times; repeat until the More Messages button disappears, indicating that all of the messages on the board are now available.

Once a stock has begun to trade, a message board will open in the Motley Fool's list of stocks as long as there's a fair amount of volume (if no one's trading it, no one will be talking about it). To find the message board for a stock within The Motley Fool, follow Steps 1 and 2 above, and look through the list of stocks by alphabetical grouping. For example, to find messages on Netscape, select Stocks M-N. On the following screens, you will need to select from a smaller alphabetical listing of folders (for example, Stocks Na-Ne) before you see the folder where a particular stock is discussed.

On the Menu: Personal Finance

There are two types of people online: those who always choose from the menu, and those who prefer shortcuts as they jump from sight to sight. If you're the type who avoids using the menus you may be missing out on the latest highlights for managing your money.

America Online staff members use the menus for each channel as a way to bring new services to users' attention. And if you haven't scrolled down the list of resources on the main menu for the Personal Finance channel (see fig. 15.6), you've probably missed a few of the newest offerings.

FIG. 15.6

AOL's Personal Finance menu will call your attention to some of the newest services available for financial management.

If you've become so accustomed to using keywords that you never see the Channels menu, you can find the Personal Finance menu by using the keyword **personal finance**.

On the left side of the menu, some of the sections within Personal Finance are highlighted; a brief description of some of the features available are mentioned with a button that will display the area. On the right side, you'll find a list of all the areas within Personal Finance. The list is displayed alphabetically after a few special items which appear at the top of the list.

One of these special items is Highlights and Suggestions. Click this choice and a menu will open with a variety of Personal Finance services (see fig. 15.7).

This menu gives extra attention to some of the Personal Finance offerings. Only a few of the items are new, but they may call attention to places you haven't had time to explore.

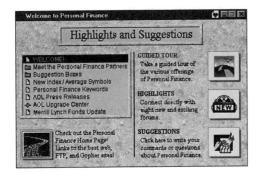

FIG. 15.7

To learn more about the latest Personal Finance offerings on AOL, select Highlights and Suggestions.

In the lower left corner, you'll find a link to a place that will almost certainly expose you to new personal finance information. Click this link and you'll see AOL Personal Finance on the Web, a page with links

to interesting sites on the Web, selected by the America Online staff (see fig. 15.8).

Each of the sites is described briefly; click any of the highlighted titles and the AOL browser will display the main page at this site. Because you'll start on a tour of the Web with this first click and you may end up losing track of where you've been, keep in mind that to return to the AOL menus, you can close the AOL browser at any time by clicking the close window button in the upper right corner.

Some of the suggestions on this page are informational resources, but others are FTP (file transfer protocol) sites that offer free software for personal finance chores. So if you like to try specialized calculators and programs that can tackle money management chores, select the link Top Internet Resources. The AOL browser will display Internet sites that will allow you to download shareware and free programs for a variety of financial chores.

FIG. 15.8

You'll find links to new personal finance resources on the Internet from the AOL Personal Finance on the Web page.

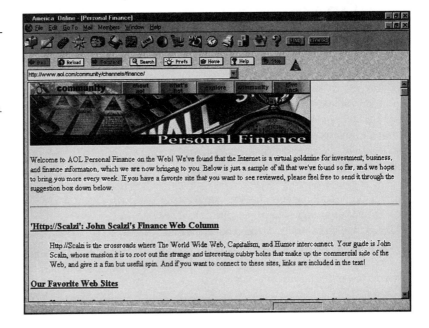

GNN's Guide to Personal Finance on the Web

One of the Web sites you'll find on the AOL Personal Finance on the Web page is the GNN Personal Finance Center. GNN is America Online's subsidiary for providing Internet access, and it runs this Web site to help users keep track of the latest Internet services available for money management.

You can reach the page by selecting the GNN link on the AOL Personal Finance on the Web page, or you can enter the keyword

http://gnn.com/gnn/meta/finance

The GNN Personal Finance Center is updated every week with new features on the Web and with new articles from GNN columnists; you'll find brief

descriptions and a link that will quickly open each site (see fig. 5.9).

To visit any of the sites, all you need to do is click the highlighted link. One of the best links you'll find on this page is WIC Personal Finance. Click this link and you'll find a Web page that is full of links to some of the most popular personal finance sites on the Web. This page has broad categories for personal finance topics—banking & credit cards, brokers, mutual funds, and more—each topic is represented by a page full of links to other Web sites. Figure 15.10 shows the top of the page. While the headline on this page is Financial Planning, this is the page that opens when you select WIC Personal Finance.

If you ever think you've exhausted all of the sources of information available online for a particular personal finance topic, visit here. You're sure to uncover something new.

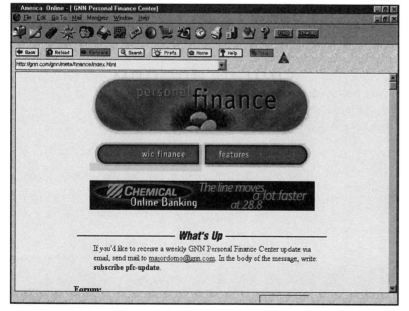

FIG. 15.9

The GNN Personal Finance Center has a new list of features every week.

FIG. 15.10

The GNN Personal Finance site lists dozens of resources available on the Web by category.

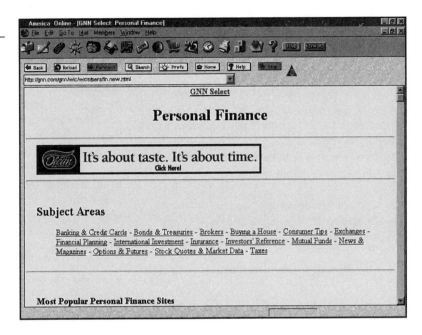

Keeping Up-to-Date on GNN Personal Finance

You can stay on top of the latest updates from the GNN Personal Finance page without even visiting the page. A mailing list is published every week, with news of the latest additions to the site. If you want to receive these messages in your AOL mailbox, follow these steps:

1. Connect to AOL and select Mail, Compose Mail. The Compose Mail window opens.

2. In the To box, enter

   majordomo@gnn.com

3. Press Tab twice to move to the Subject box. The AOL mail manager requires a subject so you can enter anything here you like; the automated listserv program that receives your message will ignore the subject.

4. Press Tab to move your cursor to the body of the message. Enter

   subscribe pfc-update

   Your screen should look like figure 15.11.

5. Check your spelling and then click the Send button.

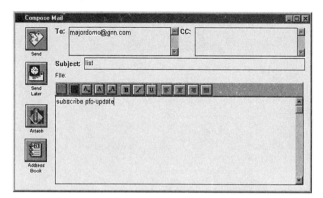

FIG. 15.11

Send e-mail to the majordomo at GNN to receive weekly e-mail updates about the GNN Personal Finance Center.

Within a few hours, you will receive an e-mail message that either confirms that you've been added to the list or reports a problem. If you have a problem, check your spelling carefully and try again. Once you've been added to the list, you'll start to receive mailings within a few days. If you find that you're not reading the messages, you can remove your name from the list by following the same steps but, in Step 4, rather than the line that begins with subscribe, use this line

unsubscribe pfc-update YourName@aol.com

and use your own screen name instead of *YourName*.

Talking to Other Small Investors

Public mailing lists are one of the great innovations that the Internet has brought to the world of communications. While Web sites provide an outlet for a person or organization to present information to the rest of the world, public mailing lists are a two-way street. People with a common interest are able to share their views and ask questions to each other without any delay. People use Internet mailing lists for just about every topic, from scientific research to hobbies.

The mail you receive when you subscribe to a public list is different from the type of professional mail you'll receive from a professional service like GNN (as described in the previous section). The messages you'll receive from a public mailing list contain messages written by ordinary users. The mailing list allows each user to share information with the rest of the group by sending just one message The mailing list manager receives the messages and then pastes them into the next mailing. The messages you receive are similar to a newsletter in their format, but they're actually a series of messages that other members of the list have written.

Persfin-Digest is a mailing list devoted to personal finance topics. Just about anything that has an impact on how people manage their money is covered, including insurance, credit cards, taxes, investments, and decisions about products to buy. Some people ask questions, other people answer, and other people add more information to the answers. Figure 15.12 shows a message from the Persfin-Digest as displayed in the AOL mail manager.

FIG. 15.12

If you subscribe to the Persfin-Digest mailing list, you'll receive the newsletter-like messages in your e-mailbox.

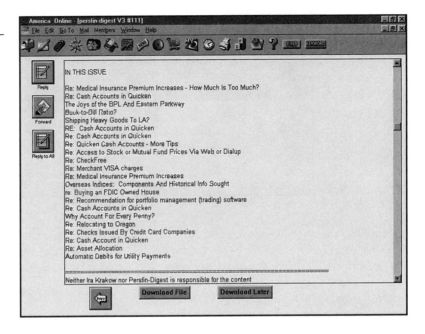

To subscribe to the list, follow these steps.

1. Connect to AOL and select Mail, Compose Mail. The Compose Mail window opens.

2. In the To box, enter

   majordomo@shore.net

3. Press Tab twice to move to the Subject box. The AOL mail manager requires a subject so you can enter anything here you like; the automated listserv program that receives your message will ignore the subject.

4. Press Tab to move your cursor to the body of the message. Enter

   subscribe persfin-digest

5. Check your spelling and then click the Send button.

Within a few hours you'll receive a mail message confirming that you've been added to the list. You'll then receive regular installments every week or so (publication is not on a set schedule; the messages go out whenever the moderator is able to find the time).

Unfortunately, some of the messages are too long to fit in your mailbox. When you receive one of these long messages, you'll see a message in the body of your text alerting you to this problem; you'll need to click the Download File button that will appear. The text of the message will be stored on your hard disk; you will then need to read the message or print it using word processing software (the message is in a text format that any word processor can read).

If you decide you want to stop receiving the messages, you'll find instructions on how to remove your name from the list in the body of every message.

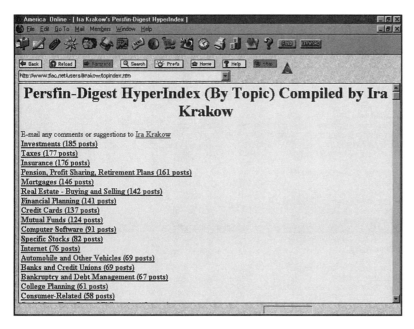

FIG. 15.13

Back issues of the Persfin-Digest mailing list at a Web site.

If you're curious about the list and want to read some sample messages, you can find back issues at the Web site run by the list manager, Ira Krakow. Enter the keyword

http://www.tiac.net/users/ikrakow

From the opening menu, select the link Persfin-Digest Hyperindex. On this Web page, you'll find recent issues of the mailing list, organized by topics. To read all of the discussion on a single topic, click any of the links (see fig. 15.13).

Keeping Up with the Latest Personal Finance Web Sites

The Persfin-Digest mailing list generates a lot of discussion about Web sites with information that can help the average consumer and small investor. Most of these sites can be visited easily from a Web site that displays a links to all of these sites. Enter the keyword

http://www.tiac.net/users/ikrakow/ pagerefs.html

The AOL Web browser will load and display the page shown in figure 15.14.

This enormous collection of Web sites may not provide the answer to every last one of your questions about earning and spending money, but it will come awfully close. New sites are added every few weeks.

FIG. 15.14

A growing list of links: Web sites discussed in the Persfin-Digest mailing list.

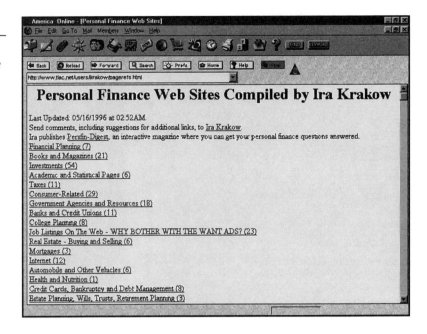

America Online - [Personal Finance Web Sites]

File Edit GoTo Mail Members Window Help

Back   Reload   Forward   Search   Prefs   Home   Help

http://www.tiac.net/users/krakow/pagerefs.html

Personal Finance Web Sites Compiled by Ira Krakow

Last Updated: 05/16/1996 at 02:52AM.

Send comments, including suggestions for additional links, to Ira Krakow.

Ira publishes Persfin-Digest, an interactive magazine where you can get your personal finance questions answered.

Financial Planning (7)
Books and Magazines (21)
Investments (54)
Academic and Statistical Pages (6)
Taxes (11)
Consumer-Related (29)
Government Agencies and Resources (18)
Banks and Credit Unions (11)
College Planning (8)
Job Listings On The Web - WHY BOTHER WITH THE WANT ADS? (23)
Real Estate - Buying and Selling (6)
Mortgages (3)
Internet (12)
Automobile and Other Vehicles (6)
Health and Nutrition (1)
Credit Cards, Bankruptcy and Debt Management (3)
Estate Planning, Wills, Trusts, Retirement Planning (3)

A

Online with the Money Guide

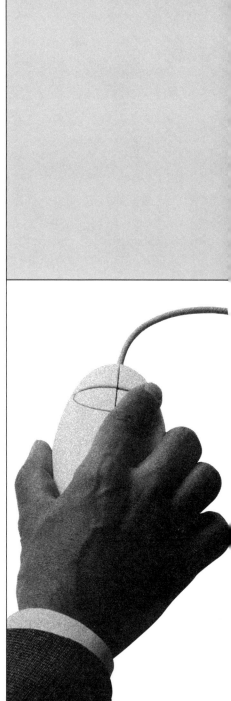

The world of online information changes so rapidly that keeping up with it is no longer possible by simply reading pages in a printed book. Fortunately, online services and the World Wide Web make it possible to keep the flow of information coming, long after you've taken this book home.

To keep up with the rapid rate of change, I maintain a site on the World Wide Web. Here you can find links to all of the Internet sites that are mentioned in this book. So rather than type in the keywords, you'll be able to click and go directly to the site. You'll also find the files for all of the spreadsheets described in this book.

You'll find this site by using a keyword on America Online (Ctrl+K) with this text:

http://www.mcp.com/que/desktop_os/money

Spreadsheet Files To Download

Also at this site, you'll be able to download the spreadsheet files that are described in this book (see Table A.1).

TABLE A.1 Money Guide Spreadsheet Files

Topic	Chapter	File name
Creating a budget	Chapter 1	BUDGET
Tracking a mutual fund	Chapter 1	MUTUALFD
Managing your portfolio	Chapter 8	PORTMAN
Comparing life insurance quotes	Chapter 9	LIFE_INS
Planning other big purchases	Chapter 11	BIG_BUY
Buying a house	Chapter 12	HOMEBUY
College savings	Chapter 13	COLLSAVE
Projecting your retirement needs	Chapter 14	RET_NEED
Saving for retirement	Chapter 14	RET_SAVE

You can download the spreadsheet in the format that works best for your spreadsheet; you'll find versions for Lotus 1-2-3, Microsoft Excel, and Microsoft Works. The files will work in the DOS, Windows, or Mac versions of these spreadsheets.

To download the file, simply double-click the file name. The America Online (AOL) browser will ask you to confirm that you want to save the file to your system. When you select the option to save the file, you'll then be asked to select a folder where the file should be stored on your system. After the file is saved on your system, you can open it with your spreadsheet software's File, Open command.

Links to the Book's Internet Sites

Because the world of online services changes so rapidly, some of the specific addresses mentioned in this book may change over time. Often, even though the address has changed, the same information is available.

To help you find the sites discussed in the book, this Web site will also include links to every Internet site mentioned in the book. Since some of these Web addresses may change, the list will be updated periodically to make sure you're able to find the information that the book describes.

That also means you won't have to type in any of those long Internet addresses. You can use the Web site as your one-stop guide to all of the sites mentioned in the book. These links will be organized by chapter to help you use the book as your online money guide.

Adding the Money Guide to Your Favorites

Because you'll want to use the site over and over, be sure to record this site in your list of favorite places.

Chapter 1 explains how to use Favorite Places at length, but here's the short course in saving this address:

1. Run the AOL software. (You don't have to sign on for this process.)

2. Select Go To, Favorite Places from the main menu. The Favorite Places window opens.

3. Click the Add Favorite Place button. The Add Favorite Place dialog box opens.

4. In the Enter the Place's Description box, type **AOL Money Guide**. In the Enter the Internet Address box, type

   http://www.mcp.com/que/desktop_os/ money

   Your display will look like figure A.1.

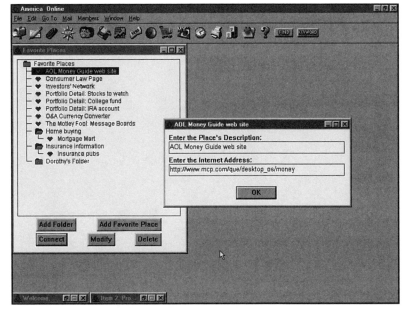

FIG. A.1

The only stop you'll need to make to find the Internet addresses mentioned in this book.

5. Check your spelling and click the OK button.
The Internet address will be recorded in your list
of favorite places.

Whenever you want to visit any of the sites mentioned in the book that are on the Internet, select Go
To, Favorite Places, and click the AOL Money Guide
listing.

B

The Banking Center

Managing your personal finances can be dramatically easier if you take advantage of the Banking Center, one of the newest additions to America Online's financial services. In the Banking Center, you'll find a list of over a dozen banks that allow you to manage your account while you're connected to America Online (AOL). You won't have to drive down to a branch office or visit an ATM to perform everyday banking routines. You can view your account balance at any time, or transfer money between accounts. You can even pay bills, saving the expense of printing and mailing checks. Probably most important to those of us whose checkbooks are often out of balance: you can use the online software to reconcile your account. If you use the Banking Center to manage your checking and savings account, you can have the peace of mind that comes from always knowing the precise balance in your account.

Online Banking with BankNOW

You can reach the Banking Center on AOL by using the keyword **bank**. From the main menu, shown in figure B.1, you can read information from the banks that participate in the program and articles about interest rates from BankRate Monitor. If your bank participates in AOL's banking program, you can begin the process of using your current account online by selecting your bank from the menus and completing the online forms. Most banks will give you access to the account within a few days of receiving your online application.

"Look before you leap into new investments. America Online has everything you need to know—you just need to know where to look, and what to do with it once you find it."

Fig. B.1

The Banking Center lists all of the banks offering online banking through AOL.

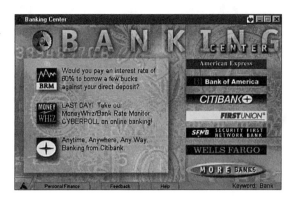

Some of the banks are listed here simply to attract your business and don't provide access through America Online. Instead, when you sign up for online banking you'll receive a disk in the mail with software you can use to dial the bank's computers directly. A few allow you to connect to their computers over your AOL connection, using their own software.

Most of the banks, however, let you use your AOL account for banking using software called BankNOW. When you establish an account with one of these banks through AOL's Banking Center—either by registering an existing account or by opening a new account—BankNOW software is downloaded to your system. The BankNOW software provides the forms you use to enter transactions, to view your statements, and to communicate with the bank. While your attention is centered on screens that display your account balances and transactions, BankNOW's most sophisticated feature is invisible. When you are transferring information to the banking network, BankNOW software encrypts all account information so it cannot be intercepted. BankNOW uses an advanced form of encryption

known as 1024-bit RSA with triple DES; that's a technical way of saying that your account information is never displayed in its original form while it's being sent over the phone line. The data is scrambled while it's moving so the transactions are safe.

You don't have to pass up on BankNOW just because none of the banks in your area participate yet. You can start a new account with one of the banks online. Many people use online banks that are located in other states; deposits are mailed to the bank, and cash is obtained from an ATM. This setup covers most banking needs everyone's favorite: cash withdrawals. Before you go ahead with a distant bank, confirm that it participates in one of the cash networks, like Cirrus or Chex, available at an ATM near you.

Since the program is relatively new, many banks around the country are still in the process of developing their presence at the Banking Center.

If your bank is not yet participating, ask a service representative at your bank if they plan to take part. They may be working on it already. Some banks plan to provide online banking through Web sites on the Internet; you'll be able to access those accounts using the AOL browser and the URL for the bank's Web site.

Less Postage, More Control

You don't give up anything by using BankNOW: you can still visit a branch and transact business in person. What you gain is the ability to manage your account at any hour, from your computer. For most people, online banking saves time and money. You don't have to write checks and mail them. After you setup a payee once, you don't have to type it in every time you pay a bill; you select the payee's name from a menu.

You save money with BankNOW if you take advantage of the opportunity to pay bills online. You can pay bills directly from your BankNOW account by completing the menus on the BankNOW software. You don't have to print a check or mail anything. The *clearinghouse* — which is basically a computer switching center that acts as the go-between for banks and their online customers—transfers funds from your account to the recipient's account. In many cases, the transaction takes place electronically, since the clearinghouse is able to access the accounts of thousands of businesses; if the party you're paying cannot receive electronic funds transfers, then the clearinghouse prints and mails the check at no charge to you.

One of BankNOW's major advantages is that it lets you schedule automatic payments. Any bill that needs to be paid monthly, such as a mortgage or loan payment, can be set up just once. From then on, BankNOW will pay the bill on time, month after month.

A Brief Tour of BankNOW

The BankNOW screen is designed to simplify your banking records but you may be disoriented at first. Once you understand the rationale behind this design, you'll find BankNOW is very easy to use. The screen, shown in figure B.2, seems to have three different checkbook registers. Each transaction you initiate begins in the OutBox and moves to the other two windows as it is processed, first by the clearinghouse and then by your bank. The three different windows are required in order to give you a very accurate view of what's happening with your account.

Fig. B.2

The BankNOW screen shows all transactions in your account as they move through various stages. You initiate payments in the OutBox, and after they're executed, they appear in the Online Statement.

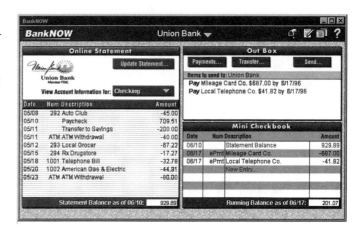

The OutBox is where you initiate payments and transfers between accounts by selecting the buttons for Payments or Transfer. Since you can do this while you're not connected to AOL, a transaction may sit here for days until you decide you want to execute the transaction. When you want a transaction to be executed, click the Send button and BankNOW will begin the process of transferring the money. Your instructions will be sent to the clearinghouse's computers within seconds.

Once the transaction has been received at the clearinghouse's computers, an acknowledgment is sent back to your system; the transaction disappears from the OutBox window and is now displayed in the Mini Checkbook window. You can consider the transactions that appear here as pending: in some cases, the transaction will be pending for only a few hours but in other cases it could be a few days. The next time you connect to BankNOW, the clearinghouse sends updated information to your system: transactions that have been executed will move from the Mini Checkbook to the Online Statement. If the transaction is still pending, it will remain in the Mini Checkbook. You can update your records at any time by selecting the Update Statement button that

appears in the Online Statement window. When you select Update Statement, you'll also see transactions that were initiated outside of the software, such as ATM cash withdrawals and direct deposits made to your account.

Throughout the entire process, you have two balances (both appear at the bottom of the display). The Statement Balance shows you the total that your bank's records indicate is now in the account; without online banking you'd need to visit a branch or phone the bank to obtain this information. The second balance is the Running Balance, which appears in the Mini Checkbook; the amount here is comparable to the total you'd have in a hand-written checkbook register. The Running Balance is the amount you'll have in the account after the transactions you've ordered are executed.

Using BankNOW won't make you rich. You'll save only a few dollars on postage and check printing. But it can dramatically reduce the amount of work you need to spend in keeping your personal finances in order and give you the peace of mind that comes from knowing exactly what's happening in your accounts.

Index

downloaded data
analyzing, 52-55
organizing, 55

downloading
Acrobat software,
255-256
art, 10-11
Big_Buy spread-
sheet, 211
Consumer Information
Catalog, 184-185
FPLAN-KWIK financial
retirement planner,
265-266
HOT spreadsheet, 40
MutualFd, 47
retirement planning
shareware, 263-266
FPLAN-KWIK finan-
cial retirement
planner, 263-264
spreadsheet files,
283-284
spreadsheets, 152
stock prices with
Historical Quotes
database, 72-73
tool on demand, 11
Treasury rates, 132

E*Trade
discount brokers, 108
TradePlus, 107-110

earnings estimates, 77
Chart-O-Matic, 78-79
First Call reports, 77
News Profiles, 78
working with reports,
77-78

EDGAR (Electronic Data
Gathering, Analysis
and Retrieval), 76-77
10-K, 76-77
10-Q, 76-77

education costs, pro-
jecting with spread-
sheets, 239-245

EEBond for Windows,
136-137

Equifax, 163-165

estate planning,
266-268
basics of, 266
professionals, 267
Web sites, 267

estimates, retirement
income, 257-259

evaluating mutual
funds' performance,
115

Excite, 204-208
searching with,
206-208

Expected Family Contri-
bution calculation, 248
Expert Add button, 32

F

FastWEB Scholarship
Search, 249-251

Favorite Place, adding
Money Guide, 285-286

Favorite Place folder
creating folders
within, 19
creating shortcuts,
18-19

Federal Trade Commis-
sion, getting credit
information from,
167-168

files, from Social Secu-
rity Web site, 256

finance planning
asset management
spreadsheets, 47-49
budget spreadsheets,
44-52
calculating
capital gains, 49-50
investment returns,
50-52
investments, 46-47
changing spread-
sheets, 45-46

cars, 194-195
electronics, 196
profiles, creating, 23
socializing, 24-30
online trading, 100-102
basic techniques,
102-103
financial services,
104-105
PCFN (or Personal
Computer Finan-
cial Network),
104-106
placing an order,
105-106
discount vs. full-service
brokers, 101
overview, 100-101
stock trade
mechanics, 102
**ordering, with PCFN,
105-106**
organizing
downloaded data, 55
investments, 147-148
**OutBox (BankNOW),
290**

P

**passwords, changing,
22**
**paying dividends,
115-116**

**PCFN (or Personal
Computer Financial
Network), 104-106**
placing an order,
105-106
**Persfin-Digest
Hyperindex Web
sites, 281**
**Personal Earnings and
Benefits Statement
(PEBS), 255**
**Personal Finance
menus, 104, 116,
275-279**
GNN Personal Finance
Center, 277
**personal finance
planning**
asset management
spreadsheets, 47-49
budget spreadsheets,
44-52
calculating capital
gains, 49-50
calculating investment
returns, 50-52
calculating invest-
ments, 46-47
changing spread-
sheets, 45-46
overview, 39-40
**personal finance plan-
ning, setting goals, 55**

**personal finance
software**
downloading HOT
spreadsheet, 40
using spreadsheets,
40-43
**personal finance terms,
keyword commands,
14**
**Personal Portfolio
feature, 143-144**
planning
for college education,
237-251
for retirement,
254-263
estate planning,
266-268
**PMT (payment)
formula, 43**
**portfolio display, Last/
NAV, 145-147**
portfolios
adjusting, 148-150
Boring Portfolio, 86
creating, 147-148
creating a spread-
sheet, 152-156
using downloaded
portfolio, 155-156
creating online,
144-145
diversifying your
portfolio, 154-155
Last/NAV, 145-147

Persfin-Digest
  Hyperindex, 281
Social Security
  Administration, 254
TRW, 163

**Social Security Adminis-
tration**
  calculating expected
    benefits, 254-256
  home page, 254
  Web site, viewing
    files, 256

socializing
  AOL mail, 29-30
  chat rooms, 24-25
  member rooms, 24
  message boards, 26
  online, 24-30

**software, upgrading,
9-10**

**spreadsheet files,
downloading, 283-284**

spreadsheet formats
  WKS, 52-54
  XLS, 52-54

spreadsheets
  arithmetic operators,
    43
  asset management,
    47-49
  basics of, 42-43
  Big_Buy, 210-212
  cells, 42
  changing, 45-46
  Collsave, 240-245
  copying formulas, 49

creating, 47-49
  using the AOL
    portfolio, 152-154
  with portfolios,
    152-156
diversifying your
  portfolio, 154-155
downloading, 152
entering data in, 43
FV (future value)
  formula, 43
for home buying,
  226-229
Homebuy, 227-228
  customizing,
    228-229
IF formula, 242
Money Guide Portman
  spreadsheet, 152
personal finance
  software, 40-43
PMT (payment)
  formula, 43
Ret_Need, 258-260
Ret_Save, 260-263
selecting, 41-42
separate cell
  addresses, 43
transferring down-
  loaded data to,
  52-54
using downloaded
  portfolio, 155-156

**Statement Balance
(BankNOW), 290**

**stock analysis, Decision
Point forum, 89-90**

**stock investment
advisors, 82**

**stock splits, adjusting,
148-149**

stock tips
  analysis (Decision
    Point), 89-90
  Boring Portfolio, 86
  chat rooms, 94-96
  Daily Pitch, 86
  Decision Point forum,
    88-91
  Decision Point's Daily
    Charts, 90-91
  Dow Dividend Ap-
    proach, 87-88
  facts check from chat
    rooms, 97
  facts checking, 96-97
  First Call database,
    91-93
  following stock market
    trends, 86-88
  Fool Ratio, 85-86
  from other investors,
    93-98
  message boards, 94
  Motley Fool, 83-88
  searching for the
    experts, 82

**stock trade
mechanics, 102**

**stock trading tech-
niques**
  ask price, 103
  bid price, 103

QUE® has the right choice for every computer user

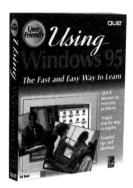

From the new computer user to the advanced programmer, we've got the right computer book for you. Our user-friendly *Using* series offers just the information you need to perform specific tasks quickly and move onto other things. And, for computer users ready to advance to new levels, QUE *Special Edition Using* books, the perfect all-in-one resource—and recognized authority on detailed reference information.

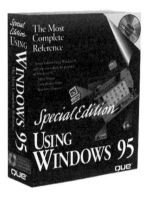

The *Using* series for casual users	*Special Edition Using* for accomplished users
Who should use this book?	**Who should use this book?**
Everyday users who:	Proficient computer users who:
• Work with computers in the office or at home	• Have a more technical understanding of computers
• Are familiar with computers but not in love with technology	• Are interested in technological trends
• Just want to "get the job done"	• Want in-depth reference information
• Don't want to read a lot of material	• Prefer more detailed explanations and examples
The user-friendly reference	**The most complete reference**
• The fastest access to the one best way to get things done	• Thorough explanations of various ways to perform tasks
• Bite-sized information for quick and easy reference	• In-depth coverage of all topics
• Nontechnical approach in plain English	• Technical information cross-referenced for easy access
• Real-world analogies to explain new concepts	• Professional tips, tricks, and shortcuts for experienced users
• Troubleshooting tips to help solve problems	• Advanced troubleshooting information with alternative approaches
• Visual elements and screen pictures that reinforce topics	• Visual elements and screen pictures that reinforce topics
• Expert authors who are experienced in training and instruction	• Technically qualified authors who are experts in their fields
	• "Techniques form the Pros" sections with advice from well-known computer professionals

Check out Que® Books on the World Wide Web
http://www.mcp.com/que

As the biggest software release in computer history, Windows 95 continues to redefine the computer industry. Click here for the latest info on our Windows 95 books

Make computing quick and easy with these products designed exclusively for new and casual users

Examine the latest releases in word processing, spreadsheets, operating systems, and suites

The Internet, The World Wide Web, CompuServe®, America Online®, Prodigy®—it's a world of ever-changing information. Don't get left behind!

Find out about new additions to our site, new bestsellers and hot topics

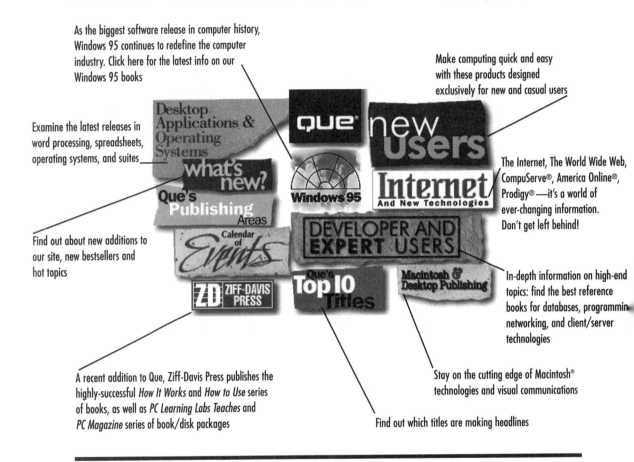

In-depth information on high-end topics: find the best reference books for databases, programming, networking, and client/server technologies

A recent addition to Que, Ziff-Davis Press publishes the highly-successful *How It Works* and *How to Use* series of books, as well as *PC Learning Labs Teaches* and *PC Magazine* series of book/disk packages

Stay on the cutting edge of Macintosh® technologies and visual communications

Find out which titles are making headlines

With 6 separate publishing groups, Que develops products for many specific market segments and areas of computer technology. Explore our Web Site and you'll find information on best-selling titles, newly published titles, upcoming products, authors, and much more.

- Stay informed on the latest industry trends and products available
- Visit our online bookstore for the latest information and editions
- Download software from Que's library of the best shareware and freeware